When the Cactus 'Blooms

CHARLES RUSSELL

Print ISBN: 978-1-64669-438-9

Cover design: Rory C. Keel (carpediempublishers.com)

Cover photo: QT Luong. Copyright © 2019

For all the young people I have coached or taught
Who brought great joy to my life

And

For all the teachers, coaches, administrators, aides, cafeteria staff and custodians

Who were my colleagues for thirty-four years

ACKNOWLEDGMENTS

I assume that most writers attempt to gain the approval of someone. That someone to me is Patricia, my wife of fifty-two years. She has inspired, encouraged, suggested, and even occasionally censored my writing. Also, publishing six novels in as many years would not have been possible without her pushing and pulling me through the difficulties associated with being a self-published author.

I appreciate Glenda Watts and Mary Danna Russell for taking the time to read the manuscript. The suggestions they provided will make it a better read.

Much credit for the professionalism of this work must be attributed to Ruth Collins who proofed the book, not only correcting errors but teaching me simultaneously.

I would like to recognize Philip Winter, long time friend and relative who has continued to provide encouragement to me through his kind words regarding my novels.

AUTHOR'S NOTE

Of course, the story is fictional but many of the situations that occur are based on actual happenings. This has been the case in my previous five novels. Living for seventy-four years, is definitely an advantage when it comes to building on past experiences.

I do not mention the name of the town where the story takes place. Being in a sparsely populated area makes it somewhat obvious but still I prefer not to name it. I will say that the setting is in one of the most beautiful regions of the state. The characters, events, and happenings in the story did not originate in the town. The factual parts of the story come from my experiences in other places I have lived and worked.

I need to mention the struggle associated with events in the book. The most concerning, involved parents losing a child. I have a number of friends who have experienced this terrible ordeal and I couldn't help but think it would remind them again of the grief and sorrow they endured. I went so far as to ask one of them if this might be the case. They assured me that it would not. Nevertheless, if such does happen, I apologize.

It was important to me that the story portrays the strength of a woman of faith who refuses to give up. For a long while, I have believed that women, in most instances, are stronger than men in the face of tragedy. More times than not, they will hold the family together.

Being an educator for thirty-four years; first as a teacher-coach and later as a high school principal and finally a superintendent, I was able to add personal experiences. As you read the book and come across unusual behavior of the characters, I'm sure you will think that surely no one would be that unreasonable. Believe me . . . they can be.

Please understand, I could fill up ten books with stories of excellent teachers, wonderful parents, and great board members but that would not be as interesting as the unique ones.

You will probably finish the book, asking why this or that wasn't settled or explained. This is the first novel in another Family Saga. Your questions will be answered in the next book.

LIFE'S LESSONS

I learn, as the years roll onward
And leave the past behind,
That much I counted sorrow
But proves that GOD is kind;
That many a flower I had longed for
Had hidden a thorn of pain,
And many a rugged bypath
Led to fields of ripened grain.

The clouds that cover sunshine
They cannot banish the sun;
And the earth shines out the brighter
When the weary rain is done,
We must stand in the deepest shadow
To see the clearest light;
And often through wrong's own darkness
Comes the very strength of light.

Author Unknown

1

ERIC

July 1976

I had a bad attitude. At least that's what everyone told me. Maybe it was true, but I could care less. The truth was that I was bored out of my mind. School was a bore, my dad was a bore, which is probably why my mother left him. My little brother was a nuisance and got on my nerves with his constant questions. I wanted to be left alone to do my own thing, hang with my friends or whatever.

Now, traveling to my grandparents, Gavin and Luta Sager, I felt like an inmate being transported from city jail to federal prison. After a half dozen calls from the principal's office last year, my dad had announced that he was through, giving up. He'd exploded, telling me I was a bad influence on my brother and nothing but trouble. Here I was sentenced—sitting in the front seat of our car, refusing to look at my dad, on the way to nowhere to live with strangers and start my junior year in a school where I didn't know anyone. Hopeless. When I tried to defend myself, his only comment was, "I can't deal with this anymore. Maybe your grandparents can make a difference."

I saw my grandmother several times a year when she came to visit. It had been three years since I'd seen my granddad since that was the last time I'd been to their ranch. He never came with my grandmother when she visited us. They were old and had to be at least fifty. They lived on a ranch, miles from anywhere in far West Texas. On the few trips to visit them, I would count the minutes until we could leave and get back to the city. I called my grandmother Dawn but had no name for my granddad since I had spent so little time around him.

I'd already considered running away and going to New York or Chicago. I could get a job and be free of all this crap. No one would tell me what to do, and I could let my hair grow down to my waist if I wanted.

My dad broke the silence. "I want you to be courteous to your grandparents."

I didn't respond.

"Did you hear me?"

"Yeah."

"I'll call once a week and check on you."

"Don't bother." I looked away from him, seeing only the dwarf mesquite, thick bushes, and cactus of every kind.

"What did you say?"

"I said, don't bother. You're going to be rid of me. That's what you want, isn't it?"

"No. I want you to be a decent human being."

That ended the conversation until we arrived at the entrance to the ranch with the rusty iron arches identifying it as the "Broken Spoke." Dodging cattle in the road we wound our way to the house. The scene before me could've been from an old Western movie—adobe every-thing—hacienda style house, a large courtyard with an old wedding cake-shaped fountain that wasn't working, and a wide veranda shading every room facing the front. Vines with orange bugle-shaped flowers strangled each post. Old stuff. We came to a stop and my dad turned to me. "Please show your grandparents more respect than other adults you've encountered. I'm sure your mother will want to talk with you. You might give her a call when you get settled."

"Why? She left us. Didn't she say something about wanting to start a new life. I'm sure she didn't mean for us to be included."

As we got out of the car, my grandmother came out the antique double doors. Small with short hair, a dark complexion, and a face that seldom smiled, she met us on the steps, giving me a hug. "Eric, welcome to our home. We're so glad to have you as our guest."

Since I didn't know what to say I remained silent. At least she didn't try to kiss me which was the case when I was younger. My granddad wasn't in sight, so I assumed he was taking his nap, like old people do. After hugging my dad, she invited us inside.

"Mom, I hope it's not too much of an inconvenience for you to keep Eric for a while."

"Certainly not. We're looking forward to it. We can always use extra help and its time we got to know our grandson."

"Is Dad around?"

"No. He's working on the fence in the South Pasture. I can't keep him in the house. He's always got to be doing something. He'll come in at sundown."

"Doesn't he have a hired hand?" my dad continued.

She laughed. "Of course not. He's too stubborn and too tight with money. He still sees himself as being thirty instead of sixty."

While they visited my mind wondered. *I'd really messed up causing so much trouble that my dad brought me out here. Maybe if I begged him and promised to be good, he would take me back with him. No, I was too proud and angry at everything to do that. Instead, I would run away at the first opportunity. Why was I this unhappy? I had some friends. I was smart, not having any trouble passing when I applied myself. My dad wasn't rich, but he had a good job and bought me nice clothes and gave me an allowance. To be honest, I didn't like myself very much, especially my appearance. I was overweight, which was an understatement. My nickname, even among my friends, was "Stubby." I hated it. If I was only taller than 5'7" the 200 pounds wouldn't look bad. Maybe 6'3" would be about right for my weight. I'd tried on several occasions to lose weight but had failed.*

My dad interrupted my thoughts. "Eric, let's get your clothes out of the car. I need to start back. It's a good seven-hour drive and that will put me late getting home. I hate to miss seeing Dad, but I can be a long way down the road before he comes in."

"That's fine. I'm sure you'll be coming back often to see Eric and y'all can visit then."

"Don't count on that," I mumbled under my breath.

After we said goodbye, she showed me to my room. The wallpaper of faded pink roses smothered it. Two canopy beds, topped with dingy white fluffy stuff occupied each side of the large window. Of course, she'd given me *their* room.

"Eric, it cools off at night because of our altitude. If you'll raise your window it'll be comfortable. We only have the evaporative unit in the living room."

It was going to have to cool down a lot to be comfortable. There wasn't a television in the room nor a radio. What was I going to do before bedtime at night? This could really be bad. I might go completely nuts sitting and looking at the walls. After she left, I lay down on one of the beds staring at nothing, wondering how I was going to survive this nightmare.

WE WERE SITTING on the veranda watching the hummingbirds attack the orange flowers when my granddad drove up in his pickup. He got out, went around to the passenger door, opened it, and lifted his dog out and put him on the ground. I remembered Max. I would play with him on my few trips to the ranch. He was much different now and as my granddad started toward the house, he limped along behind him, having to stop occasionally.

"What do we have here?" he asked, climbing the steps.

"This is Eric. Your grandson. You remember him."

He stopped, studying me. "I didn't recognize him. It looks like he's been spending too much time at the feed trough."

I didn't respond, resentment rising up consuming me. He was the way I remembered—sarcastic, mean, and angry. I tried not to think what it would be like to spend days, maybe months at this place. That wasn't going to happen. I would run away from all of this and they would be sorry.

"Why don't y'all just sit out on the porch and visit while I get supper? It shouldn't be long and will give you time to get acquainted."

Great. How could my day get any worse? She went into the house leaving us alone staring at each other. My granddad was short and stocky with a face that looked as if it had been chiseled out of stone. He wore Levis tucked into his cowboy boots and a shabby hat which he took off and dropped beside him. His gray hair was short—what we called a burr. He took out a cigar, licked around it from tip to end and struck a match against his jeans, lighting it. He sat there, glaring at me, holding the cigar in the center of his mouth, like a baby sucking on a pacifier.

I took it as long as possible before breaking the silence. "Do you smoke many cigars?"

He shifted the cigar to the side of his mouth. "All I want."

"I don't plan on being here long."

He removed the cigar from his mouth and looked at it. "Luta didn't tell me you were coming. Why're you here? In trouble with the law?"

"No, I had problems at school." I chose not to reveal any details.

"What kind of problems?"

"I didn't like anything about school. It sucked. I was bored, and everyone said I was a troublemaker. I could care less about what anyone thought. My dad gave up on me. Said y'all might do better."

Without responding, he rose and went into the house. Max who'd been sitting beside him, came over to me. It was obvious he was old with gray whiskers, and knots on his legs. I rubbed him on the head and he lay down at my feet and whined softly as if in pain.

"Eric, supper's ready," my grandmother announced through the open door.

The wooden table was large for three people and contained a ham, with a bowl of black-eyed peas along with mashed potatoes and a loaf of bread. I sat down at the opposite end of the table from my granddad who sat at the head and began to fill his plate.

"Gavin, we need to bless the food," my grandmother said.

Frowning, he put the spoon back in the peas.

"Dear Lord, we give thanks for this food and for our grandson who will be a part of our family. We pray that his stay will be a blessing for us as well as for him. Amen."

I was determined not to eat very much, but the ham and peas were so good a second helping couldn't be resisted. I was able to pass on the banana pudding for dessert. Conversation was sparse during the meal, and I was surprised at how much my granddad ate. After he'd finished his banana pudding he pushed back from the table and lit the cigar that supper had interrupted. He looked at me directly. "What're you going to call me?"

Caught by surprise, I didn't know what to say. Finally, "Granddad" came out.

"I don't like it. Try something else." He stared right through me.

I looked at my grandmother, who was frowning and shaking her head. "Gavin, please don't be like that."

"Well, I have a right to be called something better than Granddad."

At that time, I could think of several words that would fit him. Old Fart came to mind as a likely name. "What would you like me to call you?"

"My name's Gavin. That'll do fine. I don't remember what you called your grandmother."

"Dawn," I said.

"Oh, Eric, I love that name. Remember, you got the idea out of a book you read?"

"That's settled then. It's time for the news. I need to see what they say about the presidential election. After that it's *Rich Man-Poor Man*. You help Luta with the dishes."

After he left my grandmother commenced to defend him. "Eric, please understand, he's not a bad person. Gavin has never gotten over the tragedy. He's a kind man but hides it well. Let's get the dishes done, and we should have time to watch TV with your granddad."

She washed and I dried, and within a short time, we had joined the old geezer to watch television. He'd lit a fresh cigar and the room was foggy, with visibility limited. My dad didn't smoke, and I wasn't used to the odor, finding it difficult to breathe. I didn't watch any of the mini-series even though my dad and little brother never missed them. They were corny, and I considered them beneath my intelligence. My friends and I made fun of them. Halfway into the show, I went to my room. I was forced to be here but not to watch their stupid shows.

I unpacked my suitcase and hung up my clothes. I laid some pajamas on one of the beds and went to the bathroom to run water in the tub. I preferred a shower but one was not available. Removing my clothes, I looked in the mirror, hoping to see a thinner me. Instead, I looked the same as last night. I tried to suck in my stomach and expand my chest to create a smaller waist. It didn't work. The image seemed even more ridiculous. I'd let my hair grow long, which was another problem at school. It was over my ears and covered up the collars of my shirts. I'd been sent home from school a number of times and told not to come back until my hair length complied with the dress code. The last time the principal brought me to his office to address this issue, I argued with him. "Jesus had long hair and it was fine with everyone." That didn't go over well.

My friends and I pushed the limits on everything at school involving rules, including shirt tails, t-shirts with wording, hair, tardiness, and absences. Our school was large enough our schedules were arranged to keep us separated. That didn't prevent us from being together at lunch, between classes, and before school. Some would call us a gang—six of us who delighted in disturbance.

Of course, with my weight, girls paid little or no attention to me. Besides, I wasn't a jock so that contributed to their avoidance of me. I'd never been on a date and never danced with a girl. That was not a big deal for me. Why would I care about what they thought of me?

Finishing my bath and going back into my bedroom, I noticed it was still warm, so I opened the window about halfway up. Having nothing else to do, I went to bed. I lay there for what seemed like hours before going to sleep.

I woke up some time in the early morning, freezing. I closed the window, went back to bed, and before dozing off, thought, *no one should have to go through this nightmare.*

2

LUTA

R*ich Man-Poor Man* came to an end, leaving you hanging and anticipating the next show. When Gavin rose to leave the room, I knew something needed to be said before it was too late.

"Gavin, please listen to me a minute."

He turned with a scowl, sitting back down. "What?"

"We have a chance to help Cameron with his son. He'd have never brought him to us if he wasn't desperate. Cameron is your only son, and Eric is your grandson. You need to do everything possible to help him. It's obvious that Eric has problems. I believe that deep down he could be a good boy with some help."

"Has Cameron ever been around when we needed him? Now he shows up asking for our help with a troubled kid that he's given up on. Don't lecture me about what we need to do."

"Would you at least try? Take him with you tomorrow when you go to work. Give him some responsibility. You might be surprised at how he reacts."

"He's just a fat kid who's probably never broken a sweat. He'd just get in my way. Maybe even hurt himself."

I pleaded. "Please, Gavin. I don't ask for much. Do this for me."

Without responding, he got up and left the room. At least he didn't say no. Gavin could be a challenge most of the time. It took all my willpower, with the help of much prayer to maintain my sanity. He'd never understood that I also grieved. He withdrew into himself, not seeing anyone else's suffering. He'd become angry, consumed with self-pity, and remained that way. He'd not been in a church for years.

The only affection he showed was toward his dog. Now, Max was living out his last few days, and Gavin was not going to have him. I shuddered to think what that would do to him. I know he'd thought about it, but we never talked about the inevitable.

There were a few times when we relived happier memories. Gavin would seem to forget his sorrow, talking openly of specific happenings on the ranch. Then as suddenly as it began, it ended, with him drawing back into his shell. I'd tried everything from encouraging him to take a trip and get away from the ranch, to going to church with me. His response was to retreat even more, seldom going to town, and not attending any social events. The word that came to mind, not even strong enough to describe him, was recluse.

Gavin had been totally different when we married. He was jolly and fun loving, always making jokes and causing those around him to laugh. That's what attracted me to him when we first met. He did day work for my dad, Samuel Marin, along with other ranchers in the region. After finishing high school in 1937 when I was sixteen, we were married. My parents were not too happy about me marrying someone who was five years older and didn't have a steady job. However, it was impossible not to like him, and my dad came to depend on him more and more as he grew older.

Cameron was born in 1939. By the time he was a teenager, his dad had him doing a man's work. He was a handsome boy and a good athlete. His hair was dark like mine and he made a good looking man. Cameron was an immaculate dresser—always neat but never in cowboy attire.

The twins were born six years later in 1945. Macy and Stacy, were beautiful little girls and Gavin was totally different with them. From the beginning it was obvious to everyone that he was partial to the girls. I tried to tell him, first in a subtle way and later in an outright manner. He tried but to no avail. Cameron was ignored much of the time and always in the presence of the twins.

Cameron wanted no part of a life on the ranch. He finished college with a business degree and was a CPA in San Antonio. I thought he and his dad might become closer but that wasn't the case. In fact, they seemed to drift further apart. Of course, with the strained relationship throughout his life with his dad, he became a mother's boy. We talked at least once a week, and I'd make several trips to San Antonio a year to be with him and his family.

Several years after the tragedy, I considered leaving Gavin. I'd given up on him returning to even a semblance of himself. About that time, I became more active in our church and started attending a women's Sunday school class. Several of the ladies in the class became close friends, and giving up on my marriage ceased to be an option. The church family became a refuge, an escape from the unhappiness.

Gavin was never mean to me, only withdrawing into a world of sorrow, depression, and self-pity. I was glad to have Eric here. At least it would break the day-to-day monotony. Maybe we could help him and hopefully it would be good for us. At least we could try.

I watched *Johnny Carson* before going to my room. Sixteen years ago, Gavin had trouble sleeping, and suggested that I occupy another bedroom. From that time on we had slept separately. We did share the same bathroom, and he always went to bed before me, so it was available by the time I retired for the night.

Now, studying myself in the bathroom mirror, I was showing my age. My hair had started turning gray after that horrible night in 1960 and now at fifty-five, it was totally white. My most positive quality in my estimation was my complexion—smooth and dark, an inheritance from my ancestors, who had migrated from Spain in the previous century. The ranch, which contained over a hundred sections, was purchased by my granddad in 1880. He'd been a prosperous trader in Spain and came to America with the sole purpose of buying land. He told us many stories of buffalo and encounters with Indians. His favorite story retold a meeting with John Wesley Hardin in El Paso, the infamous gunfighter who supposedly killed over forty men.

I loved this ranch, and it was sad to see it not being used to its fullest. We only ran 200 mother cows and most years would purchase a hundred or so yearlings. At one time a half dozen cowboys worked on the ranch with five times the cattle. Gavin only stocked the ranch with what he could take care of, not wanting anyone else around. I hadn't pushed the issue because we were still able to make a decent living.

MY ALARM WENT off the next morning at 5:30. That enabled me to fix Gavin's breakfast and allow him to leave the house close to seven o'clock, which was good daylight. He was already up, sitting at the kitchen table, drinking coffee.

I went over and kissed him on the cheek, hoping to start the day on a positive note. "Good morning, what's on your agenda today?"

"More fence work."

"Have you given any more thought to my request?"

"Some."

"And?"

"I'll give it a try for one day. If it turns out like I think, no more."

"Thank you." I sighed with relief, appreciating even a small victory.

"You better get him up. I'm leaving after breakfast for an early start to a busy day."

I left immediately. I couldn't press my good fortune. He might change his mind. I knocked before entering, but Eric was still asleep. I went over to his bed and touched him lightly on the shoulder. "Eric, it's time to get up. You're going with Gavin today."

He moaned and turned over, covering his head with a pillow.

I shook him by the shoulder and repeated my previous statement. "Get up sleepy head. I'll have breakfast for you by the time you brush your teeth, and get dressed."

"Do I hafta?"

"Yes. Get a move on. As John Wayne would say, 'It's burning daylight.' "

I went back to the kitchen, hoping he would comply with my order, telling Gavin, "He'll be in shortly."

"I wouldn't count on it."

By the time breakfast was on the table, he hadn't shown up. I said the blessing, which I always insisted on doing, and we began eating. Midway through the meal, Eric came in, still looking half asleep. I put his plate of eggs, bacon, potatoes, and toast on the table, and without saying a word, he started eating. I kind of expected a "thank you" but maybe that would come later.

Gavin stopped eating and glared at him. "When's the last time you had a haircut?"

Instead of answering, he shrugged his shoulders, continuing to eat. He hadn't combed his hair and it was sticking out in all directions. This was going to be a challenge.

Max was lying by Gavin's chair, and he gave him half a piece of leftover toast. After that, he got up and headed for the bathroom. I held my breath, hoping he wouldn't change his mind about taking Eric.

"Eric, you do what Gavin tells you today and be nice."

He slurred with a mouthful of food. "Just like him, huh?"

"You're going to be here a while, so it would be better for you to make an effort to get along with your granddad."

Reaching for the last piece of toast, he didn't respond to my observation. He was putting a heavy layer of butter on it when Gavin came back.

"Time to go. If I'm going to feed you, maybe I can get a little work out of you. Bring the toast."

I followed them out onto the porch and watched as Gavin picked up Max and put him in the pickup. Eric squeezed in beside him. Max had always ridden in the front of the pickup, even when he was younger and could've ridden in the back. As they drove off, I prayed aloud. "Please God, for both their sakes, let this be a positive experience."

FRANK

"How much farther is it?" grumbled Riley, reaching from the backseat for her mother's Texas map.

"Maybe an hour or so." I tried to locate her in my rearview mirror.

"We've been driving for hours," wailed Aubrey, continuing to cry off and on clutching a stuffed bulldog mascot from her previous school.

"Girls, you need to be patient. We're going to a new home, and I'm excited about beginning an adventure," said their mother.

The new home and adventure my wife referred to was a small town in far West Texas where I'd been hired as the high school principal. It would be the first time we'd moved in the last six years. That was time enough for Aubrey, my thirteen-year-old daughter, to make friends she wasn't happy about leaving. I'd been passed over for a principal's position for the second time and realized it was time to move on.

The job came open late, and I decided it would be better than staying where I had no future. I'd come out alone and interviewed along with one other applicant. They offered me the job before I left, assuring me there would be an aide's position for Julie. Also, being in a remote area, they had school housing which was a big plus. The school was about one-fourth the size of my previous one and the salary was less than half. However, I couldn't be choosy this late in the year. Somehow, we would make out, and I'd be doing what I loved. Another perk was that it was so close to school starting, they agreed to pay a mover. The van would arrive tomorrow towing my old truck. For tonight, we'd brought our sleeping bags prepared to camp out.

WE ARRIVED at our new home late that afternoon. I had a key to the wooden frame house which consisted of three small bedrooms, one bath, a kitchen, and a den area. I guessed it to be about 1100 square feet. We'd left a 2000 square foot brick home with central air and heat. Silence followed a brief inspection.

Finally, Julie spoke. "We'll make it work. Won't we girls?"

"Sure, it's not that bad." Riley moved over and put her arm around Aubrey.

"I'll tell you what. Let's go get dinner at that little place on main street we passed," I suggested.

"Good idea." My wife was doing her best to lead the family toward a more positive outlook.

"I'm not hungry." Aubrey plopped down on the wooden floor.

"I'll stay here with Aubrey if she doesn't want to go," volunteered Riley.

"No," Julie intervened. "She can go and watch us eat."

It was six in the evening and virtually no activity in town. The few shops had closed and main street was vacant of cars and people. The Frontier Cafe, located at the edge of town had several customers.

"What's making that sound?" Riley asked, as we exited the car.

I answered. "Coyotes." Proof we're out in the middle of nowhere, I thought.

We found the Frontier Cafe to be a friendly place, and the food was good. Aubrey ended up eating after all. When we finished, our next stop was the high school which once again brought silence. It was small compared to what we'd left. The football stadium seemed even smaller with stands occupying only one side. The field itself had more weeds than grass and was in need of attention. No one could think of anything positive to say, not even Julie. The silence continued.

Driving around for another few minutes we saw what there was to see, which wasn't much. The highlight of the day was the sunset. Mountains and a few clouds in the west enhanced the most beautiful sunset I'd ever seen. You could visualize a cowboy galloping into it. We all got out of the car, except Aubrey who proclaimed she didn't want to be eaten by wolves. From there we drove back to an empty house, void of a television or even a radio. The electricity and water had been turned on which Julie proclaimed to be a plus. We unloaded our meager belongings, including our sleeping bags.

Julie was upbeat as usual. "Tomorrow we'll get back to normal with the arrival of our furniture and clothes."

"You brought your tennis rackets, didn't you?" asked Riley, unzipping her sleeping bag.

"Sure, but I need some balls." Aubrey continued to whine not offering to help.

"We'll find a store tomorrow, buy tennis balls, and I'll give you some practice." Riley had joined her mother in trying to create a more upbeat atmosphere.

Many parents believed they had perfect kids but Riley had to be as close as they came. She was positive about everything. She was an excellent student, loved by her teachers, played basketball and received praise from her coach, and never complained. She seldom missed church and was active in the youth group, teaching the class when the instructor was absent. Her mother and I were amazed that we could raise such a wonderful child.

On the other hand, Aubrey proved to be a challenge. Maybe we should assume part of the responsibility. She'd been beautiful from the time she was a baby, with everyone carrying on over her and telling her how cute and charming she was. Being the second child, we let things go instead of correcting her, assuming she'd eventually be like her older sister. Not so. Of course, we loved her, but she definitely made it more difficult with her attitude. One positive was the fact she liked tennis which occupied a great deal of her time and used up some negative energy that usually went toward complaining.

We went to bed early with everyone sleeping in the den on the floor. I lay there wondering if I'd done the right thing by bringing my family to the jumping-off place to satisfy my ambition. My goal was to one day be a school superintendent but before that I needed a principal's position. Maybe staying here, a year or two, would allow me to take my family back to civilization. I went to sleep hoping tomorrow would be a brighter day.

THE NEXT MORNING, after going to a donut shop and getting breakfast for my wife and girls, I went to the superintendent's office. His secretary welcomed me with a smile and said she would tell Mr. Cleburne I was here. She returned and informed me to go in that he was expecting me.

Rising, he came around his desk to shake my hand. "Good morning. Did you get settled in?"

"Not yet. My furniture should be here this afternoon."

"Ready to go to work?"

"Yes, sir. I imagine the first thing is to fill the staff if we have any vacancies."

"Unfortunately, we have several. Recruitment is a major challenge for us. The pay isn't good and we're remote. Most young people want to be closer to populated areas. We have to be careful not to accept just anyone. We've hired some real duds in the past out of desperation."

"What openings do we have at the high school?"

"Two positions. We need an English teacher who is willing to coach UIL events and do the One-Act Play. Our last teacher quit because she claimed it was too heavy a load. We also have a coach's position open who must teach math. That's going to be a tough one. We have less than 150 students in high school and are limited with flexibility when hiring staff. You might get with Coach Estates and see what can be done to fill this position."

"I'll get right on it. Where's the best area for finding teachers?" I asked.

"Of course, we're not far from Sul Ross at Alpine, and we've hired some good graduates from UT at El Paso. You can check with our Region 18 Service Center which is located in Midland. It's extremely difficult to hire experienced teachers because of our pay scale. We offer school housing which is a lifesaver for us."

"Is Coach Estates around?" I wanted to meet him and see if he had a lead on a coach.

"Should be. He works on the grounds during the summer. I imagine you can find him near the stadium today. It's been dry and our field is in bad shape. The secretary will get you a set of school and office keys.

"Frank, I'm glad to have you. I know this is a remote place, but you'll find the people for the most part, are friendly. Of course, most towns this size have a power structure. We have a number of ranches that have been here for a century. They like to think they run things, and we have to humor them somewhat but it usually works out. If you'll come by we'll have coffee, and I'll get you up-to-date on happenings in the school and community."

AFTER GETTING MY KEYS, I walked over to the high school to inspect my office. Sitting at my desk, doubt arose again, if I'd made the right decision. My pride had been hurt when I was passed over for a younger man. I'd never been promised anything but had assumed if the principal left; the job would be mine. Now here I was, about to assume a job with less money, much smaller than my previous school, and out in the middle of nowhere. Too late now. Those doubts should've come earlier. Julie was so supportive she'd never have objected to moving. She'd been promised an aide's position, but I was hoping she could find a better-paying job in the community. At least we had a rent-free place to live which didn't put pressure on us to sell our previous house. We also had some equity built up in our house so that would help us financially when we sold it. However, we were sacrificing a lot in the quality of the home we were moving into. I couldn't help but feel guilty about that.

My office was just inside the building, and a knock disturbed my thoughts. Going to the door, I found it was Riley and Aubrey. "Come in girls. What's going on?"

"Dad, can you believe there're no tennis balls in town. We checked the grocery and hardware store. I can't believe this." Aubrey collapsed into the nearest chair.

"Come with me." I locked the door behind us. We found Coach Estates on the football field, hooking joints of pipe together to begin watering. He was young, maybe thirty. He stopped working and met us.

"Coach, I'm Frank Mendenhall and these are my daughters, Riley and Aubrey."

"Very glad to meet you. Welcome to West Texas." He smiled, shaking my hand.

Aubrey giggled and stepped forward, offering her hand.

"Coach, my daughters want to play tennis, and they can't seem to find any balls in town."

"Sure, I can help. Let's go over to the field house. I bet we can rustle up some."

A few minutes later he presented the girls with half a dozen. "I apologize for the tennis courts. I haven't gotten to them yet. Weeds have grown up in the cracks and the nets are sagging something terrible. In the next several days, I'll try to get them cleaned up."

"That's no problem. The way I play, the condition of the courts makes little difference." Riley bumped her racket against her leg.

"Do you not have any help?" I asked.

"No. I'm it in the summer. The three custodians are doing inside repair work and painting some of the classrooms. The grounds are not a priority when school's not in session."

"We'll let you get back to work. Come by my office when you get a chance, and we'll talk about your coaching vacancy."

"Sounds good. Glad to meet you and your daughters."

When we were out of hearing distance, Aubrey asked, "Can girls play football? He's cute!"

"Don't be silly, Aubrey." Riley laughed, reaching over and giving her a gentle shove.

"You've got to admit it, Riley. He's cute."

"Okay. I'll admit it."

Thank goodness the mood was better today. When the furniture arrived and we were situated it should improve even more. I was impressed with Coach Estates. I'd found in my administrative duties that when you needed something done, coaches did more than their part. The fact he was working in the summer was another reason to be impressed.

AT MIDAFTERNOON the van arrived with our belongings. We'd begun unloading when Coach Estates showed up and offered to help. We received more assistance from Aubrey than at any other time I could remember.

4

ERIC

We hadn't gone a hundred yards from the house when he fired up a cigar. I started choking, rolling down my window. It didn't seem to bother Max, who was squeezed in between us. Gavin didn't say anything. We drove for several miles and the silence continued. I guessed it was going to be up to me to start the conversation.

"What're we going to do today?"

"Fence work." He mumbled, not taking the cigar from his mouth.

Arriving at our destination, he removed two items from the bed of the truck. "Do you know what these are?"

"Post hole diggers. My dad has some that he used to dig holes for a new gate at home." Maybe that would impress him.

"Do you know how to use them?"

"Sure. Nothing to it."

"If the ground needs loosening, you can use this bar to do that. I've marked half a dozen places where we need to put new posts. The holes need to be eight inches wide and twenty-four inches deep. I've marked a spot on the handles of your diggers that you need to reach for each hole. Do you understand?"

"Yeah. After I finish, what's next?"

He just looked at me and smiled for the first time. "You can sit down and rest until I come back for you at noon. Should be about four hours. I have some gloves for you in the pickup."

"That's okay. I won't need them."

"Suit yourself." Going to his truck, he left.

Picking up the post hole diggers I lifted them as high as possible before bringing them down, expecting penetration into the ground, but I only received a jolt. Looking down, maybe they'd gone an inch deep. I tried again with the same results. I exchanged the diggers for the bar and drove it into the ground a number of times, loosening the dirt. Using the diggers, I removed two inches from my hole. An hour later, I'd completed the first hole and celebrated by throwing up my breakfast. I sat down, exhausted, nauseated, and trembling. I was sick and weak. Maybe I was going to die. The sun was getting hot, and I was thirsty. He hadn't left me any water. He probably wanted me to die. Then, I was angry. I would show him! I got to my knees and stood up.

The next hole took me two hours. My hands were solid blisters and I realized that was it. I couldn't do any more. I lay down on the ground. *My dad won't even miss me when I'm gone. I can just see him answering the phone when he gets the news, and saying, "It doesn't surprise me. I didn't expect him to make it."*

I had to get back to the house. Rising, I started in that direction stumbling more than walking. Every few yards, I'd stop and try to throw up but my stomach was empty and only liquid appeared. How far was it? Could I make it? If I could just make it, my grandmother would take care of me. What was it I was supposed to call her? I fell, hitting the ground hard.

Someone shook me. "Get up. It's time for dinner. What're you doing wandering around? You only got two holes done."

THE NEXT THING I remember someone was putting me in bed, with a cold rag on my forehead and telling me everything was going to be all right. I slept all afternoon and waking, had trouble remembering what'd happened. When it came to me, I resumed my resolve to run away.

My grandmother came in just as I was about to try and get up. "Time for supper, Eric. You need to eat so you can get your strength back."

"I'm not hungry. Could you bring me some tea? I'll stay in my room."

"Okay, but if you get hungry later, let me know. I can heat you a plate."

After she'd brought me a glass of tea and left, I made it to the bathroom. The image staring at me in the mirror looked horrible. I couldn't do this again. It would kill me. I'd run away tonight, but I was too tired. Gavin must've loved seeing me suffer. I hated him. He was just plain mean. He had no right to be the way he was even if he was suffering, as Dawn had said. I'd call my dad tomorrow and demand to come home, telling him I'd have a better attitude. He'd have to come to get me—to save me.

After a hot bath, I returned to my bedroom, finding another large glass of iced tea on the long desk between the beds. I was beginning to feel like surviving might be possible. I drank the tea and went to bed, falling asleep immediately.

I WOKE up to my grandmother shaking me. "Get up, I have breakfast ready. You need to eat and get your strength back."

"I'm not hungry. Bring me something to drink."

"No. That won't work. You need to come in and sit at the table with us. Now get up and wash your face and hands, and we'll eat when you get to the table."

She left and I crippled into the bathroom, my body aching with every move. The mirror informed me my looks hadn't improved. I ran water on my hands which burned because of the blisters. I washed my face, dried off, and limped into the kitchen. The sausage and eggs didn't appeal to me in the least. All I wanted was something to drink.

"Would you like to say the blessing, Eric?" she asked.

"No."

After the prayer, they began filling their plates, but I only sipped my water. "I'm not hungry. Maybe I'll feel like eating later."

"You better eat. It's a long time till dinner, and we have a lot of work to do. We've got to feed today. It's dry and I cake the cattle every other day. After that, you still have four more post holes to dig." Gavin was apparently enjoying my future suffering.

I left the table, went into the den, picked up the phone, and put a call in to my dad. When he answered, I immediately began to plead my case. "I can't stay here another day! Please come after me. I promise to do better."

"No, Eric. I can't come now. I'll think about it and call you back in a couple of days."

I waited for him to continue, but there was only silence. "Please. I'll do better."

"I can't take off today, Eric. Maybe later but I'm not sure you're sincere about changing. Your little brother has been a different person with you gone. You'll be all right with my mom and dad. Just do what they say."

"But Dad, Gavin is trying to kill me! I can't stay here."

He laughed. "I lived and worked with him for eighteen years, and he didn't kill me."

"It's not funny. I can't believe you're laughing." I slammed the phone down.

Returning to the kitchen, I sat down, and put a small helping of eggs, one sausage, and a piece of toast on my plate. I ate my breakfast lost in my thoughts, reasoning, *I have no choice. Maybe, I can survive until my strength returns and then run away.*

TODAY STARTED out like yesterday with cigar smoke and silence. However, when we drove off it was in a different direction. We reached a cattle guard and after crossing it, he began honking his horn, continuing to drive. Cattle began to appear out of nowhere until we had a large group following the slow moving truck. Gavin reached down, pulled a lever, and something began dropping on the ground from the big can in the back.

"What's that?" I asked.

"Range cubes or cake."

By the time we'd gone farther into the pasture, a large group of cows with calves lined the road.

"That should be just about it. Now we go to work."

I didn't know what he meant by "we." I hadn't seen him do anything. Arriving at the dreaded site, I had a feeling of panic and dread, mingled with anger. He was going to leave me again.

"Well, here we are. I'll be back to pick you up in time for dinner." No doubt but what he was enjoying himself, expecting me to suffer again.

"Do you still have the gloves?"

Reaching under the seat, he brought out the gloves and gave them to me.

I got out of the pickup with the jar of water my grandmother had fixed for me and watched him drive off. Plopping down on the ground, I imagined what I'd be doing if at home. Looking at my watch, it was eight o'clock. I'd probably still be in bed until at least nine o'clock, at which time I would go to the kitchen, get several donuts Dad usually bought for breakfast, and move to the den to watch television. I'd wash down the donuts with a Dr. Pepper. After that I would relax, lying on the couch for the next couple of hours. I'd then meet several of my friends for a Number 1 at the McDonald's located three blocks from my house. The Big Mac, fries, and a large Dr. Pepper went down easy, topped off many days by a banana split. After lunch, we just hung out at someone's house, listening to music by the Bee Gees, Earth Wind and Fire, Van Halen and other popular groups. I'd be home by the time my dad and little brother arrived in the evening. My little brother, Ethan, who was six, attended a summer day care center.

My attention returned to the post hole diggers lying a few feet from me. I needed a plan to survive. I'd work for fifteen minutes and then rest for fifteen minutes. If I didn't finish, at least maybe there wouldn't be a repeat of yesterday. I wouldn't get in a hurry. I put on my gloves, picked up the diggers and marked the hole. I then used the bar to loosen the ground. I cleaned the dirt out of the hole and repeated the process half a dozen times, working slow but deliberate. After fifteen minutes, I sat down, took off my gloves and inspected my hands. Some of the soreness was gone, but they were bleeding.

I alternated between working and resting the remainder of the morning and finished all four holes. I couldn't believe I'd done it without getting sick. My plan had worked. I sat down and waited for Gavin to return. I didn't have long until he drove up, stepped out of his truck and walked over to inspect the holes. Max stayed in the truck. He took out a tape and measured them, not saying anything. After going to each hole, he started back toward his truck. I couldn't believe it. He wasn't going to say anything about my work.

He turned and looked at me. "Let's go. Get a move on. Dinner will be ready."

I followed him to the truck, angry. He could've at least acknowledge my efforts. Why should I expect anything? I was stupid, thinking he would say anything good about me.

Lunch was on the table when we arrived. I placed a moderate amount of roast and potatoes on my plate. I still wasn't very hungry. I noticed when I sat down it wasn't necessary to unfasten the top button on my jeans to give my stomach more room.

The next several days followed the same pattern, except I gave up trying to talk to Gavin. He gave me more post holes to dig and drove off in his pickup, returning in four hours. I paced myself and was able to accomplish more each day. We didn't take off Saturday like most people.

SUNDAY CAME and Dawn informed me we were going to church. I didn't object, glad to be away from this place for at least a few hours. If the opportunity presented itself, I might run away since we'd be in town. Gavin wasn't going with us and that made it even better. I'd brought a razor I used to shave the peach fuzz that was hardly visible,

hoping one day to have a heavy growth like Magnum on *Magnum PI.*
Putting on my one pair of dress pants that I brought for such an occasion, I discovered they were easier to button.

Joining them in the den, Gavin had only one comment. "You're
going to get a haircut."

5

LUTA

S unday was my favorite day of the week. I looked forward to Sunday school and church. Taking Eric with me, made today even more special. We went in my 1972 Bonneville which at four years old, was in good condition.

"Do you attend church at home?" I asked.

"Sometimes. Not very often. Dad usually plays golf on Sunday and I keep Ethan. Sometimes Dad will drop us off at a movie that's only a mile or so from our house, and we'll walk home."

"I'm proud of you, Eric, for helping Gavin. I know he appreciates it."

"He doesn't tell me if he does. In fact, he seldom says anything."

I moved to another topic. "You look handsome today."

"That's the first time anyone ever told me that."

"Well, you do and believe me, I wouldn't tell you if it wasn't so." How sad no one had ever given him a compliment about how he looked. My heart went out to him. I was going to do everything in my power to see that his self-image improved. I knew deep down he could be a sweet boy.

I attended the First Presbyterian Church and had ever since my childhood. We had an enrollment of seventy-five, however, most

Sundays our attendance was less than half that number. We had a young energetic pastor who I loved. He was positive and his sermons were easy to follow and interesting.

Eric would be in a class for high school students, and it'd give him an opportunity to meet several of his future classmates. I didn't know what to tell him when we drove up in front of the church. Probably the less I said, the better.

"Eric, I'll show you to your class and meet you before church in the sanctuary. Will that be okay?"

"Yeah. How long is class?"

"About forty-five minutes." I hoped he'd enjoy meeting some of the young people in our church.

I ARRIVED at my class wondering if Eric would fit in with the other students. There wasn't time for much thinking, as the first ten minutes was devoted to visiting about the weekly events. After that, the time passed quickly. We had a wonderful teacher who encouraged participation and discussion. Before I knew it, we were in the middle of the closing prayer.

I went to the sanctuary to wait for Eric, anxious to ask him about his class. I was early, and took a seat as people began coming in. With only a few minutes until the service began, I started to panic. Where could he be?

His teacher came in, and I stopped her as she walked by. "Eric was supposed to meet me here. Is he on his way?"

"Eric, left shortly before I did. He's a quiet young man. I tried to involve him in the discussion but wasn't successful."

"This is all new. I'm hoping he'll open up when everything becomes more familiar. Thank you, anyway, for your efforts."

Eric came in as she walked away and sat down without saying anything. "How was class?"

"Boring."

I didn't attempt any more conversation, thinking it would be futile. The sermon was based upon the story of the prodigal son. It was one of my favorite passages in the Bible. After the close of the service, I directed Eric into the line to introduce him to the pastor.

When our turn came the pastor greeted me. "How're you, Luta?"

"Fine. Pastor, this is my grandson, Eric. Eric, this is Pastor Jacob."

"It's good to meet you, Eric. Welcome to our church." Eric accepted the greeting but didn't speak.

"My, you're a big boy. Do you play football?" asked the pastor.

"No."

"You might give it some thought. I'm sure Coach would be glad to have you. From what I've heard, they're going to be short on numbers this year."

Eric didn't respond, and after telling the pastor I enjoyed the sermon, we moved on out the door.

On the drive home, I tried to start a conversation. "Are you going to be hungry today?"

"Not much."

"Do you like fried chicken?"

"It's okay."

"Did you like the pastor?"

"He's okay."

I was determined not to give up on communication. "This football thing sounds like it might be something that would interest you. Your dad played in high school and was good." Silence followed my comment, so I went another direction. "What sport do you like, Eric?"

"None of them."

"What do you and your friends like to do?"

"Hang out."

"Do you spend much time with your dad?"

"No. He doesn't have time for me. If he has a day off from work, he spends it with Ethan."

How sad, I thought. No wonder his self-image was bad. I could see, though, how Eric would not be enjoyable company with his attitude. Working toward a more positive outlook between Gavin and Eric constituted a challenge.

. . .

THE NEXT WEEK, it took all my resolve, to maintain my patience. Eric refused to talk and continued to sulk. Gavin remained the same, criticizing Eric at every opportunity, especially about his long hair. They left every morning with Max between them, came in for dinner, and went back in the afternoon. They arrived at home by sundown. Eric would eat his supper and go to his room. I attempted to get him to watch television with us, but my request was ignored. I did notice he was losing weight. His pants, which had been tight, now were loose and actually becoming baggy.

ON FRIDAY of the second week, as we were eating supper, I asked him about it. "Eric, your pants don't fit well anymore. Would you like to go into town with me tomorrow and get some that fit better? I imagine Gavin would give you a day off."

He smiled. "Yeah. That would be great."

Gavin interrupted. "I was going in tomorrow to buy fifty sacks of range cubs and was counting on Eric to help unload them when we got home."

"We should be home in plenty of time for him to help you. His pants are going to fall off if he doesn't get a size smaller." I was determined that he have some time off and new pants.

"Are you going to get him a haircut while you're in town?"

"I don't know. It depends on what Eric wants to do." Gavin was not going to leave this issue.

"Well, I guess we know how that'll turn out." He rose and left the table, his anger obvious.

Eric actually watched *Sanford and Son*, one of my favorite shows with me before going to his room.

After he left, Gavin came back into the den. "Why're you taking up for that boy? He needs discipline and to respect his elders. That's why he's here—to be taught some manners."

"No. That's not right. He needs some positive attention. To feel good about himself. Being hard on him, will drive him even further away. Isn't he doing better with his work?"

"Well, yeah. I guess so. He was terrible and had to get better. He'd never done a minute's worth of work."

"Gavin, have you told him he's doing better?"

"Of course not. He might let up and take advantage of me if I did."

"Gavin, what's your relationship with your only son like?"

"Terrible. We don't get along."

"Eric's relationship with his dad isn't good. Do you want that to continue into the type of feelings that exist between you and Cameron?"

Instead of answering my question, he got up and left the room. After sixteen years his anger and self-pity was getting old. Enough-is-enough and my patience was wearing thin. He should see what was happening and help me with Eric instead of creating more damage. I hoped and prayed he would return, at least to a semblance of his old self. If anything, he seemed to be getting worse.

EACH DAY MAX BECAME WEAKER. Gavin had to carry him up the steps when he came home in the evening. When the old dog carried the small rubber ball he once chased with such joy around with him, it required all my willpower to stop the tears. He'd been a wonderful companion for Gavin as well as myself. I dreaded thinking what Gavin's reaction would be when he was gone.

6

FRANK

I went to work immediately looking for prospects to fill our two vacancies at the high school. Of all positions, these two would be the most difficult to fill. Coaches that taught math were scarce to say the least. Teachers willing to take on the challenge of English classes, plus coaching UIL, including the One-Act Play, would be difficult to find. Also, I wanted a good theater teacher and not just someone to fill the position. I contacted the service center in Midland and asked them to post the vacancies. I placed ads in the Alpine, Midland, Odessa, and El Paso newspapers. While I waited on a response, the class schedule for the coming year kept me busy. With a limited faculty, it was a challenge to offer more than the required course offerings.

My secretary was off this month and would start back the first of August. She did come in for introductions and a visit my second day on the job. She was about my age and very outgoing and pleasant. I'd already heard good things about her from the superintendent and Coach Estates. When I told her about my wife looking for a job, she informed me that the local bank had an opening. After she left, I immediately went to our house telling my wife, since we didn't have our phone connected yet. I went back to work and she left for the bank.

. . .

THE NEXT TWO weeks I interviewed two prospects for the coaching and math position but had no response to the English vacancy. Neither one of the coaching applicants were acceptable. One was an older man who had been in half a dozen schools the last ten years, which raised all kinds of red flags. When I checked his references my suspicions were confirmed. The other one was fresh out of college which was fine, but there was something about him that made Coach Estates and me uncomfortable. Maybe it was the fact that he talked so much about himself. Anyway, we decided to keep trying even though time was running out.

The girls had settled in and had already made several friends. Julie had interviewed for the job at the bank but hadn't heard anything. We were keeping our fingers crossed it would work out. Our realtor called and she had shown our house several times, but no offers were forthcoming.

Good fortune came out of nowhere when a local boy, graduating from Sul Ross, called Coach Estates and inquired about the coaching position. He didn't have a math certification but had majored in science. Coach knew the young man and said he was solid and would like to have him. At this late date, it wouldn't be a problem to obtain a temporary math certificate for him.

I interviewed him the next day and was impressed. I offered him the job before he left my office. Coach Estates, who was present, stayed to visit.

"Mr. Mendenhall, I'm worried about the coming season. We were thin anyway, and now I've lost two more players to injuries this summer. One was in a wreck and broke his arm, the other fell off a hay truck and fractured his ankle. We're down to twenty players if everyone else shows up. Our school has lost population and our freshman and sophomore classes are the smallest in years. Our junior varsity schedule has already been canceled. We have some quality athletes, but we're just so thin."

"What kind of season did you have last year?" I asked.

"We were 5-5 but we lost seven seniors."

"Coach, is there pressure to win here?"

"Not so much. The pressure comes from certain families that feel their kids deserve special attention because they've lived here forever. I'll give you an example. I have a boy who's a senior, and his dad believes he should be the quarterback. I have a sophomore who's a much better athlete. But of course, the senior's dad doesn't see it that way. If I start the sophomore at quarterback, I can expect a great deal of criticism."

"Do you receive support from the administration and school board?"

He hesitated before answering. "Some, but you have to understand that the board members are made up, for the most part, of long time residents. They're reluctant to go against a complaint raised by one of their own. If you and your family haven't lived here for at least forty years you're viewed as a newcomer. That's just the way it is. Mr. Cleburne is a good guy, but he's been here for fifteen years and is reluctant to rock the boat. He's looking at retirement in a few years and that seems to be his priority."

"So you're worried about this quarterback thing?" I asked.

"Yes sir. Something else that compounds the problem is that the sophomore is Hispanic. You'll find that a division remains in the school and community. It's sad and frustrating but true. When we have a school election, such as for class favorites, the vote is nearly always along ethnic lines. The kids are only reflecting the views of their parents. Don't get me wrong. There are many wonderful people that live here who would give you the shirt off their backs. Many Anglos have close Hispanic friends and vise versa. Does this all sound strange to you?"

"Somewhat, however, I do appreciate you sharing this information. All communities have their challenges. Changing the subject, you haven't told me about yourself. Are you married?"

He smiled. "I have a four-year-old, and my wife is expecting in another month. We've only been here for two years. I was determined to get a head coaching job and this was the best I could do. I feel guilty about moving my family out to this remote area. The town doesn't have a hospital which means, when the baby comes, we'll need to travel to Alpine. It's kinda scary."

Listening to Coach explain his dilemma, I could see why the upcoming season made him apprehensive. Coaching football in Texas presented a variety of challenges. If I'd learned anything in my profession the last fifteen years, when it came to their own children, most parents were not objective. Without doubt, the situation here for me as a principal would present some problems. Being an assistant principal in a larger school at my last job, the principal handled the parent complaints. Most of my responsibility dealt with discipline problems that originated in the classroom.

By bringing my family to this remote area to further my career as he had, I was also experiencing guilt. I was thirty-eight years old and my career wasn't moving forward fast enough to suit me so here we were. Coach must have sensed that my thoughts had interrupted the conversation.

"Tell me about yourself, Mr. Mendenhall."

I told him about my family and career, explaining why I'd accepted this position.

"We have some things in common," he said, when I'd finished.

"Yes, it seems so."

"I need to get back to work. I finally watered the football field enough for the grass to become high enough to mow. It's less than a month until two-a-day workouts start. The practice field is in bad shape with little grass, but I haven't had time to spend on it."

After he left, my thoughts returned to how he'd described the superintendent. If I'd known the situation, would I have taken the job? It was too late to wonder about that now. Maybe his observation wasn't accurate, but not likely. Even though I'd spent little time with Coach Estates, I trusted him. Anyway, I needed to get my mind on the coming year and finding an English teacher to complete my staff.

WHEN I ARRIVED at home for lunch, Julie was beside herself with excitement. She'd received a call from the bank president asking her to meet with him at one o'clock this afternoon. If she did get the job it would take pressure off us financially and improve our morale.

Riley and Aubrey were home and aware of the good news. Riley expressed her excitement to us, but Aubrey talked about the boys she'd met at the tennis courts this morning. Her mother and I had discussed this potential problem just last night. Aubrey would be fourteen in two weeks, but she could have easily passed for sixteen. In fact, many people thought she was older than Riley. She'd always been a beautiful girl and unlike many her age hadn't gone through an awkward stage. Boys had already begun to pay attention to her which she welcomed. We'd never experienced this problem with Riley even though she'd always been a pretty girl. She was much thinner than Aubrey and late maturing. Whereas Aubrey had long blond curly hair, Riley wore her dark hair short. Aubrey's complexion was light, and Riley's took after her mother's darker skin. They didn't look anything like sisters.

In our discussion, we arrived at the conclusion that Aubrey wouldn't be allowed to date until she was fifteen. We knew she'd have ample opportunity before that and wouldn't like our decision. However, we were together on the issue and going to stand firm. Trying to be optimistic, we were hoping the issue wouldn't come up any time soon. She would be in the eighth grade this year.

We'd never had this talk about Riley. She dated a few times during her sophomore year but wasn't that interested in boys. She loved basketball and was a starter on the junior varsity team last year. She was more athletic than Aubrey and not nearly as concerned about her looks. Aubrey's only interest in sports was tennis.

I left for work after lunch and Julie headed for the bank, promising to let me know what happened. When I entered my office, the phone was ringing. Picking up, a voice said, "Mr. Mendenhall?"

"Yes, this is he."

"This is Paul Kelly and I'm calling about the opening you have for an English teacher. Is the position still available?"

"Yes. Definitely."

"I just graduated in May, and I'm looking for a job. I actually prefer theater, but my teaching field does include English."

Was I dreaming? "Mr. Kelly, would you like to come for an interview?"

"Sure. When would you like me to come?"

"As soon as possible. Where are you now?" I asked.

"In the Austin area. Today is Wednesday. Would Friday work?"

"Perfect. I'll be in my office until four-thirty. Can you make it by then?"

"I think so. It's a long way, but I can drive part of the way tomorrow and the rest of the way Friday.

"I look forward to meeting you, Mr. Kelly." I hung up the phone.

I couldn't sit here and not share the good news with someone. I left immediately, headed to the bank to wait for Julie to complete her meeting. I arrived and took a seat in the lobby. I didn't have long to wait and the huge smile as she came to meet me, told the story.

"Celebration is in order. Let's go to The Drug Store and you can treat me to a banana split."

Leaving the building, I held the door open for an older woman coming inside, who looked at me and asked, "Are you the new high school principal?"

"Yes ma'am, I am. My name's Frank Mendenhall."

She frowned. "Agnes Brossard, I teach in elementary."

"Glad to meet you, Mrs. Brossard. This is my wife, Julie. We're pleased to be here, and everything seems to be working out for us."

"Well, don't get too comfortable. Around here high school principals don't last long." She turned and continued into the bank.

7

ERIC

Attending church with Dawn wasn't bad. I had to admit she was nice and treated me better than anyone ever had, but after Sunday school I still thought about running away. In fact, I'd gone to the car before I met her in the church, to see if she'd left her keys. Strangely, I wasn't that disappointed to find she'd removed them.

The next week repeated the one before—monotony. I was up to digging ten post holes a day. Every other day we would feed. He had me driving his truck the second week while he puffed on his cigar. His truck was an automatic so I had no trouble. The only time he spoke to me was to criticize. He never let up on my hair, constantly reminding me of how trashy I looked. I didn't respond, determined not to give him the satisfaction of getting a rise out of me. Max went with us every day, but Gavin had to help him in and out of the truck, as well as up and down the steps at the house.

On Saturday, I got a break, going to town with Dawn to get some new jeans. I was having trouble holding up the old ones. I was difficult to fit since I'd been wearing a size 38 waist and a 28 length. I had to try on several until a pair of 35-30's felt good. Since they were too long and another size was not available, Dawn said she'd hem them. We left the store with two pairs of jeans and three work shirts.

We stopped by the grocery store to fill her list. It was obvious my grandmother was well liked. Everyone we saw greeted her with a smile and several hugged her, saying how glad they were to see her. I wondered what they did when they saw Gavin. Probably went the other way.

After buying groceries, we had lunch at The Drug Store. I couldn't eat all my French fries that came with my burger, which was a surprise. On the drive to the ranch, Dawn asked me if I liked my new clothes.

"They fit much better."

"You've lost quite a bit of weight. You look better, more fit."

I didn't know what to say. No one ever said good things about my appearance. People usually somehow mentioned that I was overweight. I changed the subject. "How long has Max been this way?"

"He's been gradually getting worse for the last year. I'm afraid he doesn't have much longer."

"Will Gavin get another dog?"

"I doubt it, Eric. He's so attached to Max. I believe that Max is the only thing in the world that he loves. When he's gone, I don't know what Gavin will do."

"My dad hasn't called in over a week," I volunteered, moving the topic away from Gavin.

"I'm sure he's busy with his work," she said, trying to give him an excuse.

"It doesn't take that long to call me. I thought he might miss me being around a little. It just gives him more time to spend with Ethan if he doesn't have to bother with me."

"I'm sure that's not true, Eric. Your dad loves you and only wants what's best for you. Call him tonight if you wish."

WHEN WE ARRIVED at the ranch, Gavin was waiting on me to unload the fifty sacks of range cubes. He filled up the dispenser on his truck at the feed store but kept the extra sacks for an emergency. By the time we finished, my arms were weak and aching. I sat down on an old metal milk can beside the barn. Gavin came out and stood over me.

"I see you didn't get a haircut."

"No. We had other things to do in town."

"Why do you let your hair get that long and stringy? You look like a shaggy dog. I imagine it's filthy. Do you ever wash it?"

I didn't respond, getting up and hustling toward the house.

"Did you hear me? Don't walk away when I'm talking to you!" He bellowed.

I kept walking, not looking back. I reached the house, going directly to my room. I stayed in my room until Dawn came and knocked, announcing that supper was on the table. I forced myself to eat the meatloaf, beans, and cornbread. I finished as quickly as possible but wasn't able to get away from the table until he started in again.

"I've got some sheep shears in the barn. It appears that I'll be forced to use them on you. I've looked at that mop of yours long enough. If I give you room and board then you're going to look like a human. Tomorrow's the day—before we leave for work. Do you hear me?"

I rose and left the table, escaping to my room. That was it! No more. I bathed, put on some of my new clothes, packed my suitcase, and lay down on the bed, staring into nothingness. I stayed that way for hours wondering why my life was so miserable. When I got to New York I was going to get a job and a place to live. I would make enough money to live on and maybe even save enough to buy a car. I might come back home in a few years just to show everybody I didn't need them. I would make friends in New York that wouldn't make fun of me. Dozing off, I dreamed of being in a parade on a huge flat trailer, decorated, and pulled by a red truck with everyone cheering.

When I woke up the clock beside my bed read, 2:05. Laying there, my resolve was even greater to get away. I rose, went to the closet, and got my suitcase. Being as quiet as possible, I opened my door and went into the kitchen, removing the car keys from a small hanger by the stove. Dawn always left a small night light plugged into the wall by the refrigerator. She'd left the car in front of the house rather in the garage, which was a break. I shut the car door as quietly as possible and didn't turn on the headlights until I was almost to the highway. So far, everything was going my way. I had half a tank of gas which would get me a long way from here. My dad had sent me my allowance each week and with what I'd brought with me, it amounted to fifty-six dollars. Maybe with a little good fortune, I could be several hundred miles from here before they realized what had happened. It being Sunday, maybe they would sleep late.

I'd looked at a map and determined that Highway 118 was the only route to take. It would get me to Interstate 10 and from there to El Paso, my destination. I knew the cops would be looking for the car so leaving it in El Paso and taking a bus was my best chance to get out of the area without being caught. I should have enough money to get a bus ticket to New York. I was careful not to break the speed limit since the last thing I needed was to be stopped by the cops. Several times a car passed me, causing me to hold my breath until I saw that it had no interest in me.

After an hour and a half drive, I was in Van Horn. The gauge on the gas tank read less than one-fourth. Pulling in at a truck stop I put in five dollars worth, thinking that should get me to El Paso easily. Returning to the car and opening the door to get in, two figures appeared out of nowhere—shoving me inside. One grasped me around the neck while the other got into the back seat. He let go, and something cold touched the back of my head.

The voice from the darkness was demanding. "Do what we say and you won't get hurt."

I started shaking and couldn't stop, finding it hard to breathe. "W-wh-at do y-you w-want?"

The other person had gotten into the back seat. "Just a ride. Not on the interstate. Just drive until we reach Highway 54 and turn north."

I did as I was told, and they started talking, ignoring me. "We can expect a roadblock on interstate. We should be all right on 54. We can hit 62 and go into El Paso and cross over into Mexico. They won't be looking for this car. You shouldn't have shot that guy. Now every cop in the state will be looking for us. How much money did we get?"

"A little over $2000. We can live good for quite a while in Mexico on that," answered the second man.

"He's just a kid. What're we going to do with him?" asked the other man.

Their voices lowered to a whisper, which prevented me from hearing the answer. Then I knew! They were going to kill me before we reached El Paso! Still shaking badly, it was difficult to keep the car on the road. I needed to pee. I should've gone in Van Horn but was in a hurry. I squeezed my legs together to hold it. They might decide to stop anytime and leave me. Why would they need me anyway? Besides, I could notify the law if they left me alive and was found. They could kill me and drag my body into the ditch. It might be months before I was discovered. A coyote appeared in my lights as it crossed the road. Then it hit me. They wouldn't ever find me! The varmints would eat me!

I felt the gun press against my neck and then the words, "Pull off at the next side road." I couldn't hold it any longer . . . soaking my pants and the front seat.

8

LUTA

"You better get your boy up. I'm ready to eat," Gavin stated, heading for his place at the table.

"You're not really going to cut his hair, are you? I know you were only joking."

"I wasn't joking. If he's going to live in my house and eat my food, he's going to look decent. Besides, I don't want you taking him to church today with hair that long. It's un-American to look like that."

"Well, Gavin, that's the first time I've heard someone with long hair labeled with that description."

He ignored my comment. "I'm hungry, get the boy in here, so we can eat."

It looked like one of those days. I went to Eric's room and knocked. "Time to get up, breakfast is ready." Returning to the kitchen, I put the plates of bacon, eggs, and toast on the table.

Something made me go to the front door and look outside. My car was gone. Maybe I'd put it in the garage yesterday. Going directly to Eric's room I knocked, called his name, and opened the door. The bed hadn't been slept in! I opened his closet door and it was empty! Oh, no! He's gone. A trip to the garage, confirmed what I already knew. Going, to the kitchen, I told Gavin.

He jumped from his chair. "What? You mean he stole our car and left?"

"He took our car, Gavin. I wouldn't say he stole it."

"I'm calling the law!"

"Gavin, please listen to me. Maybe we can catch him in your pickup. He probably hasn't been gone long. Let's not get the law involved." He paid no attention to me, dialing a number on the phone in the den. He was talking loudly, and it wasn't difficult to hear what he was saying.

"Yes, that's correct. Gavin Sager. Our car's been stolen. My grandson took it . . . I don't know how long he's been gone . . . It doesn't matter if he's my grandson. I want to press charges . . . Just a minute. Luta, get me the license plate number."

Briefly, I thought of refusing but followed up on his demand, listening as he read it to the person taking the report.

"I have no idea where he might have gone. The kid's crazy, spoiled rotten, and there's no telling what he'll do."

After hanging up, he stared right through me. "Are you satisfied now? When they catch him, he's gone from here. If he's not put in jail, then he's going home where he belongs. You should've never allowed Cameron to put him off on us. He's not our problem. Are you going to say something or just stand there?"

By now, I was crying. "You've become a mean person, Gavin. Trying to help our grandson was the right thing to do. You're wrong and you've become an angry and bitter person. I keep thinking you'll return to the way you were, when we still had the girls, but that's not being realistic. You like the way you are, and pitying yourself makes you feel better and makes everyone around you miserable. I'm taking the pickup and looking for Eric. You can go or stay here. It makes me no difference."

I expected a response but received only a startled and confused look. I walked outside, not glancing back. I opened the pickup door to get in and Gavin came out of the house, so I waited. My first stop was going to be the police station in town, maybe they already had information.

"Yes. A suitcase but that doesn't mean they took Eric. I'll give it to you before you leave."

"Do you have any idea where they took the car?"

"They were last seen at the truck stop in Van Horn late yesterday. Officers interviewed workers at the truck stop, and they had no recollection of a boy resembling Eric. The two men probably took the car and traveled I-20 to here where they were apprehended."

"We're going to spend the night here in El Paso at a motel. After we check in, I'll call the station and give you my number in case something comes up during the night. My mom and I realize this could turn out bad and we're worried out of our minds."

"I understand and I'm sorry you're having to endure this. It took me awhile to place you, but years ago there was a case this department assisted with, involving your sisters. I can't imagine how terrible this is for you."

Cameron sighed. "Yes, it brings back memories."

I felt helpless. Darkness invaded the emptiness and we left the police station, frightened and discouraged.

9

ERIC

Then it came to me—what I had to do. It had to be quick before we came to a side road. My headlights revealed a shallow ditch on each side of the road. I glanced at my speedometer which read sixty. I reached down, turned off my lights, and drove into the ditch not slowing down. The car bounced half a dozen times, but I managed to stay in my place, hands clutching the steering wheel, which was not the case for my passengers. One came flying over the seat and the other hit the top of the car! When the car finally came to a stop, I dove out, running across the highway into the dark. I heard cussing and then several shots rang out with sounds like bees buzzing around—bullets! I didn't stop, thinking they might be in pursuit. I ran until giving totally out—collapsing.

Looking back, there was no sign of life. No moon. Only tiny stars blinking in the darkness. I must've run for at least a mile, maybe two. My pant legs were full of thorns with some going through and into my leg. I sat down and pulled out as many as possible while resting. After a short time, I moved on, determined to put as much distance as possible between me and those renegades.

Later as it began to get light, signs of life were nowhere in any direction. Vegetation was scarce with only different types of cactus and prickly, thorny stuff that stuck or grabbed me whenever I got near it. I must be miles from any town. No one would live in this desolation. I didn't dare go back, thinking the two men might not have gotten the car running and would still be there. They were desperate, having already shot and maybe killed a man.

As the sun began to move higher, I became thirsty, imagining how good a large glass of water with lots of ice would taste. I'd messed up in the worst way. Failing in my attempt to run away would make Gavin hate me even more. Dawn would probably give up on me, and it wouldn't surprise me if they sent me to a youth detention center. I'd heard of those. My dad didn't want me back. All this might not make any difference. I was getting weak, and with no water it would only be a matter of time until I couldn't go any further. Then it occurred to me that if it hadn't been for the hard work, digging post holes, I'd never have been able to escape from the two thugs. A month ago, running a hundred yards would've caused me to collapse. The killers would've followed and shot me dead. Unbelievable, I thought. What a joke . . . to be indebted to Gavin.

By midafternoon, I was staggering. I prayed aloud. "Please help me God. If you'll help me, I promise to be a better person. Don't let me die out here. I should've been in church today instead of running away." Continuing to pray, my movement became slower and slower. Finally, able to go no further, I sat down as the sun was setting. When darkness came, lying down, my last thought was, *no one would find me soon enough.* I dreamed, hearing voices sounding as if coming from a great distance, encouraging me—*you can make it, Eric. You have to keep moving. Don't give up.*

SOMETIME, during the early morning, I woke up. A noise and movement to my left terrified me. They found me! Rolling up in a ball, I waited for the sound of a gun and bullets hitting me but heard only a "moo", followed by another, and then another. Cows and more cows surrounded me. I relaxed, cows had to have water. There must be water close by.

At first light, the cows moved off to my left, and I followed them. Feeling better, my legs had more strength as we moved south for the next hour. Then the windmill appeared in the distance. I began to run, tripping and falling twice before reaching it. There was not enough wind to turn the vanes but the water in the trough was cool and wonderful. I put my head under, coming up laughing. How could water taste so good? I sat by the windmill for two hours, returning to the trough several times to drink again. Milling all around me, the cows paid little attention.

Now what? Should I leave the windmill and try to find civilization or stay put, hoping someone might come along? I had no way to carry water. No houses were in view. Maybe the road leading to the windmill would also lead to a house or at least a highway where someone might give me a ride. I rose, drank one more time, and started walking west, hopefully to someone or someplace that could help.

I was hungry. How long had it been since my last food? "Thirty-six hours," I mumbled, answering my own question. I'd never gone that long without eating. Constantly having to pull them up, my new pants were loose. I could see no sign of life. After walking three more hours, I sat down and rested. Maybe I'd never get out of here. Suddenly, I remembered the dream. Where had the voices come from? Was it Dawn? No. Who then? I wasn't giving up. At least, I was alive. I'd be dead and probably breakfast for the coyotes if not for my escape from those criminals.

Continuing on, my mind focused on a Big Mac, large fries, and a Dr. Pepper with lots of ice. After that, maybe a large strawberry shake, my favorite. When and if I did find someone to help me, my trouble would just begin. Gavin would want me sent to jail. My dad probably wouldn't care what happened to me. Dawn was my only hope.

I wondered what happened to the car and the two guys. They were probably in Mexico by now, if they were able to get the car running, after I ditched it. I actually was kind of proud of myself. I couldn't have done it a month ago.

To get my mind off my stomach, I tried to imagine what Gavin would say when he saw me. At least he didn't get a chance to cut my hair off. I wondered if my dad had even bothered to come out here after they told him about me leaving. If he did, would he take me home or leave me? I'd failed in my attempt to get away and wouldn't get another chance. Why was I even thinking about Gavin or my dad? I might never get back. Out of a puff of dust in the far distance, a speck of a truck appeared, coming this way.

THE MAN who found me owned the ranch and was checking on his cattle. He was nice and after arriving at his house, his wife fixed me a large breakfast of eggs, sausage, and biscuits. They'd seen my picture on the news and were aware of the fugitives, who they informed me, had been killed by officers in El Paso. They notified the police in Van Horn that I'd been found and also called the house where Gavin answered. I didn't hear what he said and was afraid to ask. They did inform me that a Highway Patrolman was on his way to take me into Van Horn where I would meet my grandmother and dad. They suggested that I lie down on their couch and rest until the patrolman arrived. I took the offer and was asleep within minutes, dreaming again of images in white, singing as if to celebrate.

I woke up to someone gently shaking me on the shoulder. I must've been asleep for some time since my ride was already there. He introduced himself as Trooper Crawford and asked me if I was ready to go home.

"Yeah," I replied, not yet fully awake. I thanked my rescuers and we left. On the drive back, the trooper was curious about my last two days, asking me how I was able to escape.

I explained what had occurred, omitting how terrified I was. "That was a brave thing to do, and it probably saved your life. These were bad guys who had nothing to lose."

"Will I be arrested for taking my grandparents' car?"

"I doubt it. I don't know of many grandparents who have their grandchildren arrested, no matter what they do."

"You don't know Gavin," I said, under my breath.

"From my calculations, you probably walked at least 25 miles. You must be in good physical condition."

I then told him about digging post holes for the last three weeks.

He nodded. "That'll do it if anything will."

Silence followed giving me a chance to think. *I hadn't realized there were so many nice people. The man who found me, and his wife, were kind and did everything to make me comfortable. The trooper was kind and complimentary at the same time, treating me with respect—then the dream. I didn't expect that type of welcome from my dad or Gavin.*

We arrived at Van Horn, going to City Hall where the police station was located. Dawn and my dad were not there since they had further to come than we did. The trooper shook my hand, wished me the best, and left. I couldn't ever remember an adult offering to shake my hand.

I didn't have to wait long before my dad and Dawn arrived. She hugged me. "Oh, Eric, we were so worried. I prayed you would be safe."

My dad even hugged me, not as tight or long as Dawn. "Thank goodness you're safe."

After telling them I was hungry, we went by the truck stop to eat before leaving town. We ordered our meal, then Dawn started in with the questions. I repeated my story of what happened beginning at my abduction, leaving out the part about sneaking out of the house and taking the car.

"You drove into the ditch going sixty miles an hour? It's a wonder you weren't killed," said my dad, actually looking like he cared.

"I had to do something. They planned to kill me anyway. How was your car, Dawn?"

"It had a bent fender and that was all. The car was the least of my worries. We decided to leave it in El Paso so we could come after you together. Gavin can take me back to get it later when things settle down."

Finishing our meal, we started our trip back to the ranch. I tried to sleep but kept thinking of having to face Gavin. He might attack me. At the least, he'd have the police waiting.

10

FRANK

My applicant for the English and theater position was sitting in my office at two o'clock on Friday. He was everything and more than I'd hoped for. A recent graduate, he'd been in numerous college theater productions. He had all the right answers. I liked him immediately. I'd always favored youth and enthusiasm, especially when it was accompanied with modesty and respect. Discovering that his mother was an elementary teacher and he came from a family of educators, added to my positive impression.

I showed him around the campus, including what would be his classroom and the auditorium. I knew that he'd expected much finer facilities, but he didn't seem disappointed.

When we returned to my office, I couldn't help but ask him his reason for applying in this area. Not that I wasn't pleased, it was just strange to me.

"Growing up we lived in small remote communities, and I'm comfortable in that environment. That's where I wanted to begin my career."

I asked him to give me a few minutes to check his references, suggesting that he might drive around town. After he left, I called three of his references who all gave me glowing recommendations, repeating the descriptions; creative, intelligent, enthusiastic, and dependable. He was gone longer than I expected, causing me to be concerned that he might have left town. I was waiting on him in the open doorway when he returned, offering him the job.

He was pleased with the availability of school housing and promised to be moved in by the week before school started. I told him if he wanted to stay the night, the school would pay for a motel room. He declined the offer, saying he'd planned to drive part of the way back today.

After he left, I sat at my desk thinking about my good fortune. My new job was off to a good start with my two new hires. The elementary teacher we ran into at the bank, with her negative comment about high school principals not staying long, didn't bother me. More than likely she had a bad attitude about everything.

I had been disappointed at being passed over for a principal's position in my last school. We had over 600 in high school, and being in a suburban area, were growing every year. It should've been a perfect place for advancement. I'd considered asking what the problem was but decided against it. I'd never been social and that was likely partly responsible. I did my job and didn't attend many functions in the community. My few friends weren't in a position to help me professionally. Not playing golf, as did most of the administrators and board members that lived in the community, didn't help me politically either. The fact was that I had never been athletic even in high school, instead playing a trombone in the band. I was in several theater productions and thoroughly enjoyed it, which was probably the reason for being determined to have a good program here.

I could've been described as boring to anyone who knew me. I enjoyed reading, working in my yard, and spending time with my family. There was nothing about me that would stand out in a crowd. I was just a normal-looking middle-aged man who, upon meeting, the next day you probably wouldn't remember.

I met Julie my junior year in college when she was a freshman. Her math teacher had suggested that she receive tutoring since she was struggling. I happened to be the person her professor recommended since I had taken his class the year before. Maybe she was impressed. I'll never know. She passed the class and the rest of the story is history.

After I graduated, Julie and I had married. She was tall, with a dark complexion, and athletic, the opposite of me. She'd completed two years of college and had always wanted to finish her degree, but Riley came along and financially we were not able to afford the expense associated with it. Julie continued to work at a savings and loan after Riley was born, only taking off a few months. The same was true when Aubrey was born. She was a wonderful wife and mother, and not a day went by that I wasn't thankful she came into my life.

We had attended the First Presbyterian Church the last two Sundays and were due to join this Sunday, transferring our membership. Julie and I had attended the Presbyterian Church from the time we were married. The congregation was much smaller than we were accustomed to, but everyone had gone out of their way to welcome us. The pastor had been to visit us our first week in town, and we were impressed with him.

Julie was due to start her new job at the bank Monday. I was pleased with how everything was going thus far and my family was adjusting better than expected.

I was about to leave my office and conclude a positive week when Coach Estates came in.

"How's it going, Coach?"

"Not good. I just found out that two brothers on the team are moving which puts me at eighteen if everyone shows up. We start workout two weeks from Monday."

"Sorry. My day's gone better." I smiled, telling him about my new hire.

"Mr. Mendenhall, I've been thinking all day that the best thing might be to resign and get a job out of education. I could make more money and it'd be easier on my family."

"Don't do that. It's too late in the year and we couldn't find a replacement for you. Breaking your contract would follow you from now on. Also, you'd be letting the kids down, even if you do have only eighteen."

"It's hopeless. We may not be able to field a team the way we continue to lose players."

"The only thing that will make it hopeless is if you leave."

"I have an offer to go to work for Exxon and live in Odessa, making twice the salary."

"Coach, decisions come up throughout our life that we make based on what's right or wrong. I've only known you a few days, but you're not the kind of man that makes a decision you know is wrong. Don't sacrifice your values because you are in a tough situation. You're young and most of your career is ahead of you."

He didn't respond for several minutes. I held my breath. "I'll let you know something Monday morning. That'll give me and my wife time to talk about it and reach a final decision."

"Coach, we've only known one another a few weeks, but believe me, if you'll stay, I'll support you through this season. We'll make it somehow, and when the year is over you can leave and do whatever you wish."

"I believe you, Mr. Mendenhall, however, at this time I'm in a panic about the coming season. You'll know something Monday morning," he stated, getting up and leaving.

I couldn't believe this. How could things go from great to terrible in a five-minute conversation?

SATURDAY WAS SPENT MOPING AROUND the house, worried about what Monday would bring. Julie tried to cheer me up, after finding out what the problem was.

"Frank, no use worrying about it. That won't help a thing. Can't you refuse to accept his resignation?"

"Sure, but he could still leave. I could turn him into the Texas Education Agency and end his career but that wouldn't help the school. All we can hope for is that he will stay on his own."

"Why didn't you tell the superintendent?"

"He couldn't have done anything but worry. Besides, I have the feeling that Coach Estates doesn't have much respect for him, and his involvement in the situation might have done more harm than good."

"Well, look at the positive for a minute. You're pleased with the young man that will teach English and theater."

"Yes, definitely. But can you imagine, with only two weeks remaining before football starts, being without a head coach? Remember, we're living in a small community in West Texas where football is the big event."

"You haven't forgotten we're joining the church tomorrow, have you?" she asked, changing the subject.

"No. I haven't forgotten you begin work Monday, either. It might help to think of something besides my own problems. Are you nervous about your new job?"

"A little. After seeing what it will include, everything should go fine. Mr. Swenson, the president was nice. After I get my first check, it'll be necessary to go shopping for some new clothes."

"I imagine you are dreading that," I said, smiling.

She came over and kissed me. "I can handle that. Just like you can handle this situation with the coach."

COMING OUT OF HER BEDROOM, Aubrey pranced around the den in a pair of high heels. I was hoping they were her mom's. When she was out of our hearing, I had to ask. "Are you going to let her wear heels?"

"Yes. It's going to happen sooner or later. Actually, if you'd have seen the swimsuit she picked out that I bargained her out of for the heels, you'd be pleased."

"When did all this bargaining happen?" How had I missed this event?

"Before we moved. We went shopping to improve her attitude about leaving her friends. That's when we bought the heels."

"What's this about a swimsuit?"

"She chose one that wasn't appropriate. She was already in one of her moods because of the move. I suggested she get the heels instead of the bathing suit and she went for it. Pretty smooth, huh?"

"The heels make her look much older."

"You should've seen her in the swimsuit!" she replied, her eyes growing large.

"Why didn't we have to go through this with Riley?"

"They're different, Frank. That's the only way I know to say it."

The girls came into the room, ending our discussion. They both looked beautiful. Riley had on very little make-up, but Aubrey made up for what she lacked.

Riley asked if she could drive and I consented, riding in the front with her. She had her beginner's license and would get her permanent in a couple of months. She was an excellent driver, and I was looking forward to the time she could chauffer Aubrey around.

The church service was good, and our ceremony went smoothly. People were friendly, and it was twenty minutes before we could return to our car with everyone extending a welcome. On the drive home, Julie had a suggestion. "Let's celebrate today and go to Pecos. We can take in a movie and maybe find a mall and do some shopping."

"What are we celebrating?" I asked.

"Everything. Our new home, friends, and church. We have so much to be thankful for and I want to concentrate on that."

"It's seventy-five miles to Pecos," I reminded her, knowing already that was going to be our destination.

"So? Riley can drive and it'll be good practice."

When Julie decided upon something, it was almost impossible not to go along. She was working on me to get my mind off tomorrow morning, but it wasn't a bad idea. With school about to begin, we wouldn't have much time for family outings.

"What about it, girls?"

"*Rocky*!" Aubrey exclaimed. "We've got to be the only people in the world who haven't seen it."

"I agree," said Riley.

"I guess that settles it then."

EVEN WITH THE LONG DRIVE, the day was a success. Traffic was virtually non-existent, and Riley received almost three hours of driving time. The Academy Award winning movie was worth the trip, and for a few hours I was able to forget my problem. On the trip back, my worry returned as I tried to determine what could be done in case Coach Estates went through with his resignation.

11

LUTA

We were on our way from El Paso to Van Horn. Eric had been found by a local rancher and was safe. Thank God. I'd prayed off and on all night. The officer that informed us he'd been found, assured us that he wasn't injured. It was an hour and half drive, and Cameron and I had plenty of time to discuss Eric's situation.

"I honestly, don't know, Mother. I've tried everything to reach him and nothing works. What worries me is his negativity. Ethan has been a different little boy since Eric's been gone. I'm open for any suggestions."

"He was doing better until Gavin started in on him about his hair. He'd actually opened up a little with me. Eric's main problem, Cameron, is his self-image. He's self-conscious about his weight and also the fact that he doesn't receive anything positive. I'm not trying to blame you. I know he doesn't give you reason to be complimentary. Sometimes you just have to exaggerate his good points. I believe that would lead him to having a more positive outlook."

"Finding something good to say to him is a challenge but I'll try," he said, void of enthusiasm.

"If you take him home with you, do you think that might change?" I was hoping for a more positive reply.

"I don't think so. Would y'all be willing to let him stay with you and start school here? It's already the last of July and less than a month until school begins. For some reason, I believe that would be good for Eric. Maybe it's because going to school here gave me such good memories."

"We could try. The problem, of course, is Gavin. I know that Eric will not want to stay with us because of him."

"Could you talk to Dad about it?"

"I've begged and pleaded with your dad to be reasonable with Eric and it hasn't helped. I guess it wouldn't hurt to try one more time. I really believe that Eric has good qualities. He just needs someone or something to bring them out in the open."

ERIC WAS WAITING for us at City Hall in Van Horn when we arrived. I hugged him, saying how happy we were that he was safe. Cameron hugged him, also, but I couldn't help but notice it was with little feeling. We ate at the truck stop before starting home, with Eric telling us of his escape and being found by the rancher. I'd thought he was in danger, but after listening to his story, it was obvious he was fortunate to be alive. He said nothing about taking my car and running away, and we didn't bring up the issue until we were nearly to the ranch.

"Why did you run away, Eric?" his dad asked.

"Gavin was going to cut my hair."

"You do realize what could've happened to you?"

"I guess so."

"Eric! You could've been killed! Surely you realize that," I exclaimed.

"Yeah. I know it. What's Gavin going to do? Put me in jail?"

"No. He's not going to put you in jail . . ." I didn't complete my statement. I won't allow it.

"I'm not staying here. I'll run away again. Gavin hates me, and the feeling is mutual."

His dad nor I responded to his declaration, both of us probably thinking that settled the issue. We rode the remainder of the way in silence. Driving up to the house, I knew something was wrong. Both of Gavin's pickup doors were opened and he sat on the porch, holding Max. As I walked closer to the house, I could see Gavin was crying. He cradled Max like a baby, and it was obvious he was dead. All my anger and frustration with Gavin disappeared, and I started crying also. For the past sixteen years he'd clung to that dog as a replacement for the twins. Now he was gone. I moved next to him and pulled his head against me as he continued to cry softly.

Cameron gently took Max from him, carrying him to the pickup. Eric stood off to one side, watching his granddad. "Let's go inside, Gavin, and I'll make us iced tea." I helped him up and guided him through the door. I sat him down at the table and started the water boiling. "I'm sad too, but we had him for sixteen years. He's not in pain anymore."

Gavin spoke quietly, almost in a whisper. "It happened on the way back from feeding. He just lay down in the front seat, put his head in my lap and died." He wiped a tear away. "I don't know what I'll do without him."

I didn't know how to respond. I put ice in some glasses and poured tea for us. Eric and his dad hadn't come into the house. We sat in silence with Gavin not touching his glass. I didn't know what to do about bringing up the subject of Eric.

"I don't understand why everything has to die. If God is so great why does he let it happen and make everyone suffer?" he asked, not looking at me. "Why did God take our beautiful little girls on that horrible night? It makes no sense."

"I can't answer that, Gavin. We just have to trust Him and have faith."

"I don't trust Him. All he's done for me is take away the things I love."

"I'm sorry you feel that way. In times of suffering the most comfort we have is from faith. A belief that there is something stronger than our sorrow that offers hope for the future. I believe that Gavin." He was silent as he got up and went to his room.

Gavin didn't come out for supper nor did we see him before bedtime. Eric, his dad, and I visited while we watched television. We stayed away from conversation involving Eric's escapade.

"How long can you stay, Cameron?"

"Today is Monday and I need to be back in my office Wednesday. Ethan is staying with a friend, and I don't want to leave him any longer than that."

"You need to bury Max before you leave. I doubt if Gavin is able to do it. I would suggest that you put him beside the girls. I'll ask Gavin in the morning if that will be okay."

The twins had been buried in the family cemetery. My parents and grandparents were buried there as well as other family members.

"Eric and I will do that in the morning, then we'll need to leave after lunch," he said.

Glancing at Eric, he smiled for one of the few times since arriving at the ranch.

WHEN I WENT into the kitchen the next morning, Gavin was not there. He was always up before me, drinking coffee when I came in. I started breakfast and then went to his room. He was still asleep. I shook him. "Time to get up, Gavin. Breakfast will be ready in a few minutes."

Finally, I got a response from him. "Leave me alone. I'm tired."

Unbelievable, I thought. He never sleeps late.

Returning to the kitchen, I found Cameron was sitting at the table. "What's the deal with Dad? He's always the first one up in the morning."

"I have no idea. He said he was tired. Breakfast will be ready in a few minutes. You might get Eric up."

"It looks like Eric will be going with me. No use leaving him here to run away again." His disappointment was more than obvious.

"I'm sorry, Cameron. I wish it would've worked out."

"We tried, Mother. That's all we can do. After breakfast, Eric and

I'll take Max to the cemetery and bury him. Did you have a chance to ask Dad if that would be okay?"

"No. He just said he was tired and that was it."

When Eric came in, he was in better spirits. "What's for breakfast? I'm hungry."

"Sausage, eggs, biscuits, and gravy," I said. "Your dad's favorite."

"That sounds great."

Cameron then explained to Eric their plans to bury Max in the family cemetery beside the twins.

"No problem. I'm good at digging holes." It disappointed me that he didn't exhibit at least a little sorrow over Max dying.

After breakfast, I went back to check on Gavin and he was still asleep. So strange, I thought. He never stays in bed. Returning to the kitchen, I told Cameron that Gavin was still asleep.

"That's strange, Mother? He never stays in bed."

"After losing Max, he's devastated. I didn't know how he'd react when it happened. It appears that he's going to withdraw. Maybe that's better than anger." I hadn't given up on his returning to a semblance of the man I married. Maybe, I was optimistic and it would never happen, but it was hard to imagine living the rest of my life with him being the way he was. Eric needed to stay with us, mostly due to his dad who didn't even seem to be aware of the way he treated Eric.

I WENT with them to bury Max. The cemetery was located at the back of the ranch hugged by two low lying hills in the stillness of a little meadow, protected from the elements on three sides. As we approached, Eric and Cameron settled into a hush.

Cameron whispered reverently. "I'd forgotten what a beautiful place this was, Mother."

We moved over to where our little girls were buried. There was ample space at the foot of the graves. We'd brought tools for the digging and watched in amazement for the next hour as Eric went to work. He didn't let up until he had a hole that was adequate to house the tool box that Max would be buried in. I'd wrapped him in his favorite blanket that he slept on when we placed him in the box, before leaving the house.

They lowered him into the grave which was at least four-foot-deep and then Eric filled in the hole with the excess dirt, piling it up in a mound. I kept waiting for Cameron to praise Eric for his work but finally gave up, saying, "Eric, thank you. That was a wonderful job and makes me proud."

His dad remained silent. I thought how difficult that must be for Eric. I know he was intent on making an impression. We stood a few minutes as if something needed to be said about this wonderful companion. Surprisingly, Eric provided the perfect eulogy. "He was a good dog."

When they returned to the pickup, I stayed behind. It's been sixteen years, and I still miss them every day. Strangely, most of the time, I remember them as little girls, full of life, always giggling and running through the house. I'd always heard that parents never get over losing a child. I believe that. They would now be in their 30's and we'd have grandchildren. Stacy had loved the ranch, riding her horse at every opportunity and pitching right in when it was time to work the cattle. Gavin had always said she could run the branding iron better than any of the men. I have no doubt but what she would've insisted on staying even after being married. Macy, on the other hand, had little interest in the ranch. She talked constantly of getting away and moving to a city where as she put it, "civilized people lived."

They disappeared on the way home from a party and were not found for a week. Seven days of pure hell. Tears welled up every time my mind went there—precious lives ended by a monster who was never found. He was still loose, maybe continuing to take the lives of innocent children and tear apart families. I hated him. Forgiveness was impossible. Never!

I stumbled back to the pickup, blinded by the tears.

Eric was behind the wheel. Cameron got out and I sat in the middle between them. As we started back to the house, I was determined that Cameron say something positive to Eric. "Go by the last set of post holes you dug to show your dad, Eric."

"We really don't have time," Cameron said. "It's a long drive home, and we need to get on the road. The next time we come out, he can show me."

Again—my son demonstrated his lack of interest in—his son.

Unspoken words accompanied us until we arrived at the house. "Eric, get your things together. I don't have all day either, so make it quick." Cameron sounded more like a sergeant giving orders to a recruit than a father.

12

ERIC

Some things never change. I was a nuisance to my dad, plain and simple. It wouldn't take me long to pack. I didn't remind him that most of my clothes were already in my suitcase. They'd been given to them in El Paso.

I was sitting on the edge of the bed when Dawn came in and sat down beside me. She put her arm around me and pulled me close to her. "I love you, Eric. You know that, don't you?"

Nodding my head, I believed she really did love me. Probably the only person in the world who did.

"Please listen to me, Eric. I need your help. Your granddad is still in his room, refusing to come out. I've got to have help with the ranch. Tomorrow is the day to feed, and I can't do it by myself. If you'll stay and help me for a few days until Gavin gets over losing Max, I'll take you home. I promise."

"I don't understand how anyone could be that upset over a dog dying. After all, it was just a dog."

"No, Eric. It was more than that. On the day of our girls' funeral, we discovered a little scrawny puppy in the bar ditch that someone had abandoned. I always believe God put that puppy there for us. We took him home, nourished him, and for the past sixteen years he and Gavin have been inseparable. Of course that puppy was Max and when he died it was like reliving our girls' deaths."

I couldn't say no. She'd been nice to me and besides no one had ever said they needed me. "Yeah, I'll stay and help you."

"Thank you. I'll go tell your dad."

I followed her to the kitchen where my dad was drinking a glass of iced tea. She relayed the information to him, and he didn't try to hide his approval. "That's good news. I believe it's for the best. Are you going to run away again?"

I couldn't resist the jab. "No. Dawn needs my help and wants me to stay with her, unlike you."

He ignored my response. "I need to get on the road. I've got a long drive ahead of me."

He probably wanted to get away as soon as possible in case I changed my mind. Within fifteen minutes of his announcement—he was gone, leaving Dawn and me sitting at the table.

"Eric, do you know if the range feeder needs cubes?"

"I don't know but I'll go check."

"That would be good. We may need to make a trip to the feed store to get it filled."

The dispenser was about one-third full and reporting this to Dawn, she said we had better go to town. We left immediately, and she asked me to drive. It took about twenty minutes and upon arriving, she told me to go with her into the office. She addressed a man behind the desk. "Willard, how're you today?"

"Good. Do you need a load of cubes?"

"Yes. This is my grandson, Eric. He may be coming in for feed in the future. It's okay for him to charge to my account. He's helping me out."

"Is Gavin sick?"

"He's not feeling well. A couple of days' rest should get him back on his feet."

I left the feed store feeling more important than at any other time in my memory.

. . .

THE NEXT WEEK PASSED QUICKLY, and my responsibilities increased. Dawn sent me to town several times. I guess she'd given up on Gavin because Wednesday we went to El Paso and got her car. I drove the truck home, and she followed.

Gavin seldom came out of his room except to eat and then had little to say. He didn't mention my hair one time. Most of his conversation consisted of one-word answers to Dawn's questions. To my knowledge, he hadn't left the house since Max died. Dawn informed me that she was going to ask the doctor to come for a home visit. She couldn't convince Gavin to go into town.

The doctor came out the day after Dawn contacted him to examine Gavin. I wasn't there but she gave me a report when we were alone that evening. "His blood pressure is high, and the doctor prescribed medicine for that as well as an antidepressant. Whether or not he will take the pills, is anyone's guess. The doctor wanted to see him again in three days to check his blood pressure. He indicated that I needed to bring him to the clinic. I'll try but I am not optimistic.

"It's also time to wean the calves. They'll follow the pickup into the pens but separating them requires additional help. We usually hire several of the high school boys. I thought Gavin might be up and going but now it doesn't seem like it. I'll make some calls tonight and try to get help. This is Thursday and football starts in a few days, so we need to get it done this week since the boys that we get usually play. We'll try to get it done Saturday. We always mark the calves and put them on feed for several months before selling them, however, due to the circumstances this year, I'm going to sell them immediately."

I felt the anxiety rise in me. "How many boys will it take?"

She thought a minute. "I think me and you, plus three more can get the job done."

I would be forced to have to associate with people who were strangers. I didn't know about being around other boys my age. In the past, I stayed with my small group to prevent ridicule. I didn't see how this would be any different. At least they wouldn't know that my nickname was "Stubby." Regardless, my life story continued to be written —outsider. I wondered if they would've heard of my running away?

Probably. I answered my own question. My grandmother was the only person that had ever seemed to care about me. My friends and I hung out together because it was an escape from the crowd and gave us a feeling of safety. I knew their friendship was superficial and had little meaning, serving only as a refuge for an outcast.

I'd only been here for five weeks but was not the same person physically. I'd weighed at the feed store on a set of scales which showed 180. Most of the weight I'd lost came from my stomach. My arms were bigger and more firm. I'd always been built like a pyramid with large legs, hips, and waist but my shoulders were not broad enough to fit the bottom portion. In elementary school, before becoming overweight, I could actually outrun everyone in my class. Observing myself in the mirror the night before, I didn't look like the same person that had arrived at the ranch. My face was even thinner and with my newly acquired tan, my previous classmates would've had a difficult time recognizing me.

Dawn, interrupted my thoughts. "We'll pen the cows and calves tomorrow and be ready Saturday, to separate them. We can do that easily enough without additional help. I'll show you what your job will be before the other boys arrive. I know that you're not familiar with this kind of work, but you'll do fine.

"Eric, I'm sorry for not being able to take you home. I know that's what you want, but Gavin is still not able to do anything. I wish there was something that could be done to get him out of this slump. Honestly, I don't know what to do."

"I don't mind staying longer, Dawn. My dad doesn't want me anyway. He wouldn't care if I never came home."

"That's not true, Eric. Your dad just doesn't see you the same way I do, but he loves you. I know he does."

"He has a strange way of showing it," I mumbled, softly enough that she didn't hear me.

DAWN INTRODUCED me to the three boys from town when they arrived early Saturday morning. I concentrated on their first names only, hoping to be able to remember them. Bobby Lee, Roger, and Luis were their names. They were all smaller than me, in weight at least. Of course, Luis was Mexican. There was little time to visit since we went to work immediately. The cattle were in a large pen but there was a narrow chute leading to a smaller one. It was my job to operate the gate leading into the smaller pen. Six or eight cows with their calves were run into the chute and it was my job to let the cows out while the other guys kept the calves in. It was difficult at times and on more than one occasion, I let a calf slip through with their mother.

Dawn reassured me each time it happened. "Don't worry about it, Eric. You've got the hard job."

We stopped at noon with Dawn predicting that we had separated about half of them. She'd cooked the night before and we had a roast with potatoes and apple pie for dessert. Sitting down at the table, she said the blessing. Filling our plates, we fell into silence. Dawn broke the awkwardness by asking the boys if they were ready for football to start.

"Yes, ma'am, I guess so," said Bobby Lee.

"We only have seventeen players this year. We've lost several to injuries over the summer and two have moved. Coach has already cancelled our junior varsity schedule," Roger added, reaching for more potatoes.

Luis looked at me. "Are you going to school here?"

I shrugged. "Don't know."

"Do you play football?" Roger asked.

"No. Never have."

"Basketball?" Bobby Lee questioned.

"No!" I answered sharply, wanting to turn the conversation away from me.

"What sport do you like?" Roger fired off another question. "Almost everyone here is involved in something."

"None of them," I retorted.

My grandmother came to my rescue. "Eric attends a large school and many of the students are not involved in an activity."

Luis seemed amazed. "You mean they don't do nothing?"

"They have numerous electives, including after school work programs, which some students choose to do." Dawn continued to defend me.

"I can't imagine going to school and not playing sports. I play football, basketball, and run track. School would be a bore without them," Luis announced.

I was getting tired of this. Downing my food, I got up and left, going outside to wait until they finished. I hated jocks. All they had done was make fun of those who were not part of their little group. I'd only been outside on the veranda a few minutes when Luis came out.

"Your grandmother's a good cook. She's also nice. I've been out several times to work for them. Your granddad is not as nice as she is. He's hard to work for."

I smiled, feeling better. "I know. I've been here nearly a month."

"Why isn't he helping us?"

"After Max his dog died he seldom comes out of his room."

"When my dog died, I didn't act that way. It's strange."

Finally, someone else felt like I did. "Yeah, I guess so. I don't understand either."

"I bet you have a lot of pretty girls in your school, Eric?"

"Yeah, I guess so." I needed to come up with another answer and stop using the same comment.

"Are there many Mexican girls?"

"Sure, and Black girls also."

"Do the Mexican boys ever date the white girls?"

"I never noticed if they did." I thought, *what difference would it make?*

"You did good on the gate this morning. That's a tough job," Luis said.

"Thanks."

"I hope you go to school here. Maybe we could be friends."

I didn't know what to say. No one had ever offered to be my friend. Hesitating, I finally responded. "Sure, why not?"

The other guys came out, followed by Dawn, before we could continue.

13

FRANK

I woke up at one o'clock, again at three o'clock, lay awake until four o'clock and gave up, rising as quietly as possible and going to the kitchen. Julie kept reminding me that worrying wouldn't help. But I couldn't heed her advice, even though she was right. I would find out this morning if we had a football coach for the coming year. I didn't know the first thing about football, having never played, but I did know how important it was, especially in small towns. Most citizens had a son, grandson, nephew, cousin, or even a great-grandson playing football. If not, they probably had a special interest in someone who played in the band or was a cheerleader. At the first of the week, the talk was of the coming game and at the end of the week it was about the game itself. Academics were supposed to be the priority. But on Friday night no one in the stands was talking about math or science.

I sat, drank coffee, and worried until Julie arrived. "Did you sleep any?"

"Some. Not much."

She filled her cup about half-way then added milk. "Do you think he'll stay?"

"One minute I do, the next, I don't. He can double his salary and not have to worry about fielding a team on Friday night. With only seventeen players, he might have to cancel the season. He's terrified. He's young and not thinking about his future and what he has spent so much time preparing to do. I know he's a good man, but at the moment he's in a panic mode."

"Have you given any thought to what you'll do in case he leaves?"

"Sure. The chances of finding a coach that would be acceptable at this late day would be slim to none. The assistant coach is older and according to Coach Estates wouldn't take the job under any circumstances. The other coach will be the young man that graduated from college less than three months ago. He couldn't be considered. I just have to hope that Coach Estates stays."

"Are you regretting taking the job?"

"No, but I should've been more selective. I had my feelings hurt when they passed over me and was determined to leave. If I'd had more patience, a better job would've become available. What about you? Do you regret moving out to this remote area?"

"Of course not. It's going to be a grand adventure. I have a good job and the girls are adjusting. Things will work out. You'll be a wonderful principal and everyone will love you."

I laughed. "There's never been a high school principal that everyone loved."

"Anyway, I start my new job today at the bank. We can be thankful for that. You'll need to check on the girls since I won't be home. I don't worry about Riley, but Aubrey's another matter."

"No problem. Will you be home for lunch?"

"I should be. If not, there's sandwich stuff in the fridge."

I KNEW the answer before Coach ever spoke a word. His pregnant wife and little girl were with him when he came into my office. Also, his sheepish look told the story.

He handed me a sheet of paper. "I'm sorry, Mr. Mendenhall, but here's my resignation."

"Are you sure about this?" I asked, trying to hide my disappointment.

"My wife and I gave it a lot of thought and prayer, and we feel it's best for our family. I hope this doesn't put you in too much of a bind."

Damn—now he has me cursing, which I never do. How much more of a bind could I be in with two weeks left until football started and no head coach? I didn't respond. They rose, we shook hands, and they were gone. My attitude toward coaches had always been positive but this would put a damper on it. I sat there and tried to understand. It was obvious his wife was involved in the decision. It was understandable that being in Odessa, close to a doctor, would influence her thinking. The extra money would be important with an addition to the family. But giving up a career because of one season that hadn't even begun was ridiculous. Now, I had to give the bad news to the superintendent before someone else informed him.

Entering his office, his secretary greeted me, saying that she would tell Mr. Cleburne I was here. She came back immediately and said he would see me.

I went in, and after a brief greeting, informed him about Coach Estates' resignation.

He stood up, red-faced, placing his hands on his hips, like an umpire about to eject a coach from the game. "You mean he resigned effective immediately! He can't do that. It's too late."

"Yes. I tried to talk him out of it but was not successful."

"Did you inform him of the consequences of leaving this late in the year?"

"No. I don't believe a threat would have done any good. He has a job offer in Odessa with an oil company and was determined to leave."

"Well, I'm not going to allow him to get away with it. The school board will be upset and expect us to do something. The president of the board has a senior who will start at quarterback. He's going to be livid. I'm going to turn him in to the Texas Education Agency." He sat back down, turned, and reached for a copy of the Texas Education Code on a shelf behind his desk.

This was not going as I'd expected. I had no desire to punish Coach Estates for his decision even though he was wrong. It would accomplish nothing except to damage his career if he decided to return to coaching. When I conveyed my thoughts to Mr. Cleburne his response was surprising. "If that's the way you feel, the school board meets tomorrow night, and you can explain it to them. What do you plan on doing about filling the position? It's only two weeks until football starts. This community loves its football."

I sat there amazed at what he was saying. Not, "What are *we* going to do?" but "What are *you* going to do?" The total responsibility rested on me.

I tried to keep the bitterness out of my voice. "I'll get to work on trying to find a replacement. It will be difficult."

I left the office wondering how, after being here only a few weeks, I could be in this predicament. Now, I understood what Coach Estates had said about the superintendent. When I met with the school board to explain my situation it wasn't going to be a good way to start my school year. I was supposed to have a honeymoon period with the school leadership, but it appeared that had flown out the window.

O N   M Y   W A Y out of town, I stopped at the bank, telling Julie what had happened and my plans for the day. She tried to be encouraging but didn't succeed. I was in Alpine within half an hour and at the college a few minutes later. I found the athletic office easily and entering, interrupted a coaches' meeting.

"What do you need?" asked the man at the blackboard who was leading the discussion.

I turned to leave. "I'm sorry to interrupt. I can wait until you're finished."

"If you're selling something, there's no need for you to wait. I'm through buying for this year." He seemed young to be the head coach.

"No, I'm not a salesman. I'm a high school principal at a neighboring school, and I have a problem. I was hoping you might be able to help me."

His tone softened. "Sure. Just give us fifteen minutes, and it'll be time for a break. I can visit with you then."

I waited in an outer office, thinking what a long shot this was. At least, there was a chance the coach knew someone who was looking for a job. After all, it was all I could think of at the moment. Desperate was too mild a word to describe my situation. It was half an hour rather than fifteen minutes before the coach came out of the meeting, introducing himself. "Mason Beckett," he announced, offering his hand.

"Frank Mendenhall."

"What can I help you with, Frank?"

I explained my problem, beginning with my arrival and starting my new job. Coach Beckett listened without interrupting until I paused, waiting for a response.

"Estates shouldn't have quit this late, no matter what. I'm surprised and disappointed. I didn't know him well, but he seemed like a good guy. Now, he's put the school in a tough situation. Nothing's left this late but rejects that nobody wants." He stared at the wall, as if talking to himself.

"Can you think of anyone that might be interested? Even someone who's not in coaching now?" I tried not to sound too desperate.

"I know a person you could contact that lives here on a ranch. I'm reluctant to give you his name. I played football with him at Texas in '69 when we won the National Championship. He went on to try out for the Cowboys but was cut in the second round. He never got over it. Football was his life. Unfortunately, he didn't have to work for a living, coming back here to the ranch. His parents were well-off and about all he's done since returning is drink. Seldom is he seen sober. He was my friend and a hell of a defensive back but was devastated at not making it in the pros. The only thing that has kept him going is his wife, who continues to put up with him."

"Would he be interested?" My heart skipped a beat.

"I have no idea. He did graduate with a degree in education so he'd be qualified. If you'd like to talk with him, we can go out to his place, after we finish our meetings. We should be through in about two hours. He's the only prospect I know, and it would be a huge gamble. On the positive side, he's knowledgeable and capable of doing the job if he could leave the bottle alone."

"It's worth a try. Right now, there're no other options. I appreciate it and will wait for you."

THE COACHES' meeting lasted for three hours until a few minutes after one o'clock. I heard him tell the other coaches that they should return at three. We took my car, and on the way out of town, stopped at the Dairy Queen and ordered burgers, fries, and drinks to go. We headed south and it was no problem to eat and drive, since we didn't meet a car. I asked him how he ended up in Alpine.

"After graduating in 1970, I stayed on at Texas with Coach Royal as a graduate assistant for two years. Then I took a job as an assistant coach at a AAAA school outside of Dallas. The head coach retired after my first year, and I was promoted to head coach. Having outstanding athletes, I was fortunate enough to win the state championship. I wanted to coach at the college level and this job came open. I was young but having a reference from Coach Royal and a state championship was enough to offset my age. So here I am. I love it out here and hope to stay and build a winning program. What about you?"

I reviewed my career for him, explaining my decision to take a principal's job in this area late in the year. I didn't tell him about the superintendent's response to Coach Estates leaving and my scheduled visit with the school board tomorrow night. However, he was more aware of the challenge than I realized.

"Cleburne's not a strong superintendent. You won't get much help from him. There aren't many schools out here and word gets around. The boy that you've hired is a good one. He played for me the last two years and is as good as they come. Of course, going back to his hometown will have some disadvantages, but he'll make it fine."

"Coach, tell me more about this guy we're going to see."

"Carter Duncan had it all; speed, strength, and savvy. I'm surprised he was cut by the Cowboys. I would've laid odds that he made it. He was a captain and leader on our '69 National Championship team. Of course, when you reach the pros it's a whole new level. We were friends and still are, I guess. He seldom comes to town, but his wife and mine visit frequently. I've tried to help him but found it to be a waste of time. He's received support from many people, including his mother, wife, and other family members, but no one has been able to reach him. I understand he helps out on the ranch which is large, about the only kind you find out here. You'll discover that land owners have influence in this country. I'm sure Carter's family was another reason for my being hired at Sul Ross."

This was the second time I'd heard about the influence of landowners. I didn't know whether this was good or bad. I would find out soon enough. We arrived at the ranch, driving under a huge arch with the name DUNCAN spanning the width of it. A large two-story house sat about four hundred yards from the entrance, with a smaller brick home located behind it. Coach pointed it out as our destination.

We parked out front, with three dogs greeting us, barking and wagging their tails. A woman answered the door with a warm greeting for my companion. "Mason! Come in. What brings you out here?"

"Is Carter home?"

"Yes. We just finished lunch. He's in the den."

We followed her into the house before any introductions were made. The den was huge with leather chairs and a large couch. Carter was sitting in one of the chairs with a Coors in his hand. He had a three-or-four days' growth and it appeared his long hair hadn't seen a comb in at least that many days. He rose and shook hands with Coach.

"Mason. Good to see you."

Introductions were made and his wife, whose name was Vicky, told us to make ourselves comfortable, while she brought us iced tea. Carter and Mason carried on a conversation about their college days and Texas' upcoming season until Vicky returned with our drinks.

Carter caught her arm as she went by. "Honey, bring me another beer."

She frowned but returned a few minutes later with a beer, giving it to him and sitting down.

He took a long drink from the beer and wiped the foam from his lip. "Now, what brings you and this stranger all the way out here?"

Coach Beckett went right to the point. "Mr. Mendenhall has a proposition for you. Please listen to him before you say anything."

Once again, I started from the beginning and continued through the resignation of Coach Estates. I tried not to sound desperate but to present it as an opportunity for him to return to football. When I finished, he took another drink of his beer before responding. "I'm not interested."

Silence followed until Vicky, asked, "Why? It sounds good to me."

"I wouldn't know anything about coaching high school kids. I'm a rancher now. That's all in the past."

"Mr. Mendenhall, could you let Mason and me visit with my husband for a few minutes in private?"

"Sure." She led me into the kitchen and returned to the den. Looking at my watch, it showed 2:05. An hour later she still hadn't returned. Finally, at 3:30 she came back asking me to join them. Going in and sitting down, Coach Beckett said that Carter wanted to ask me some questions.

"Would I have to teach classes?"

"Yes. Your schedule will include four physical education classes. You'll be able to work with the junior high athletics also, which is scheduled for first period. That will allow you two conference periods which will give you time to perform your duties as athletic director."

"Is school housing available?" Vicky asked.

"It will be as soon as Coach Estates moves, which I assume will be immediately."

"Will I coach anything but football?"

"Yes. The staff only has three male coaches for all sports and one female for girls' basketball. You'll need to divide the assignments between the three of you. I understand that the older coach on the staff has been coaching high school boys' basketball but that still leaves junior high basketball. We also have track and tennis. It'll be your responsibility to distribute the coaching duties evenly."

"When would I report for work?"

"The board meets tomorrow night. I would submit you as my

recommendation to replace Coach Estates at that time. If accepted, you would go to work immediately."

He frowned. "They probably won't approve your recommendation."

"Carter, I have to assure them that you will be a good example for our students. Coach Beckett has told me of your past, but I'm willing to take a chance on your rising to the occasion and making a positive contribution to our boys and girls. I know you have the ability to do that, but you need to tell me you'll make the effort."

Ducking his head, he muttered. "I know a change is needed in my life. Maybe this is my chance." Looking up, he finished. "I'll do my best. I love football and being involved again excites me."

Vicky didn't attempt to hide her approval. "Mr. Mendenhall, if you hire him, I'll see that he comes to work looking like a professional employee."

"I'll let you know tomorrow night after the meeting. I need to get Coach Beckett back to town. I've already taken too much of his time."

Vicky followed us to the door in tears. "Thank you. Maybe this is what he needs, and my prayers have been answered."

On the drive back to town, I kept thinking about the board meeting that awaited me with its challenge.

14

LUTA

When I went into the kitchen early Monday morning, Gavin was sitting at the table drinking coffee. "Good morning, I'm glad you're up. We need to talk about the livestock. A buyer is coming out this morning to make an offer on the calves. What would be a good price?"

He stared down at his coffee. "Don't know. Haven't kept up with the market."

"How many of the older cows do we need to replace with heifers?"

He continued to look down at his coffee. "Have no idea."

"Gavin, you need to snap out of it! I can't do this by myself. When're you going to come out of your room and join us again?"

Without answering, he rose and went back to his sanctuary.

THE CATTLE BUYER arrived later that morning, and we reached an agreement on the sale of the calves. The price we settled on was forty-four cents a pound for the 181 weanling calves. They would be weighed after pick-up and we would get paid within a week. We could expect a check somewhere around $22,000. We always culled our herd at this time, selling some of the older cows and keeping an equal number of heifer calves for replacement. Since Gavin wasn't going to help this year, I didn't follow this procedure. After paying our feed bill, we should be able to meet living expenses and have some left over. Due to some better than average years, we did have a reasonable savings account. Still the ranch was not living up to its real potential. We should've been making at least three times that amount.

Gavin continued to stay in his room most of the day, however, he did join us for dinner and supper and even watched television with us that evening. He ignored Eric, for the most part, seldom participating in the conversation. He wasn't taking his medicine, as I'd expected—finding his pills in the bathroom medicine cabinet, unopened. I hadn't been able to convince him to return to the doctor. I'd finally given up and stopped my nagging.

I was proud of Eric. I couldn't have done without his help feeding, and he'd done well the day we weaned the calves. School was going to start in a few weeks, and hopefully he would be willing to attend. His birthday was coming up on August sixteenth, and I wanted to do something special for him. He didn't have any friends here, but surely I could come up with an idea. He'd spoken several times about Luis, the boy who had helped us separate the cows and calves. I had two weeks to work on it.

The trucks arrived on Wednesday, August fourth, to pick up the calves we'd sold. Eric and I were at the pens watching them load, and Gavin appeared without either of us realizing it.

"What's going on?"

I was surprised to see him. "They're loading the calves we sold."

"How much did we get?"

"Forty-four cents."

He glared at me. "That's all? We should've gotten at least fifty cents."

I stood there, too angry to speak. It was like he had woken up from a dream. Evidently he was back to normal. I was hoping when he returned from his mourning he would be different. So much for that.

He looked at Eric. "You still haven't got a haircut."

"No. I'm not going to either."

"We'll see about that."

One of the men loading the trucks came over to where we stood. "That's about it, Mrs. Sager. We'll be pulling out shortly."

"You're not going anywhere!" Gavin said, angrily.

Looking confused, the trucker asked, "What?"

"You're not leaving with my cattle. I didn't agree on the price. They're worth more than forty-four cents."

"Mister, I just haul cattle. I don't buy or sell them. The deal was made Monday between Mrs. Sager and the buyer." The trucker looked beyond Gavin to me.

I knew something had to be done. "Gavin, we need to talk privately." I approached the truck driver. "Would you excuse us, please?"

Gavin walked away but I followed him and continued. "The deal has been made. You didn't even come out of the house when the buyer was here. I tried to talk with you about selling the calves and it was useless. Now, you show up making demands and embarrassing me. The calves were sold for forty-four cents a pound which was a fair price. They're leaving on the trucks because I've given my word." Mumbling, he started back toward the house.

I apologized to the trucker before he left. Eric hadn't said anything since his exchange with Gavin. I asked him if he was okay.

"Yeah, I guess. He's back to his old self. You told me when he could help you with the ranch I could go home. You gave me your word. I'm ready to go now."

I was afraid of that happening. Just as Eric's attitude was improving and he was feeling better about himself, Gavin had to ruin it. I had no choice but to keep my word to Eric. "We'll leave first thing in the morning. I'm sorry. I'll miss you. You've been a tremendous help."

"Gavin's mean. He hates me and I don't want to be around him."

I had to get his mind off Gavin. "Let's go into town, Eric. Since you're not going to be here for your birthday, I want to buy you something. It's about dinner time and we can eat at the café."

"Suits me. Anything to get away from him."

. . .

I HAD no idea what to get him for his birthday. Maybe he could tell me what he would like. Of course, there weren't a lot of choices in a small town. We did have a Bartlett's Hardware Store that stocked a variety of goods. On the way into town, I asked him if he had something in mind for a birthday present.

"Not really, I haven't thought about it. Birthdays have never been a big deal at our house."

"The hardware store has a good stock of fishing gear. What about a rod and reel?" I remembered what Cameron liked when he was Eric's age.

"I've never been fishing."

"Eric. You'll be seventeen and have never been fishing?"

"No, never. I watch it on TV sometimes. It looks like fun."

Suddenly, I was angry at Cameron. He never took the time to take his son fishing. Every dad should take his son fishing. My heart went out to Eric. No wonder his self-image was poor.

We ended up going to the hardware store and getting him a rod, reel, tackle box, and other supplies that would allow him to be ready to go fishing at the first opportunity. We actually had a large pond on our ranch that was well stocked with bass and catfish.

We ate dinner at a small café, and staying in the mood, had fried catfish. I asked Eric if he was looking forward to going home.

"Not really. It's better than staying here, though, and being harassed by Gavin. I don't like school and dread it starting. It's boring. My dad doesn't want me and my brother is a pain. Of course, my mother left us, so that tells the whole story of my relationship with her. I've liked being here when Gavin left me alone. For the first time in my life, I felt needed and useful to someone. I guess you could say, I liked myself more."

"You've helped me, Eric, and I still need you. Wouldn't you consider staying just a while longer?"

"No. I don't want to be around Gavin. You promised I could go home when Gavin was able to help you with the ranch. I want to leave tomorrow."

"Yes, and I'll keep my word to you."

I should've known this would happen, but was hoping for a different outcome. We finished eating and then drove to the ranch, lost in our own thoughts. As we entered the house, I didn't see Gavin. He must've been in his room. I'd expected a confrontation. I had dirty dishes left over from breakfast and went to work on them. After finishing, I looked out in the court yard, and Eric was practicing casting with his new rod and reel. I thought, how sad. His dad had spent many days fishing when he was growing up. The ten-acre stock pond on our place could be labeled a small lake, it was so large. Seldom did Cameron return to the house without a full stringer from the time he was big enough to fish.

Returning to the kitchen, I heard a loud thump. Puzzled, I went to Gavin's door and called his name. When he didn't answer, I opened it and saw him lying on the floor, clutching his chest . . . gasping for breath.

15

ERIC

I had just made one of my longer cast into the yard when I heard my grandmother call. Her voice was too loud. I knew something was wrong. Going inside, I found her in Gavin's room, bent over him. His face was white. He was having a hard time breathing.

"I think he's having a heart attack! Help me get him to the car. We have to get him to a doctor as quickly as possible."

I took hold of one arm and her the other as we struggled to get him to his feet. From there we had to virtually drag him. The steps were a problem, and we came close to dropping him several times. Finally, we reached the car and put him into the backseat.

"Eric, you drive and I'll stay back here. We need to get there fast. Don't worry about the speed limit."

The tires spun. Reaching the highway, I continued to increase my speed. Afraid to look at the speedometer, we were at the outside of town within fifteen minutes. I asked Dawn where we were going.

"Turn right at the light and the doctor's office is two blocks down."

As we drove up in front of the building, Gavin's breathing became worse. Dawn jumped out of the car and ran into the building, coming back in seconds with the doctor. He took one look at Gavin and said an ambulance would be called immediately to take him to Alpine to the hospital.

It was amazing how quickly the ambulance arrived. Dawn announced she would ride with Gavin and instructed me to follow in her car. I couldn't keep up, following at a distance and finally lost sight of the ambulance. There were signs in town showing directions to the hospital and by the time I found it, Gavin had already been taken inside. I went in the door labeled "Emergency" and found Dawn in the waiting room.

"Eric, they took him to ICU. The doctor said he would notify me as soon as they knew something. All we can do is wait."

The clock on the wall read 3:15 and looking at it every little bit, time dragged by. At a few minutes after five the doctor returned. With a solemn look, he gave us information about Gavin's condition. "He's had a heart attack and from all indications it's severe. We believe surgery will be necessary, so the best option is to move him to Midland. I'll need you to sign some papers, allowing us to proceed. We need to get him there as quickly as possible, so I recommend that we transport him by helicopter. Would you agree to that?"

"Yes, whatever you think."

Twenty-four hours later a doctor in Midland explained the outcome of the surgery. "He made it through the operation fine. We had to do a quadruple bypass. We anticipate there is quite a bit of heart damage. We'll know more in a few days. The next forty-eight hours are critical. We're going to keep him in ICU for the time being. Do you have any questions, Mrs. Sager?"

Dawn was rattled and couldn't think clearly. "No, not right now."

"He will need rehab after we get him up and around. He experienced a severe heart attack. Like I said, it's going to be a few days until we know more. At the moment, we're doing all we can for him."

"Thank you. When can I see him?"

"Probably in a couple of hours but only for a short time."

"I can't think of anything else to ask. Thank you again."

Dawn returned to me. "Eric, we might as well find a place to stay. I noticed a motel a couple of blocks from here as we were driving in."

I didn't know what to say. I'd spoken terrible about Gavin and here he was, maybe on his death bed. I wanted to say something to encourage my grandmother but after all my remarks about him, I felt stupid. We left and secured a room at the motel. As she was about to leave again for the hospital, I managed to get something out. "I'm sorry, Dawn. I hope he gets well." Of all the things to do, she hugged me.

"I know you do, Eric. You're a good boy, and I love you. I'm so glad to have you here with me."

Now, I really felt bad. How could anyone be that nice? She left for the hospital. I stayed in the room and watched a fishing show on TV.

THE NEXT DAY Gavin was moved to a regular room from ICU. The doctors were pleased with his recovery but emphasized that he did have considerable damage. I'd not gone to see him, but Dawn kept me informed with the updates. My dad called several times but hadn't come to Midland, saying he was really busy.

Pastor Jacob, from Dawn's church showed up later that day which was Friday. His smile made you feel like he had known you for a long time. I wish I was as tall as he was, guessing he played some major basketball at his high school, but maybe his reddish brown curly hair made him look taller than he really was. He had on jeans and a t-shirt with a church logo on it and didn't resemble a preacher. I was impressed that he would drive three hours to visit Gavin but realized it was more for Dawn when he spent little time in Gavin's room.

"Is there anything I can do for you, Luta?"

"Maybe. Eric, would you be willing to ride back to the ranch with Pastor Jacob. The cows need to be fed. I believe you can do that. I know you're bored sitting around here. I can't leave Gavin now. Maybe later."

This caught me by surprise. "Sure. I can do that."

"Pastor, would you be willing to let Eric ride with you back to town and take him out to the ranch?"

"No problem."

"Eric, here's some money to get groceries. I'll call you each day to see how you're doing. If something comes up, you can call me at the motel early in the morning or after eight in the evening."

I couldn't believe this. She was going to trust me to look after things on the ranch. I'm not going to be a disappointment.

We left within the hour and surprisingly, the pastor didn't talk about religion. He talked about his parents and his experiences in high school and college, never once telling me I needed to attend church. We were at the ranch by five that afternoon.

"Eric, if you need any help, let me know. Here's my phone number. I enjoyed visiting with you. Your grandmother depends on you so don't let her down."

I thanked him and after he was gone, went to Gavin's truck, started it, and drove to the pasture where the cows were located, and began putting out range cubes for them. They were starved and came running. There's no way I can describe the feeling that came over me from feeding hungry cows that were depending on me.

Dawn called me that night, and I told her about feeding. She thanked me again and asked if I could stay for awhile until Gavin recovered. I told her that was no problem, but she did have a condition. I would have to start school which I agreed to do.

PASTOR JACOB SHOWED up the next day, which was Saturday, looking like anything but a pastor, especially with his jeans and tennis shoes, inquiring about how things were going.

"Good. I fed yesterday and everything seems to be okay."

"I wish the same could be said for me. I can't come up with a sermon for Sunday. I don't know what the problem is. This happens occasionally but thank goodness, not often. You know what helps me?"

"No."

"Going fishing. It seems to open up my mind. Would you go with me?"

"I guess. I don't know anything about fishing though."

"Doesn't matter. Luta lets me fish in her pond. We can go there."

We loaded our fishing gear in the back of Gavin's truck. Pastor Jacob gave me directions since I'd never been on the part of the ranch where the pond was located. Driving up to it, I was amazed at its size. It was huge, bigger than some lakes I'd seen. A small boat had been pulled up on shore, which we pushed down to the water. There was no motor, only two oars. I sat in the back and he pushed us out, jumping in quickly to avoid getting wet. With each of us rowing, he pointed to several trees sticking up out of the water as our destination.

"Eric, let's try some artificial bait first and if we don't catch anything, I brought some worms. I have several spinner baits which are usually good. If you'll give me the end of your rod, I'll tie it on for you."

I watched him cast and retrieve his lure before throwing out my line. I tried to copy his movements as closely as possible. After about a dozen casts, he yelled. "I got one!" With his rod bent, he reeled in a nice fish.

"Eric, throw as close to those trees sticking out of the water as you can. The bass like to hang out around them."

On my second cast, I felt a tug on my line and jerking to set the hook, reeled in a bass. It was not as big as the pastor's, but I can't remember being so excited. I'd caught a fish! After two more hours we had kept a total of eight bass, releasing some of the smaller ones. Pastor Jacob said the smallest would weigh two pounds and the largest about four pounds. I'd never had so much fun in my life.

We cleaned the fish at the house on a board placed on the tailgate of the truck. He showed me how to fillet them so you wouldn't be bothered with bones. The water hose was long enough to reach. When we finished, sixteen nice fillets were stacked on the tailgate.

Pastor Jacob grinned. "Ready for the frying pan. Eric, you come to my house after church tomorrow, and we'll have fresh fish for lunch. Emily is a great cook, and this will be some good eating."

I hesitated before answering, but the day had been wonderful, and it wasn't possible to say no. "Sure. What time?"

"It takes about half an hour for the church to clear out. About 12:45

would be great. You can come, eat, and leave. You don't have to stay for a social visit."

"I'll be there." After he'd left, I began to doubt my decision. What if he started in on me about religion? After all, he was a preacher even though he didn't look or act like one. He was young, not like all the preachers I'd known. He seemed like a real person. He probably expected me to be in church tomorrow. Maybe that was the reason he asked me to eat with them. It'd put pressure on me to attend the service. He didn't strike me as the type of person who would do that, but could I trust him?

Dawn called that night saying Gavin wasn't doing well. He'd had a bad day and the doctors were concerned. I told her about going fishing and Pastor Jacob inviting me to his home for a fish fry.

"Eric, that's wonderful. It's been several months since he came fishing, but he's always welcome. He's such a nice young man. Are you going to church?"

"Probably not. My dress pants are too big. I always wear Sunday clothes to church."

"Oh, Eric. Jeans will be fine. He was nice enough to take you fishing and invite you for dinner. You should go to church."

I tried to change the subject. "When're you coming back to the ranch?"

"I need to come back for more clothes but don't want to leave Gavin. If he improves within the next few days, I'll come back at least for a few hours."

We visited awhile longer before ending the call. I ate a sandwich for my supper, without a dessert, determined to keep my weight off. I watched television for a couple of hours, concluding my evening with one of my favorites—*Starsky and Hutch*.

THE NEXT MORNING, I woke up with a great idea. I would go fishing again today. That would give me an excuse not to attend church. I could fish for several hours and still have plenty of time to make it in to eat lunch with Pastor Jacob. My excuse for not coming to church could be that I had to feed. Pleased with my decision, I dressed, grabbed a bite to eat and was at the lake by the time the sun was coming up. It was a beautiful morning, and I couldn't wait to get on the water and start fishing.

Within a few minutes, I had the boat in the water and rowed over to the trees where we had fished yesterday. The water was so calm the anchor wasn't needed to keep the boat in place. I started casting my lure and retrieving it and expected to catch a fish at any time. After a dozen casts—nothing. This was the case for the next hour, and confused, I couldn't understand why I didn't catch a fish. Maybe they'd moved to another area. Following this thought, I rowed out to the middle of the lake. The wind had picked up, and I had to use the anchor to keep the boat in place.

On my third cast in my new location, I hooked something. It had to be huge, since my rod was bent double. Excited, I stood up to get more leverage. I was about to catch a really big fish and as it was brought closer to the boat, I leaned over trying to see it. Suddenly, the boat tipped over! Dropping my rod and reel, I was in the tank going under. Panicking . . . I came up struggling to stay above water. The shore looked miles away and the boat was sinking!

16

FRANK

"Frank, you'll do fine," Julie said. "This isn't the first time you've addressed a school board."

"I know, but this is different. I have to ask them to approve my recommendation to hire a drunk. Most people with a drinking problem go to rehabilitation—not a school house to teach and coach young people. I should have my head examined."

"You've always been a good judge of character. If you hadn't thought he could do the job, you wouldn't have offered him the position."

"I was desperate and not thinking clearly." I continued pacing from one end of the den to the other.

"Do you want to back out, Frank?"

"No, of course not, it's too late now. Besides, I don't have any other option. I'm just ranting out of frustration. A new principal shouldn't have to face these problems."

My beautiful wife came over and kissed me. "Just be yourself. If anyone can do it, you can. I believe in you."

"I better get on over there. I'm hoping the executive session will be first and my part will be over." I left not feeling any better.

· · ·

THE BOARD MET in a vacant classroom at the high school the first Tuesday of each month. Today was August 3. Only four of the seven were present when I arrived. Mr. Cleburne introduced me to the ones there, even though we'd met previously at my interview for the principal's position. I took a seat in a chair on the front row. It wasn't difficult to identify their professions. Two had on dress slacks and two had on jeans with a cowboy hat. Within a few minutes two more arrived and introductions were made. Not nearly as conspicuous, they had neither boots or a hat but were wearing jeans. After waiting another ten minutes the meeting was called to order. I assumed one board member was going to be absent.

Mr. Cleburne gave a short prayer and the meeting began. For the next three hours, sitting there and listening, it was all too obvious that Mr. Cleburne was not going to make a decision. The board voted on everything from a supply of toilet tissue to a lawnmower, with Cleburne taking a neutral stance on any issue that came up. The meeting was dominated by the board president who put his cowboy hat back on after the prayer and didn't remove it again. The most alarming decision was the vote of 4-2 not to grant the elementary principal's request for additional supplies for his teachers. Slade Loughton, the president spoke for the dissent, saying the teachers could purchase additional supplies if needed from their own pockets.

Finally, after a break was taken, where the weather and cattle prices took up most of the twenty minutes, the board went into executive session to hear my presentation.

Cleburne told the board that I had recommendations for three positions to fill. He asked me to give the board information about the applicants. I started with Mr. Kelly, knowing it would be more positive, explaining how fortunate we were to get such an outstanding applicant this late in the year. I conveyed his excellent references. I finished and asked if there were any questions.

"Couldn't you find anyone with experience? We haven't had much success with first year teachers." I'd already seen that Loughton took issue with about everything.

"This late in the year, I was fortunate to find an applicant as qualified as Mr. Kelly."

He wasn't going to take my word for it. "Did you have any other applicants?"

"No. He was the only one I had." I couldn't believe the questions. What was it with this guy? I was thrilled with getting Mr. Kelly.

I moved on to my next applicant, the first year coach that had just graduated from Sul Ross, Steve Adams. I had little information about him except my interview and Coach Estates' recommendation. The response was totally different from Kelly's.

"Steve's a fine boy. He was an outstanding athlete for us." That was the only comment from Loughton.

Now for the difficult proposal of our head football coach and athletic director. I was hoping that Cleburne had gotten in touch with each board member and told them about Estates' resignation. That was not the case. When I mentioned Coach Estates resigning, Loughton exploded. "You mean he just resigned, with football beginning within a few days?"

"Yes. That's correct."

"Estates can't do that! It's got to be against the law. He broke his contract. What're you going to do about it?"

I didn't know how to respond. I took a deep breath and in a calm voice tried to explain our position. "We can't force him to stay. I don't think we want to hold him here against his will. He's young and impulsive. He's just looking to tomorrow and not into the future."

Loughton continued to rant. "I want something done. He needs to be punished for leaving us high and dry this late. Isn't there some action we can take?"

Cleburne offered a solution. "We could report him to the Texas Education Agency for violating his contract. I'm not sure what they would do, but some action would be taken against him."

Finally, another board member, spoke up. "I can't see where that would do any good. For sure, Estates was wrong to leave, but trying to punish him won't help us. Mr. Mendenhall, is there any chance of finding a coach this late?"

"Yes, with the help of Coach Beckett at Sul Ross, I have someone who'll take the job." I told them about my visit with Carter Duncan and his willingness to accept the position. I did go into his drinking problem and concluded by saying hopefully that would be corrected. I wasn't overly positive but at the same time told them what they already knew—we had no other choice.

"What kind of offense is he going to run?" asked Loughton.

"I have no idea." *That's not in my job description*, I thought.

"He'll probably run the *Wishbone* like they did at Texas when he played on the National Championship Team." He looked at me like I was a student who'd given an incorrect answer.

"Did you play football?" He demanded.

"No." I didn't trust a lengthy answer.

He looked appalled like he couldn't believe it. "I see."

His response indicated I might not be qualified as a principal in his school. It took all my restraint not to respond. What stopped me was, I noticed several other board members had ducked their heads in embarrassment. He was a bully that much was clear, and the other members couldn't or wouldn't stand up to him.

Loughton perked up like the good news just dawned on him. "My son's going to be excited to hear that Duncan will be his coach. We watched every game that Texas played on TV that year."

The board spent the next hour discussing gossip about several teachers in the district. Needless to say, when we reconvened in open session my three applicants were approved. Concluding one of my most frustrating experiences since entering the profession, I made it home a few minutes after midnight.

DUNCAN WAS in my office before noon after calling him the next morning with the news. He looked like a different person with his hair combed and a clean shave. He was wearing dress pants with an expensive sport shirt. I was almost impressed until the thought crossed my mind that he'd probably already downed a beer or two.

"What do you plan to do first?"

"Today is the fourth and that only leaves us twelve days until we have our first workout. I need to meet with the other two coaches and go over our offense and defense. I also need to become familiar with the personnel. Hopefully, I can get help from the older coach. I've met Steve previously and he should work out great. As soon as possible, I need to get a letter out to the boys, conveying my expectations and welcoming them to a new season. I need to go over our equipment and determine its condition. I'd like to see an athletic budget if there is one.

I have to admit his answer was impressive. I gave him a set of keys to the building and to the field house, tempted but resisting to remind him, he was now an employee of the school district and should at all times conduct himself in a professional manner.

My secretary had come back to work Monday and within three days, I realized how fortunate I was to have her. She actually took the sting out of the board meeting when she welcomed me.

"Morning, Mr. Mendenhall. How was the board meeting?"

"Frustrating, Mrs. Kraal."

"I'm not surprised. Loughton doesn't have the sense God gave a piss ant. His brain has probably taken the shape of a football. He thinks his son, who plays quarterback, is great. He has a daughter, and you wouldn't even know she existed. The other board members don't have the courage to stand up to him. The result is he practically runs the school."

"What about Mr. Cleburne?"

Instead of responding, she just frowned and shook her head. She confirmed what I already knew, but at least someone else recognized the challenge of working in this school district.

Mrs. Kraal came to work dressed to the hilt, in the latest fashions. I'd discovered that when given work, she finished it quickly and accurately. Maybe I was looking for something positive, but from every indication, she was going to be an efficient and loyal secretary. I didn't have time to worry about the school leadership. School was due to start in a little over three weeks, with in-service on August 19, and a teacher work day on the twentieth.

. . .

THE NEXT TWO weeks flew by. I met a number of my teachers who were positive and eager to start school. Of course, there always seems to be an exception. The high school English teacher came into my office, introduced herself, and began complaining. No, complaining is the wrong word. A better fit is whining.

"Mr. Mendenhall, football spends money I need for my classroom. It's a disgrace. You need to do something about this. Coaches make more money than I do. It's not fair."

I sat there mystified that a grown woman could sound like a five-year-old complaining about having to eat their vegetables. When she dragged out fa-fai-fair, I almost became nauseated. Patience—I kept repeating over and over. She finally left, with me thinking about the teachers who came by who were positive.

Mrs. Kraal came into my office. "Well, you met Parton. Isn't she a ray of sunshine to brighten your day?"

"She complained about several things, mostly coaches."

She laid a page for me to sign on my desk. "You couldn't satisfy her with a chocolate bar the size of a brick."

"I hope she's a good teacher."

Picking up the signed paper, she offered her view of the English teacher. "Okay, I guess. In my opinion too much grammar and not enough literature."

I CHECKED on Coach Duncan several times and so far so good. He'd carried through with his plans, conveyed to me on his first day. Finding him in the field house alone, I sat down for a visit. He did say that only seventeen players had reported for workouts. He didn't seem too concerned. I asked him about his other two coaches and how practices were going.

"Like I told you earlier, Steve is going to be good. Coach Bryson has his own ideas about everything. I think in time he'll see what we need to do. He's older and set in his ways, but I need him to get with the program. Workouts are going fine. It's difficult with so few players, forcing us to do half-line scrimmages rather than full team. We're running the *'Bone* on offense, but I don't have a fullback so that's a major problem. Our defense looks good. The kids are tough and aggressive. I thought you might come to one of our practices."

"I've been busy getting ready to start school. Coach, I know nothing about football. You'll need to bear with me."

"Mr. Mendenhall, that's not bad. I'll get more than enough advice from one of the school board members. I've already heard all about him. His son's a senior and plays quarterback."

I moved to something more positive. "Have you gotten settled into your new residence?"

"Finished up this weekend. Vicky is being a real trooper about moving to a small house after she's been used to our place."

"Are you enjoying yourself thus far?" I held my breath, hoping for a positive response.

"Immensely, more than I expected. I love football and being involved again, even at this level, is exciting. I missed the competition and the game itself. I know it's going to be tough with only seventeen players."

"What about the ranching?"

"To be truthful, I wasn't doing that much. The ranch will still be there. My parents, especially my mom, have been supportive. I needed football and a purpose in my life. After being cut by the Cowboys, I was devastated. I'd been involved in football for ten years. It'd been my life and then suddenly it was gone. Plus, it had a negative effect on the relationship between me and my dad."

"Your wife seems to be a nice lady."

"She's wonderful, and the only thing that's kept me going. She wants children, but we haven't been successful. We've considered adoption but haven't made a decision."

We made idle talk for a few more minutes, and I left him to his work. On the way back to my office, I thought, *he may work out after all.* It was obvious he was glad to get back into football. He was positive even though his chances for success this year didn't look promising.

. . .

I WAS WORKING LATE in my office on the Wednesday before our in-service meeting the next day, preparing a presentation for my teachers, when Julie called.

"Frank, Aubrey's not home yet and it's almost six o'clock. Riley said she was on the tennis courts when she came home from shooting baskets in the gym. I'm worried about her. She's not at the tennis courts, and I can't imagine where she went."

I left immediately, checking around the school, hoping to find her visiting with some of her new friends. There was no sign of her.

Arriving at home, I found Julie in a panic. "Where could she be? She knows not to leave with anyone. She's been told to come straight home from the tennis courts. Riley, do you know anything you haven't told me?" Julie gave her a stern look. "Riley Jean."

"There were some boys hanging around the courts. Older boys." Riley added.

"Did they have a car?" I was beginning to get the picture.

"There was one parked there," she answered.

"Come with me." Julie beat both of us to the car.

"Riley, you tell me if you see the car." I ordered as we drove through town.

Riley was quiet until we drove by the The Drug Store, a local hangout for teenagers. "There it is." She pointed to a car that was empty.

"Stay in the car." I saw them immediately when I entered. Audrey was sitting with two boys in a booth toward the back. When she saw me, a look of surprise, which turned to terror, appeared. I was at the booth in three strides.

"Come with me, Aubrey Lee." I didn't have to tell her twice as she scuttled out of the booth. By the time we reached the car, she was crying and apologizing.

"I'm sorry. We just went for a coke. They told me we wouldn't be gone but a few minutes."

No one else said a word until we stopped at home then Julie gave the order. "Aubrey, go to your room."

Julie and I were left alone in the kitchen, since Riley wanting no part of this had gone to her room. Julie was on the verge of tears. "What're we going to do, Frank? Riley said those were high school boys. She didn't mind us, but thought we wouldn't find out. She planned to be home before Riley but stayed too long, probably at the encouragement of the boys."

After a lengthy discussion, we decided on a month's grounding. That would mean coming straight home from school, not leaving the house except when accompanied by one of us, and not talking on the phone. In order to present a unified front, both of us talked to her, explaining our concern and the punishment. The session lasted half an hour and both of us wondered if we made any sort of impression.

17

ERIC

I treaded water, realizing my work boots were pulling me down. I went back under, pulling off one boot and then the other. I started swimming toward the shore, tiring quickly realizing that it was hopeless. My jeans were heavy and making my efforts more difficult. I pulled them off, having to go under water again.

I struggled toward the bank, *no way can I make it to shore. I was going to drown and it might be days before they found my body. Please GOD help me.* Then I remembered my strategy digging post holes. Take your time. Don't get in a hurry. I stopped swimming and treaded water, regaining my breath. Then I continued with a side stroke I'd learned years ago in swimming lessons. It required less effort. Every few minutes I floated on my back. I stopped looking at the bank because each time it didn't seem any closer. Finally, I was exhausted and couldn't go any farther. I shut my eyes and gave up, knowing this was the end. I started sinking feet first and suddenly felt the bottom! On tiptoes, with my head barely above water . . . I walked with more of my body coming out of the water every few yards until I reached land. I collapsed, gasping and sobbing.

I must've lain there for an hour. Then staggering toward the truck, I stopped and sat down several times to rest. My legs weak and wobbly, refused to go but so far before giving out.

I reached the truck and for the first time, thought, I must be a sight in my underwear, t-shirt, and no shoes. Then it struck me. I'd sunk the boat, along with my new rod, reel, and tackle box with all my fishing supplies. My boots and pants were at the bottom of the lake and my billfold was with them. The money that Dawn had given me for groceries was in my billfold. My driver's license was also gone. How could I be so dumb? If I'd gone to church none of this would've happened. How was I going to explain this to Dawn?

Glancing down at my watch to see the time—it was gone. In the lake at the bottom. I drove to the house, thankful that no one was there, went in and saw I had time to make it to lunch at the pastor's house. I put on clean clothes and drove to town. I was early and waited in the truck going over the events that had happened since arriving at my grandparents. Gavin had been terrible to me, forcing me to do hard work and not having one good thing to say. Dawn had been the opposite, encouraging and complimentary. I'd almost died twice and each time had begged God to save me, yet instead of going to church, went fishing. Gavin hated me, but I realized if not for the hard work, I wouldn't have survived either ordeal.

The pastor and his wife arrived. We went inside, and he and I visited while she prepared our lunch. I didn't mention my recent catastrophe. The fried fish was great, and the pastor never asked why I wasn't in church, increasing my guilt.

FOR THE NEXT several days I never left the ranch. My meals were made up of what was in the house, consisting mostly of canned goods. I thought constantly of how to tell Dawn about the boat sinking and losing my personal belongings. Every explanation seemed more foolish than the previous one. I decided that the only thing to do was tell the truth. The difficult part was that she'd trusted me to stay by myself and take care of the ranch. I'd proven that I couldn't even take care of myself.

When I returned from feeding on Wednesday her car was parked in front of the house. I don't ever remember dreading anything as much as facing her with my blunder. She met me at the door, hugging me. "Eric, I'm so proud of you for taking care of everything. My goodness, you've lost more weight."

"How's Gavin?" I wondered how he was, but self-conscious about the fishing incident, especially after her praise.

"Much better. That's why I came home. He's walking some each day. Before I left, he went to the end of the hall and back."

"When's he coming home?" I stalled dreading my confession.

"It'll be at least two more weeks and then he can't do anything physical for another three months. I'm hoping you'll stay and start school here. Eric, I really do need your help."

I guess now was as good a time as any. "I need to tell you something, Dawn. You may not want me to stay after you hear it."

"Don't be silly, Eric. It can't be that bad."

We sat next to each other at the kitchen table, and I told her everything. I began with my decision to go fishing rather than to church and ended with lunch at the pastor's house. She didn't say a word throughout my entire story. I finished and felt a heavy load lifted.

"You could've drowned. Thank God you were able to make it to shore. I'm not angry with you, Eric, only thankful that you're safe. Did you learn anything from this experience?"

"Yeah. Never stand up in a boat." The second it was out of my mouth I knew it was the wrong answer.

"That's not what I mean, Eric. Did you learn anything from this experience?"

"I was wrong in not going to church. The pastor had invited me for lunch, and the right thing to do was attend the service before eating with him. I made a bad choice. It was a selfish decision, and I paid for it."

Smiling, she seemed satisfied. "Now, that's more like it. The first time we're in town we'll replace your fishing equipment. I'll give you some more money before leaving for Midland. I plan on returning tomorrow. Your birthday's next Monday, and I'll be back before then and bake you a cake. How does that sound?"

"Good." I couldn't believe anyone would be that nice to me especially after I'd messed up so bad. Maybe I could make it up to her someway.

"Have you talked with your dad lately?"

"No. Not since I was in Midland and he called you. You let me talk with him a few minutes. I'll stay and help you until Gavin is able to get back to work."

"Thank you, Eric. You know that means starting to school here?"

"Yeah, I guess so."

"Good, that's settled then."

On Friday, after Dawn went back to Midland, I had a visitor. Luis, who'd helped us wean the calves from their mothers showed up just as I was leaving to feed. It was good to see someone, and I invited him to go with me. As we drove out of the yard, he took out a package of Beechnut and put a big wad in his mouth.

"Want a chew?"

It looked good. "Sure, why not?" He passed the package to me and I took out a large pinch of the stringed tobacco, cramming it in my mouth. I'd watched it done a number of times. I bit down and felt the juices filling up my mouth.

Luis rolled his window down and spit. "Good stuff, huh?"

I couldn't reply. My mouth was full. I tried to spit out my window and at least half didn't make it outside. "Mm-un," was all I could get out. Actually it didn't taste bad.

I soon found out the purpose of his visit.

"Are you going to school here?"

I was able to answer but swallowed some of the juice. "Yeah, it looks that way."

"Did you ever think about playing football? We only have seventeen boys."

"No."

"It's fun. Girls like boys who play football."

"I don't know the rules." I was getting tired of these questions. Besides girls wouldn't like me regardless, even if I played football.

"You're big and strong. We could use you."

I had to spit again and got more out the window this time. "Not interested."

Luis didn't mention it again but shared a lot of information about himself. He actually liked school and was looking forward to it starting. He had a girlfriend, but they had to sneak around because she was white and her parents would've thrown a hissy fit if they'd found out. His dad worked on a ranch and his mother in the school cafeteria. He had three older brothers and a younger sister. His brothers had already graduated and left for larger towns where better jobs were available.

When he questioned me as to what my interests were, I was embarrassed and had to think before replying, swallowing more tobacco juice. "I like to fish and dig post holes."

"You're kiddin'! Nobody likes to dig post holes. That's hard work."

I was beginning to get dizzy. "Well, I like fishing better."

"Do you have a girlfriend?"

"No. Girls don't like me because I'm fat." I began to sweat.

He laughed. "You gotta be kiddin'! You're not fat. Have you looked at yourself in the mirror lately?" He removed his tobacco and threw it out the window.

Thankful, I did the same. "I've been fat a long time."

"Well, believe me, you're not fat now."

The pickup was spinning around, and I had broken out in a cold sweat. I was deathly sick. I was going to throw up. Somehow, I had to hold it until Luis was gone.

We arrived back at the house and before Luis left he had a request. "Would you do one thing for me?"

"What?" I couldn't hold it much longer.

"Come to a football practice. Just to watch. We start two-a-days, Monday. Morning practice begins at 7:30 and afternoon begins at 4:30."

"Sure." I would agree to anything to get him away from here. As soon as he had his car pointed in the direction of the highway, I started throwing up. Everything I'd eaten during the day spewed out on the ground. I went to my knees, unable to stand. I'd never been this sick. Finally, I just had the dry heaves. Nothing was left. Shaking, I made it into the house and bathed my face in cold water. I'll never do that again, I thought.

I WENT to church Sunday and actually arrived early. Pastor Jacob came to my seat and shook my hand, saying he was glad to see me. I felt important and looked around to see if people were watching. I sat on the back row by the aisle and just before service began, a man, woman, and two girls came in and sat down in front of me. The taller of the two girls turned, smiled, and said hello. Was I imagining things or did she just smile at me? A girl had never smiled at me.

I couldn't tell you anything about the sermon but spent the entire time studying the back of the tall girl with black hair. She was dark as Luis and could've been a Mexican. Maybe she was. I didn't care. She'd smiled at me.

When the last hymn was sung and we were dismissed, the man turned and introduced himself as Frank Mendenhall and the lady as his wife, Julie. He pointed to the girls as his daughters, Aubrey and Riley.

I didn't know what to do. He offered his hand and I shook it. "Eric Sager." I managed to get out.

"Eric, will you be attending school here?"

"Yes. Probably so."

"What grade?"

"Junior." I mumbled.

"Great, I'll be your principal and Riley here will be a classmate."

She smiled at me again. I needed to say something, but what? I just stood there.

"It was good to meet you, Eric, and I look forward to seeing you in school." He left, with his family following. Stupid me. I could've at least said bye. They probably laughed at me when they got out of church.

On the drive home and most of the afternoon, I kept thinking of the girl smiling at me—of her as that girl—her name was Riley. She probably smiled at everybody. Her sister didn't smile at me. She was taller than me and thin. No, not thin, just looked like an athlete.

I went to the full length mirror in my bedroom and studied myself. Luis was right. I wasn't fat. I didn't have a stomach any more. My face was tanned and smooth, free of any pimples. I smiled and my teeth were white, and for the most part, straight. What was wrong with my looks? I was plain, nothing to set me off from anyone else, except my long hair. Would cutting my hair improve my appearance? I tried to imagine what it would do to my looks. Maybe it would make me look taller and older.

I took off my shirt and inspected my chest to see if hair was showing or if any was appearing on my stomach. Nothing. Smooth as a baby. Rumor was that if you shaved your chest and stomach, hair would start growing. I had dark fuzz on my face which I needed to shave every third day. I took off my jeans inspecting my legs. They were large. Big thighs and calves but not much hair. I found a tape measure in a kitchen drawer. I wrapped it around my waist drawing it tight, thirty-four. I moved up to my chest, thirty-eight. From what I'd read there should've been a ten-inch difference. I turned around and determined that my butt was too large. I measured my thigh, twenty-four. My bottom half was way out of proportion to my top half.

DAWN CAME HOME, Sunday afternoon, just as she said she would to celebrate my birthday. She made my favorites for supper—T-bone steak, baked potato and hot rolls. Of course, she made another favorite, chocolate fudge-icing cake. She even had candles and sang happy birthday to me. Even though she'd already bought me the fishing stuff (twice), she gave me a pretty blue-wrapped present, which turned out to be some beautiful high heeled cowboy boots. It was the kind I'd been hoping for, to make me two inches taller. I couldn't believe it when she took pictures of everything like it was some big deal and to me it was. While she was here she washed and ironed school clothes for me so I'd be ready for the first week. I wondered if most mothers did these things for their kids.

18

LUTA

I had plenty of time to think on the three-hour drive back to Midland. I was pleased with Eric's progress. He'd made a mistake but was honest in telling me and taking responsibility. Now, if his self-image would improve and he could make some friends, school could be a positive experience. Eric had been a blessing. I was fifty-five years old, and for the past sixteen years Gavin had been making my life miserable. Eric, being here, had given me something else to think about and work toward. I'd been lonely and didn't realize it until someone else was around. I didn't know how his heart attack would affect Gavin or even if it would make any difference. It was two weeks until we could go home, and I'd know by that time.

There was little traffic and I was at the hospital by midafternoon. I heard laughter coming from his room and was surprised to find he had a visitor.

"Luta, this is an old friend from my younger days, Lance Wagner. Lance this is my wife, Luta."

"My, my, Gavin, how did you land such a beauty? I never remember you dating anyone who looked like this." His face lit up and stepping forward, offered his hand.

I returned the smile. "Pleased to meet you, Lance."

"Believe me, the pleasure is all mine," he said, holding on to my hand.

"Lance lives here in Midland and owns an oil company. We haven't seen one another for years. He subscribes to our local paper and saw I was in the hospital. We've been reminiscing about old times before we married."

"Sounds like they were happy times. I heard the laughter before I reached the room."

Lance winked. "Gavin and I were a couple of rounders all right. Made many a mile together."

"Yes, indeed we did."

"I better be going. I'll come back to see you again in a day or two." He squeezed Gavin's shoulder and moved toward the door. When he went by me, he reached out with an arm and hugged me. "You take care of my old friend, now."

I was shocked, maybe offended, I couldn't decide which. I didn't remember being hugged by a stranger. Gavin was in a talkative mood after he left.

"Isn't he something. I couldn't believe it when he walked in. I actually recognized him after all these years. He's probably one of the wealthiest men in this area. He lost his wife a couple of years ago, and I'm surprised he hasn't married again. He was always quite a ladies' man."

"How do you feel?" I was still trying to figure out Lance's intentions.

"Fair. I had to ask for a pain pill last night."

"Has the doctor been in today?"

"Just missed him. He said I was doing good and tomorrow could start therapy. He's still insisting on me staying two more weeks. I was hoping a week would do it."

He seemed to be in a good mood so now might be the time to bring up Eric. "Eric's doing a good job of taking care of things at the ranch. We're fortunate to have him. He's lost more weight and looks good plus he's agreed to start school here. I've seen a change in him for the good."

"Has he got a haircut?"

"No, not yet. I'm sure he will before school starts."

"He'd better. He's not staying in my house when I get home if he hasn't."

"Gavin, I couldn't have gotten you to the hospital without Eric. We had to practically drag you to the car. The doctor said that you wouldn't have lasted much longer without medical care. Doesn't that matter to you?"

"Ah, the doctor was exaggerating. They all do. I'll be up and going in no time, and Eric can go home."

I didn't argue with him. It was no use. He was never going back to the way he used to be, before we lost the girls. I stayed until he'd eaten supper then I went back to the motel.

There was a Denny's next to the motel where I'd been having my evening meal. Breakfast was coffee and a donut, with lunch being a sandwich in the hospital cafeteria. Tonight while I was waiting for my order to be filled, my thoughts returned to Gavin's friend, Lance. I had to admit his compliments were nice and made me feel good.

I never considered myself beautiful. But looking in the window from my seat in a booth, maybe he was right. My skin was dark but smooth, and my face was more oval than round. Everything fit together —my nose, mouth, teeth. My neck was slender. Did the gray hair make me look older? Maybe I'd get a rinse put on it. I'd never had problems with my weight. I was five feet two inches and had weighed between 105 and 110 ever since I could remember, except of course when I was pregnant. I smiled and looked even better. I hadn't smiled enough in the last sixteen years.

THE NEXT MORNING after Gavin had his breakfast, the physical therapist came to get him. He was young, probably in his mid-twenties, slender, with hair down to his shoulders. He was friendly, and I liked him immediately.

"Morning, Mr. Sager. Ready to go to work? It's a beautiful morning, and we're going to start you on your road to recovery. I hope you had a good breakfast, you're going to need plenty of fuel."

He turned to me. "I'm Jenson. I'll be seeing a lot of y'all the next two weeks."

"Luta. Pleased to meet you."

"You his better half?" He had a Robert Redford smile.

"Yes. For thirty-nine years."

He turned his attention back to Gavin. "Up and at 'em big guy. Times a wasting."

Frowning, Gavin rose and put on his robe. He didn't say a word as he followed Jenson out the door. I knew they'd be gone for some time and didn't want to sit in the room and stare at the walls. Out of nowhere, I had a desire for a new outfit. I seldom spent money on myself but today was going to be different.

I drove across town to a mall, located a Dillard's store, and went shopping. I splurged and bought two new outfits. One was a teal shirt-waist dress with a slim, black patent-leather belt. The other was a brilliant blue pant suit with a white polka dot blouse and a tailored blue jacket, fitted at the waist and slightly gathered at the back. I could probably wear both all year round. Coming out of the mall it occurred to me that I might look like a stunning peacock with my choices. I smiled.

By the time I returned to the hospital, Gavin was back in his room. He was lying on his bed, moaning. I asked him if he was hurting.

"Just tired. I've never been so exhausted."

"Do you want me to call a nurse?"

"No. I just need to rest."

He slept for the next two hours, and I began reading James Herriot's latest book, *All Things Wise and Wonderful*, which I'd purchased at the mall. I'd read his previous works, which were nonfictional accounts of his experiences as a British veterinarian. I was excited to find his most recent publication.

Gavin's rest and my reading were interrupted by his friend, Lance, who seemed to float into the room without knocking, carrying flowers and a package.

"How's everybody today?" He didn't notice or seem to care Gavin was asleep.

Gavin didn't wake up immediately, and he turned his attention to me.

"Afternoon, Luta. I hope you're doing well today. I thought I'd drop by with some flowers to perk up the room and bring you a little something. Sweets for the sweet." He presented me with the package which contained a large heart-shaped box of chocolate candy.

I didn't know what to say and settled on. "Thank you."

He flashed a big smile. "You're welcome. It'll give you something to do while you wait for this big lug to get well."

Gavin was awake by now. "Lance, you're back."

"Brought you some flowers, friend. This place needs brightening up. Also, brought a box of candy for your pretty lady."

Gavin frowned. "That was thoughtful of you."

Lance spent the next hour talking, mostly to me, ignoring Gavin except occasionally glancing his way. He talked about himself and his rise in the oil business. He bragged that he had started with nothing and with little help, had been able to form his own company. He now had over one hundred employees and did work throughout the Permian Basin. He asked about me, and his interest heightened when he discovered the ranch had been handed down from my family.

"Really? So old Gavin married a pretty girl and got a ranch to boot. He always was ahead of the game."

Finally, he turned to Gavin. "So, what's the prognosis for you? Will it be back to normal or will you have to watch what you do and take care of your ticker? I've known some men who seldom noticed a change in their lives and others who couldn't walk up a flight of stairs. I imagine you have some kind of idea which category you'll fit into."

"It's too early to tell." Gavin's usual sparkle for Lance had diminished.

"Well, I'll be here for you if you need anything. You remember that. I better be going now. I'll see you in a day or two."

"What the hell's going on?" Gavin asked, no sooner than Lance was out the door.

"I don't know. He's your friend."

"Looks like to me he's more interested in your welfare than mine. I'd just as soon he didn't come back. Where were you when I got back from therapy?"

"I did some shopping and had dinner at the mall."

"What'd you buy?"

"Some new clothes."

"What's the occasion?"

"Nothing special. I just wanted something new. I haven't bought anything this year." Why should I have to have a reason, I thought?

An older, heavy-set nurse came in and interrupted us. "Need to check your vitals." She placed the blood pressure cuff on his arm. "Little high. You been to therapy today?"

"Yeah. I'm tired."

"Jenson take you?" She removed the cuff and straightened up.

"Yeah. Him and his long hair."

"Isn't he a doll? If I was twenty years younger, well maybe thirty years younger, I'd be following him around. He's still single, you know."

"Doesn't that mop of hair bother you?" Gavin looked as if he was questioning her sanity.

"Of course not. It's sexy." She finished adjusting the bed. "You better be careful criticizing Jenson around here. That'll get you in trouble."

After the nurse left, he continued to grumble about Jenson's long hair.

THE NEXT SEVERAL DAYS, I could see a gradual improvement in Gavin. He went to therapy twice a day and it made a difference. By the fourth day, he wasn't nearly as tired and was in better spirits. Amazingly, he'd ceased to criticize Jenson who was impossible not to like. I actually believe that Gavin began looking forward to therapy. Jenson was upbeat and always positive, which seemed to be contagious.

Lance had been back twice, staying an hour each time. I was embarrassed at the attention he gave me. On his last visit, as he was leaving, he reminded Gavin that if anything happened to him, he would look after me. When he left, Gavin was irate.

"I can't believe him! What's it called? Not flirting. I know—he's hitting on you. Why would he do that? I figured him to go for someone younger."

Anger started at my feet and traveled to my brain. "Gavin Sager! Maybe he appreciates experience, coupled with good looks. Anyway, I'm not so old. You're the most inconsiderate person I've ever known. I left the room not giving him a chance to respond.

I didn't return that evening.

THE NEXT MORNING, I ate breakfast at Denny's and returned to my motel room to finish my book. I was in no hurry to get to the hospital. At eleven o'clock there was a knock. Opening the door, it was Jenson.

"Morning, Mrs. Sager."

"Jenson, is something wrong?"

"No, not really. Gavin wanted me to check on you. He was worried since you didn't come to the hospital last night or this morning."

"I'm fine, Jenson. I'm sorry you had to interrupt your day to come see about me."

"No problem. I'll let Gavin know you're okay."

"Thank you. Please tell him us old people need plenty of rest."

He smiled like he understood. "I'll do that."

I went back to reading my book, finished it, and ate dinner before going to the hospital, arriving at a few minutes after two. Gavin was asleep or pretending to be. I sat down in the chair and waited. After a few minutes he opened his eyes and turned toward me. "I'm sorry."

19

FRANK

I was in my office by six o'clock the first day of school, which was to be an In-Service Meeting for teachers. I wanted plenty of time to prepare my presentation to the high school faculty that was scheduled for one o'clock in the afternoon. I planned to convey my expectations and express my philosophy about each area of education including discipline, curriculum, instruction, grading and extra-curricular activities.

First thing this morning, Mr. Cleburne would address the faculty after which we would have a motivational speaker. It seemed that motivational speakers were always scheduled at the beginning of school. In my opinion, we would be better served to save them until the spring when they were needed more. Most teachers and administrators were excited about the opening of a new school year.

I'd about completed my presentation when the phone rang. Mrs. Kraal wasn't in yet so I answered.

"I wanta talk to the principal." So much for courtesy, I thought.

"This is he."

"The air conditioner is broken in the band hall, and the kids will burn up when practice starts. I called Cleburne and he said to get in touch with you. It needs to be fixed immediately. Band practice starts today and it must be a hundred degrees in here. If it was the field house you probably would've already fixed it."

Welcome to the principal's job, I thought. "I'll see what can be done."

"You do that." Click.

Thank goodness, Mrs. Kraal arrived, and I asked her who to get in touch with about a maintenance problem.

"I'll call Snuff. He's a custodian and does most of our maintenance. What's the problem?"

"Band Hall. I received a call that the air conditioner wasn't working."

"Probably Wister, he's always complaining about something."

"My first upset parent."

"Wister's not a parent, he's the band director. You haven't met him?"

"No."

"Gripes about everything. He's been here so long that many of the kids' parents had him. Threatens to retire every year. We all keep hoping."

The day started at eight o'clock in the cafeteria with coffee and pastries. It was a shock to see so few people in a faculty meeting. I'd gotten acquainted with most of my teachers already, plus the other two principals. By the time Mr. Cleburne addressed the group, I'd met everyone in the room, including the elementary teacher who reminded me that high school principals didn't last long here.

Cleburne spoke for fifteen minutes, telling us how fortunate we were to be here and what a wonderful school district we had. Loughton, the president of the board was there and Cleburne asked him if he had anything to say. He spoke a few encouraging words and finished by saying. "If you don't like it here you should leave." Looking around the room, you could tell by the expressions that he was despised.

The motivational speaker was good and received a positive response from his audience. We broke for lunch, and I went home rather than dining at one of the three eating places in town. Julie was already there and started quizzing me immediately. "How was your morning?" She asked, while putting a couple of sandwiches together.

"Fine. Our speaker was good. Everyone was nice, and I met all the teachers, including those from the junior high and elementary."

"What about your coach?"

"I thought he smelled like liquor and panicked, but decided it was his after-shave."

Bringing the chips over, she continued. "What about the rude elementary teacher?"

"She was there. Looks like she pretty much runs the elementary school."

She finished her questioning while cleaning up the kitchen. "You ready for this afternoon?"

"I think so."

"You'll do great." She gave me a peck on the cheek before she walked out the door.

MY FACULTY MEETING was held in the library. There were an even twenty teachers in attendance, and it took me a minute to get their attention. When I began my presentation, Coach Bryson, the older man on the staff, was reading a newspaper. I thought he would put it down but was surprised when he didn't. "Coach, put your newspaper up."

With a scowl, he put the paper down but didn't look at me. He was going to be a problem. From that point the meeting went well, and I was satisfied up until I asked if there were any questions.

"In the past, my classes have been grouped according to ability." One of the teachers pointed out. "It enables me to challenge my better students without having to slow down for the others. Will we continue to group?"

"No. There will be no ability grouping."

"But that's what we've *always* done."

"Not this year. All students will learn together. We're not going to separate according to ability. I feel strongly about this."

She argued. "I have a son who has a chance to be a Merit Scholar.

This means he'll be limited because the slower students will prevent him from being challenged. Elementary and junior high both group."

"Mrs. Parton, I'm not a proponent of grouping students according to their ability. We're not going to do it at the high school as long as I'm the principal."

"I'm just wanting what is best for the students." She was determined to have the last word and I allowed it.

"Any more questions?" I hoped this ended the discussion.

No one spoke up so they were dismissed to work in their rooms. I went back to my office, waited an hour, and then visited every teacher in their classroom. Some were working while others chatted. They seemed surprised I would come by their rooms. They might as well get used to it. A priority for me was visibility. That included visiting classrooms every week if possible.

The two story building was old with wooden floors. A furnace supplied heat through pipes in the floors. Each room had a window unit for air conditioning. I also went out to the band hall, located in a one room facility separate from the main building. I guessed it had been built within the last ten years since it had central air and heat. The band director was talking to someone I figured to be the custodian that doubled as the maintenance man.

"It's going to be unbearable in here," Wister complained.

"It'll take several days for the part to get here. I can't do anything without it." Snuff couldn't have been clearer about his problem.

"If you'd have gotten on it sooner we wouldn't be going through this."

"We've been trying to get the buildings ready for school to start. We're short-handed and have worked ten to twelve hours a day." Snuff had more patience than I would've had.

They paid little attention to me, in fact, they may not have even known I was present. Wister was big and round, probably 300 pounds, red-faced and wearing coveralls. Snuff was small and much older, probably in his late sixties, wearing khakis and a work shirt that was soaked with sweat. I decided to make my presence known.

"Problem?" I interrupted.

Wister turned around and looked surprised. "You could say that."

"We live in a remote area and it's difficult to get parts. I can't fix the air conditioner until the part gets here." Snuff repeated.

"I'd just like to get some consideration around here." Wister whined, appearing to be Mrs. Parton's student.

"I noticed a large industrial fan when I was in the Ag shop. Couldn't we just borrow it a couple of days until the air conditioner's repaired?" I suggested, hoping this would satisfy Wister.

"I guess that would be better than nothing."

"I'll get it moved over here." Wister wasn't satisfied but at least it shut him up.

I accompanied Snuff to the Ag shop, introducing myself on the way. "Is Wister always this difficult to work with?"

"Yep. Worse most of the time. He has his own little kingdom and thinks the world revolves around it. He's been here twenty-five years. Came right out of college and stayed."

"How long have you been here?" I was taking longer steps to keep up with him.

"Eleven years. We moved from Dallas. Got tired of the city and wanted to slow down. Had enough years as a custodian in a large hospital to take retirement. Still needed to work so here I am, listening to that blow hard, Wister. I enjoy my work though, especially the kids. Being around them keeps me young. I know all the kids in high school by name. I lost my wife four years ago and they're sorta my family now. I guess that sounds silly."

"No, not in the least." I liked this little man immediately.

The Ag teacher was in his room and readily agreed to loan the fan to the band hall. Several of his students, who were due anytime to go look at prospective show animals, would move it over there. He was young and totally opposite from Wister. We left and Snuff walked back to my office with me or rather I followed him.

"Puckett's a good one. If you need anything he's always willing to help. He was a college bull rider, and as I understand it, a good one. There's a funny story about him his first year here. When he interviewed, the board asked him if he was through with rodeo, not wanting it to interfere with his teaching. Puckett said he was, however, he couldn't resist entering the bull riding at Pecos on their big July Fourth Rodeo. Sunday's *Pecos Enterprise* had his picture on the front page riding a bull he won on. He survived the incident—thank goodness. The kids adore him. He works harder and longer than anyone, including the coaches."

I felt better after visiting with Snuff and meeting Mr. Puckett. I ended my day going to football practice. It was a shock to see only sixteen players taking calisthenics. A few students and adults were gathered around the field to watch, including Riley, who came over to where I was. She had on her gym clothes and probably had been shooting baskets.

"Hi, Dad. How's your day going?"

"It's been interesting."

"Dad, you remember the boy we met in church? He's here today at practice and I've been talking to him. Actually, he hasn't said much. I guess you could say he was doing more listening. Anyway, I feel sorry for him. He seems lonely and out of place. I suggested he come out for football. He's friends with Luis and came to watch workout at his request."

"Riley, when you make up your mind to get something done, it usually happens." I laughed. "I would say that Eric will join the football team."

"Would you ask the football coach to invite him to play?"

"Sure. I imagine he'd welcome another warm body."

"Dad, I made another friend today. Her brother plays quarterback, and she's in several of my classes. Her name's Becky and she's so nice."

"Good. I'm glad you're making friends even though it doesn't surprise me." That must be Loughton's daughter, Mrs. Kraal mentioned, he didn't know existed.

Riley left in the direction of Eric. She was something else—always considering others. She could be a great missionary.

Coach came over when they took a water break. In his coaching shorts he looked totally different. It was obvious from the first look that he was an athlete. He walked with a spring in his muscular legs and his height and weight were more noticeable.

"Afternoon, Coach. How's it going?"

"It could be better, but I'm not complaining. The kids are willing and doing everything I ask. We just have so few. We can't stand any injuries, and we have to limit contact. The kids are tough so that doesn't bother me. See that little Mexican boy at the end of the water line. That's Luis. He's only a sophomore but has much more ability than the senior quarterback. I'll warn you now, if I play him at quarterback ahead of the senior, we're going to catch hell."

"Loughton's son?"

"Afraid so. Loughton's son is big and slow. He needs to be playing end. You know the saying that the 'apple doesn't fall far from the tree?' That's not true in this family. The kid is as nice and polite as can be. The *'Bone Offense* needs a quarterback that can run. Luis is quick as a cat and can throw the ball."

"What're you going to do?"

"Put the best eleven on the field in their best positions. My wife reads the Bible daily and prays. I'm going to ask her to put me at the top of her list."

"I almost forgot, Coach. Riley asked me to request that you invite that big boy over there to come out for football." I pointed at Eric.

"Sure. I noticed him right off. I watched Riley shooting baskets in the gym. I wish she could play. She'd be an awesome split end. Thanks for coming out to practice." He left and headed in Eric's and Riley's direction.

20

ERIC

I put off going to workout until August 19, which was a Thursday. When I arrived, practice had already begun. I spotted Luis immediately. In his uniform, he appeared to be larger. This was the closest I'd ever been to a football player. I'd watched several professional preseason games on TV since deciding to come to practice. I was beginning to understand some of the rules. I was trying to decide whether to sit down on the grass or keep standing when someone called my name. I turned and my heart jumped up into my throat. It was her!

She smiled. "It's good to see you again."

She had on gym shorts and a t-shirt, stained dark by sweat. I thought girls perspired, but she was sweating. She was tall, dark, and beautiful.

I didn't know what to say. Finally, I mustered up, "Hi, good to see you."

"Are you ready for school to start?" She cocked her head to one side seeming to be interested.

"I guess so." I replied, looking into those dark brown eyes.

"Why don't you come out for football?" she asked.

I shrugged, without answering. Unlike me, she was confident. She probably realized I was nervous. I kept trying to look away but couldn't take my eyes off her for very long.

"I heard about your granddad. How's he doing?"

"He's better. They're coming home in a few days."

"You must've been busy taking care of the ranch while he was in the hospital."

"It wasn't that bad." I felt good about my answer.

She repeated. "You need to join the football team. They need more players."

"I'll think about it."

"There's my dad. I'm going over and talk to him. I'll see you later."

I watched her every move as she walked to her dad. Who was I kidding? She wouldn't give me the time of day. Would playing football give me a chance? I'd never had a girl pay the least bit of attention to me. I sat down in the grass and pulled a stem, putting it in the corner of my mouth. Maybe if she came back it would look cool.

When practice ended, Luis came over. "What'd you think?"

"You don't have many players."

"I know. That's why you need to join us. I saw Riley talking to you. What did she say?"

"Asked me why I didn't come out for football."

"See. What did I tell you? Girls like jocks. If you'll wait for me to shower and get dressed, you can drive us for a coke. I'll give you some more advice about girls."

"Okay. I'll be in my truck." As Luis started back toward the dressing room, I tried to imagine what I would look like in a football uniform.

As I walked toward my truck, someone shouted. "Wait up a minute, Eric."

I turned and saw it was the coach.

"I'm Coach Duncan." He greeted me with a smile and a handshake. "I want to invite you to come out for football. As you saw we're short-handed and could use some help."

I hated to just come out and say no. "Coach, I've never played football. I don't know anything about it."

"You can learn."

"I'll think about it." I kept saying that.

"Just give it a try for a couple of weeks. If you see it's not for you, then quit."

"I'll let you know something Monday, the first day of school." It would give me time to come up with some excuses.

"Sure. That's fair enough." He turned and trotted off.

I COULDN'T DECIDE what to do. All weekend whether or not to play football, dominated my thoughts. One minute, I was going to say yes— the next minute no. I was afraid they'd laugh. I had no idea how to put on a uniform, but Luis would help me. They would see I was dumb. Coach might even be sorry he asked me to join the team. But then, there was Riley who wanted me to play. She was the only girl who'd ever given me any attention.

Dawn called me Sunday night, and I told her about trying to decide whether or not to come out for football. She was excited and encouraged me to accept the coach's invitation. She told me again about my dad playing football and how good he was. She asked me to call her tomorrow and let me know what I decided. Before I went to bed, I laid out my best pair of jeans and favorite shirt. I slept little, tossing and turning, still undecided. I would talk to Luis again. Maybe he could relieve some of the doubt.

Afraid I would oversleep, I set an alarm clock for six. After dressing, I fixed a piece of toast. It was only seven. Hoping to catch Luis before school started I left early. However, I wanted to avoid Coach, since I still hadn't made a decision. Parking my truck at the front of the building, I spotted Luis with a group gathered by the flag pole. I headed that way. Suddenly one of the boys pointed at me, with the group breaking into laughter. They were making fun of me. Was it the way I was dressed? Maybe they knew about me running away and making a fool of myself. I changed directions and went directly through the front doors.

In the principal's office, the secretary directed me to the counselor. I needed to get a class schedule. I sat down with Mrs. Fields who was nice, causing me to feel comfortable and wanted, and we filled out my schedule. I didn't sign up for athletics seventh period but instead took Algebra II. No way was I going to play football now. She assigned me a locker. Of course, I had nothing to put in it.

The first bell rang and I went into the hall feeling dumb and lost. Students started filing in and I began looking for my first period class, which was chemistry. I started on the bottom floor, going from room to room. I finally asked another student where the chemistry classroom was located. He directed me to the second floor, Room 10. There were a dozen students or so already seated and visiting with one another. I took a desk on the back row attempting to hide. The teacher came to where I was seated.

"You're new. I'm Mr. Fowler and your name is?"

"Eric Sager."

"Welcome, Eric. We're glad to have you."

At least he didn't laugh at me. Books were passed out, and he went over his rules including the grading system he used. The students were attentive and courteous with their questions. If all my classes would go like this one, maybe I could get through the day.

My next class was American history, and the teacher was one of the coaches I'd seen at practice on Friday. Being one of the first to arrive, I again took a back seat. The teacher made eye contact but didn't introduce himself. Students started filing in and one of the last was Riley, who smiled at me and selected a desk on the front row.

The teacher, who said his name was Coach Bryson, was short with little hair and a big belly. He began going over the rules in a much different fashion than Mr. Fowler. He appeared to be angry and the rules were more like demands. Mr. Fowler hadn't mentioned a dress code, but Bryson made it part of his classroom rules. When he finished he looked directly at me.

"What's your name?"

"Eric Sager."

"Your hair doesn't comply with the dress code. Before you come back to my class, you need to get it cut. Where did you attend school last year?"

"San Antonio." I muttered.

"Speak up!" He demanded.

"San Antonio!" I said, louder than necessary.

"Are you getting smart with me?"

He's going to make an example of me, I thought. I was right back in my previous school where everyone looked down on me. I wasn't going to sit here and take it. My resentment and anger rose. "No. I'm just trying to understand what your problem is. Why pick on me?"

"Get out! He yelled, coming toward me. "Don't come back until you get a haircut and your attitude improves."

I got out of my seat and started toward the door, having to go around Bryson. When I passed him he bumped against me. I made it out of the room and exited the building through a side door, going to my truck. I left—promising myself I would never return. Nothing had changed since last year. Other kids laughed at me and the teachers hated me.

I expected someone to try and get in touch with me, so I spent the remainder of the day driving over the ranch looking for places in the fences that needed repair. I remembered where the cemetery was and spent some time there thinking of Max. I was still confused as to how the loss of a dog could create that much devastation.

While looking at the twins' graves, the wind picked up and the strangest feeling came over me. I had a chill but it wasn't cold and the hair on the back of my neck stood up. I felt something behind me and turned around quickly, finding nothing. The wind blew harder. The cap I was wearing flew off. After chasing down my cap, I left quickly, confused and afraid.

I was only a few months old when the twins were killed. Of course, I'd heard the story but not until a couple of years ago. My dad finally told me what happened. He warned me never to mention it around my grandparents.

My mind kept returning to what happened at school today. I attempted thinking of other things to keep my mind off the incident. I'd actually thought it was going to be different. But having Riley witness what happened was my life's low point.

I stayed out until it was nearly dark before returning to the house. I wasn't hungry and turned on the TV but couldn't sit still to watch anything. I walked from room to room rehearsing what to say when I called Dawn. From the den, I noticed car lights coming up the road. Dawn had already heard what happened and was coming home. I went to the kitchen and sat down at the table, trying to organize an explanation. The knock at the door brought me back to reality. Dawn wouldn't knock. I went to the door, opened it, and was shocked to see Coach Duncan.

"May I come in, Eric?"

Unable to answer, I stepped back to allow him room to enter. He still had on the clothes he wore to practice.

"I came to check on you and see if you were doing all right."

"I guess so. It was a bad day at school. I'm not going back."

"Have you eaten, Eric?"

"No. I wasn't hungry."

"Good. I haven't had time to eat either. I brought us a pizza. Let me get it," he said, going back to his car.

What was going on? He was probably going to try and talk me into coming back to school. No way was that going to happen. He returned with the pizza and followed me into the kitchen.

"Luis gave me directions to your place. I actually found it without getting lost. I'm starved. Here, there's plenty." He slid the box over to me.

For the next few minutes, nothing was said while we ate. I thanked him for the pizza, hoping he would just leave and not give me a lecture.

"Tell me about your day, Eric. From the beginning when you arrived at school."

I hesitated and then told him about the group pointing at me and laughing. I explained that had always been a problem. Other students made fun of me.

"That reminds me of a funny story, Eric. I was a senior at Texas University in 1969. We had high hopes of playing for a national championship. The upper classmen were confident. You might say even arrogant. We made it hard on the incoming freshmen. I mean we didn't haze them—we just gave them all kinds of hell. We had this guy from a little town that had probably, 250 total population. The mascot for his high school team was the gorilla. Can you imagine that? Anytime he came around we would make these grunting sounds. Sometimes we would get down on all fours and scoot around him. We worked out a week in shorts and continued to harass the freshmen, especially Gorilla Boy as we called him. The second week we put the pads on. We went on the field yelling, 'new meat,' referring to the freshmen who we planned to punish.

"Coach didn't believe in easing into contact. We went directly to drills that were physical and meant to test our toughness. The first drill had one offensive lineman and a ball carrier pitted against a defensive player. The freshmen lined up to take their turns at the defensive position. Well, you can imagine what happened. They were blocked on their butts most of the time and when they weren't, the backs ran over them. One of the last to go was Gorilla Boy, and when he took his place the grunts started. What happened next was something to see. The offensive lineman charged Gorilla Boy and he shucked him off like he was a fly. Then he put his head square in the chest of the runner and exploded, knocking him on his back. The silence was only broken by the runner gasping for breath. Gorilla Boy or Stan, his real name, went on to play on that National Championship team as a freshman. The joke actually turned out to be on us."

"What was it like to win a National Championship?"

"I can't explain it, Eric. It meant so much at the time and even more today for the ones who played. I was fortunate enough to be named to the All American Team as a defensive back. I didn't want football to end. It had been my life."

"What did you do after you graduated?"

"I was drafted by the Dallas Cowboys in one of the later rounds, however, I thought my chances were good. I made the first cut, but the saddest day of my life was being cut in the second round. I came home devastated and thinking of myself as a failure. I wasn't interested in the ranch or anything else. I thought about trying out with another team but decided against it, fearing another rejection.

I couldn't believe he was telling me all this. What possessed him to confess all this to me. He answered me quickly.

"I have trouble talking about it. Maybe it would help if I did it more often. You need to understand, Eric, that we all have our problems. I didn't face my problem but instead started drinking. In doing so, I lost most of my self-respect. If we deny our problems, they will not go away. You had a bad day. I can't start to tell you how many bad days I've had since learning that my career was finished. I'm determined to have good days and stop worrying about not achieving my dream. I have a wonderful wife and hopefully one of these days we'll have children.

"I've taken up enough of your evening. I enjoyed the visit even though I did most of the talking. I'll see you tomorrow." Then he got up and headed for the door.

21

LUTA

F rom Eric's first few words, I could tell something was wrong. He asked about Gavin and said everything was good at the ranch. He then hesitated. I had to ask him about his first day of school.

"It was horrible. It reminded me of how my school year began last year. Students laughed at me and a teacher put me down in front of the class. I left, not intending to go back."

"Are you still planning on not returning?" I asked, holding my breath.

"I'm confused. I don't know what to do. Coach Duncan came to see me earlier tonight and brought pizza to share. I expected him to try and convince me to come back to school and join the team. He never mentioned what happened to me at school and didn't ask me to return. Instead he told me about some of his experiences. It was almost like he needed to talk with someone. It made me feel special for him to tell me personal things about his life. I kept expecting him to encourage me to come back. When he left all he said was, 'I'll see you tomorrow,' like he knew I'd be in school. It's almost like I don't have a choice. Why would he care about me, Dawn?"

"I've known Carter Duncan all of his life, Eric. My dad and his granddad were the best of friends. I watched him grow up and followed his career. He's a good man who's had his share of problems. After being cut by the Dallas Cowboys, he became a heavy drinker. I believe he saw a chance to help you and is trying. He knows from experience that putting pressure on you won't work. I truly believe that he'll be disappointed if you're not in school Monday."

Eric stayed silent, so I continued. "I know you're discouraged, but this was only your first day at a new school. I wish you'd give it another chance. I can't make you, but it would please me. Carter is interested in you, the fact that he shared his own problems with you, proves that."

"Yeah, I felt sorry for him. It's hard to believe he played on a National Championship team and made All-American and was still disappointed. I think he was trying to tell me he had worse problems than mine."

"You're probably right. He still didn't tell you the whole story which involved his dad but maybe I'll share that with you later." After we ended the call, I still didn't know whether he would go back to school.

GAVIN CONTINUED TO IMPROVE. When the doctor came by Tuesday, he said Gavin would be released on Thursday if everything went well. That would be August 26. I was more than ready to get home. With the good news, I decided it was an opportunity to tell him about Eric. I attempted to make as little out of it as possible, but Gavin picked up on it immediately.

"He got into trouble the first day of school and left?" Gavin stated, in the form of a question.

"Yes, but I've been praying that he'll return today. I don't know the whole story of what happened. He didn't share that with me even though he did tell me about Coach Duncan coming to visit him."

"Carter was a good boy and a heck'uva athlete. I'm surprised they could talk him into coaching here. He sure doesn't need the money."

I was caught off guard by Gavin's response, expecting him to come down on Eric something terrible for leaving school. I shouldn't have been surprised though. A gradual change had occurred in Gavin's attitude. He'd become less angry and I attribute one hundred percent of the improvement to Jenson. He was kind yet firm with Gavin and scolded him when he became negative. I think he tried to find fault with Jenson but found it impossible. In my opinion, he finally gave up and accepted him, and was now even trying to please him with his efforts.

"I'm just hoping he went back to school today." I repeated.

"You've done all you can. It's up to him now. He's stubborn like his dad and I guess—me."

Jenson came through the door interrupting us. "Ready to go, Big Guy? We've got work to do. I heard you only have a couple more days so we need to get a move on and have you ready to walk out of here into a new life."

He turned to me with his charming smile. "How're you today, Mrs. Sager?"

"Good. Ready to go home."

"I'm going to miss you and Gavin. It's been fun, and he's turned out to be a good patient."

"We appreciate what you've done for Gavin." That was an understatement.

"Thanks. Just doing my job which I love."

After they were gone, I sat down, thinking how fortunate we were to have Jenson for our therapist. I'm convinced that no one could've reached Gavin the way he did. Jenson told me when I ran into him in the cafeteria one day Gavin had shared personal information with him including the death of the twins. It amazed me that he would open up to someone after all these years. I was afraid to expect a change in Gavin when we went home, even though it was obvious here in the hospital.

My thoughts turned to Gavin's friend, Lance, who had continued to come back every few days. He'd returned on the pretense of visiting Gavin, however, I received most of the attention. It was embarrassing. I started leaving the room when he arrived and not returning until he left. He must've gotten the message because he quit coming. If nothing else, his attention bolstered my confidence. For years no man, including Gavin, had found me attractive.

My thoughts kept being interrupted by whether or not Eric had gone back to school today. I'd been determined to wait until after school to call but finally my curiosity won out. I'd call the high school office and ask the secretary if he was present. I had the school number and could use the phone in the room. I picked up the phone, dialed, and waited nervously as it rang—once, twice, three times, until a voice answered.

"Principal's office. May I help you?"

"Yes. This is Luta Sager."

"Luta! How're you today? This is Cynthia. I bet you're calling about Eric. He's in school today."

I breathed a sigh of relief. "Thank you so much, Cynthia. I was worried sick."

"Luta, we have a good principal who cares about the students. It didn't take me long to determine that. How's Gavin? He's been on our prayer list at church."

"Improving. Hopefully, we'll be coming home Thursday."

"That's great news. Do you want me to tell Eric you called?"

"No, that's not necessary. I'll call him tonight. Thanks again, so much."

After hanging up, I relaxed, leaning back in the cushiony chair, waiting for Gavin and Jenson to return. I said a prayer of thanks.

THE NEXT COUPLE of days dragged by but finally Thursday arrived, and we waited anxiously. The doctor didn't make his rounds until noon, coming in and sitting down in the one other chair.

"I would like to visit with you for a few minutes. I always try to be completely honest with my patients. Mr. Sager, you held up well during the surgery and are improving, however, you need to understand that your heart suffered considerable damage. You have a chance of living many more years, but it will require you to limit strenuous activities. I know that Jenson has pushed you, and we have carefully monitored your progress. You'll need to be careful not to exert yourself past a certain point and to limit stress. You'll be on medication for the rest of your life, and it is vital for you to be consistent in taking it daily. Of course you shouldn't smoke or drink alcohol. You will also need to follow a diet low in fat and maintain your weight. Do you have any questions?"

"Is that all the good news?" Gavin asked with sarcasm.

"No, Mr. Sager. The good news is you survived a severe heart attack and have a chance to continue to live. If you had not gotten to us as quickly as you did, another heart attack was imminent. You had a ninety-percent blockage in your main artery. You're going home today and it will be your choice, no one else can do it for you."

"Thank you for your honesty and for the care you've given Gavin."

"You're welcome, I'm just doing my job." He left the room.

Alone, Gavin started complaining. "I don't understand why this happened to me. I've taken good care of myself."

"How old was your dad when he passed?" I knew the answer but wanted to remind him.

"Fifty-two."

"I imagine heredity had a lot to do with it."

"I'm ready to go home."

"Good. Me, too. As soon as we get the paperwork done, we should be able to leave." Sadly, I could tell his attitude was returning to normal.

We didn't have to wait long until a nurse appeared with papers for me to sign. She was accompanied by a male nurse who was pushing a wheelchair. I'd bundled up Gavin's clothes, and we were about to leave when Jenson came bursting in the door carrying a hat box.

"Just made it. I was afraid of missing you. Are you ready to go home?"

I walked over and hugged him. "We are. Thank you, Jenson, again for all you've done for Gavin."

"Appreciate it, Jenson. Come see us if you're ever out our way," Gavin said, extending his hand.

"I brought you something, Big Guy." He handed the hat box to Gavin.

"Got me a hat, huh?"

Gavin took the box, opened it, and a tiny chocolate colored puppy lay nestled in a yellow, flannel baby blanket.

"She's a lab and just a few weeks old. I got her at the pound. You may have to feed her with a bottle."

Gavin reached into the box and gently picked up the puppy, holding it against him. Tears rolled down both cheeks as he tried to speak.

22

FRANK

Mrs. Kraal stood in my doorway. "Mr. Mendenhall, Coach Bryson would like to see you."

"Send him in."

I'd already decided from the first time we met that Bryson was going to be a problem. Before he said a word, it was evident he was angry. He didn't bother with an introduction or small talk, getting right to the point.

"I don't want that boy back in my class. He's a smart ass, and I don't tolerate his kind. Besides that, his hair is in violation of the dress code. His first period teacher ignored that fact. In my class I make no exceptions."

"What boy are you talking about?" Of course, I already knew the answer.

"Sager. I kicked him out of class yesterday for getting smart with me, and he's back today. I brought him to the office. I don't want him back in my class," he repeated.

I already knew about the incident and was hoping it would work itself out. I should've known that was only wishful thinking since these types of occurrences never solved themselves. Riley had told me what happened. She ordinarily wouldn't have said anything, but she was furious with how the teacher treated Eric.

He continued without pausing to take a breath. "I want him sent home until he gets a haircut, and then he has to apologize to me before coming back to class."

"No, Coach, it doesn't work that way. I'll talk to him about his hair and give him a few days to take care of it. He lives with his grandparents who are out of town due to medical reasons. We're not going to send him home. He needs to be in school. You're going to let him back in your class, immediately."

"So, you're not going to support me? That figures. I'll be talking to some of the board members. If you let them, these kids will be running the school."

"Do what you need to do, Coach. Now, do you have someone watching your class while you're down here?"

He marched out without saying a word. Eric was still sitting in the office, and I motioned for him to come in. "How's your granddad?"

"He's doing good. They're coming home Thursday."

"That's good news. I'm glad to hear that. You can go back to class."

"Bryson doesn't want me in his class."

"It'll be fine. Go on back to class now. Come by after school and tell me how your day went."

It's strange how getting ready to start school is a busy time, but when it starts everything kind of takes care of itself. Coach Bryson and Eric were the only ones to be in my office. Most confrontations that occurred between a teacher and a student can be attributed to the student. Occasionally the opposite is true, as I believed was the case in this instance. I felt sorry for Eric. From what I'd seen he needed encouragement and understanding. I've found that it's not unusual for a teacher to make an example out of a student the first day of school in order to instill fear in their students. My guess is that Coach Bryson chose Eric to accomplish this goal.

I made a point to be out in the hall between classes, alternating between the first and second floor. It discouraged students from being late to class. I noticed several couples who stayed together as long as possible before moving to their respective classes. I didn't visit any classes—that would come later.

The second day ended without any major problems, and Eric came by my office as I'd requested. I invited him to come in, but instead of sitting behind my desk, I sat in one of the two other chairs, facing him. I'd found communication to be easier when I wasn't behind my desk.

"How was your day?"

"Not bad."

"Make any friends?"

"I talked with Luis. He's a friend. I thought they were laughing at me yesterday. He said they were laughing at Mrs. Abbot who's big time pregnant. One of the other boys said she must've swallowed a watermelon seed this summer which everyone thought was funny."

I smiled, thinking the young homemaking teacher was going to be the target of many jokes this year. Her baby was not due until around the first of the year, and we'd already talked about how much school she would need to miss.

"Riley's nice. She talked to me today and said she was glad I came back."

"I agree even though she's my daughter."

"Is that all? I need to get home and feed before dark."

"You're a good boy, Eric. You know that don't you?"

Looking surprised, he muttered. "Thanks."

After Eric, left, I walked through the building and visited with several teachers who'd stayed late. Each one, with the exception of Mrs. Parton, said they'd had a good day. She reminded me again that she was not happy with mixing the low achieving students in with regular students. I didn't respond to her complaint, afraid of ending my day on a bad note.

WHEN I RETURNED to my office, Mrs. Kraal, said the superintendent had called and wanted to see me. His office was located in a building on campus within easy walking distance. A few minutes later, I was told by his secretary he was expecting me.

"Frank, how was your day?"

"Good. Everything went smooth."

Frowning, he commenced. "I received a call from a board member this afternoon. He was concerned about an incident at the high school."

"What was that?" *So this is what the meeting is about,* I thought.

"A teacher had a discipline problem with a student and didn't want them back in class. The student was disrespectful and was not in compliance with the dress code. The teacher requested he not be allowed back into his class until he got his hair cut and apologized for his behavior. According to what the board member was told, you allowed him to go back to class. I told the board member I would look into it and get back to him."

"Yes, that's correct. I did allow the student to return to class. He lives with his grandparents, and they're out of town until Thursday because of medical reasons. The student will get his hair cut within the next several days. As far as being disrespectful, I don't know about that. From my understanding, Coach Bryson instigated the whole thing. I didn't appreciate him coming into my office making demands. Is it customary for Coach Bryson to go directly to a board member with his complaints?"

"Coach Bryson has been here a long time. He's friends with several board members. Can't we settle this issue without things getting out of hand? Maybe you could take the boy out of his class until he got a haircut. Coach Bryson is a stickler for enforcing the dress code which is commendable in my opinion. After all, there's no use having one if it's not followed. I hate to start the year with a controversy. I like for everything to run smoothly."

I sat there too stunned for words. What had I gotten myself into? He was asking me to give in to Bryson, because he was friends with a board member. The student was not even a consideration. Was this the manner in which all small schools operated? I remained silent, not knowing how to respond.

"Take care of this, and we'll get our new school year off right."

"I just need to think about this." I was out the door before he could respond.

BY THE TIME I was back in my office, my shirt was soaking wet, even though it wasn't that warm. I'd always sweated when stressed. I shut my door, propped my feet upon my desk and wondered what to do. Give in or start the school year off with a controversy. Compromise everything I believed in to please Cleburne. The student came first— always. That was the number one rule in my world. That was and always had been my philosophy. To me leadership meant being the strongest person in the building. Not physically, but having the strongest beliefs. I couldn't tolerate Bryson overriding a decision that was meant to benefit the student, even with the support of a board member and superintendent. What board member? I could guess and probably be right on.

A knock interrupted me. "Come in."

"Sorry to bother you, Mr. Mendenhall."

"No problem. What do you need, Mrs. Kraal?"

"I've been a secretary for ten years, and the principal has always called me Cynthia. It's fine with me if you do, also."

"No. You'll be Mrs. Kraal, as long as I'm here. That's my way of showing respect for you and keeping everything on a professional level. You deserve that title. Believe me, you'll do enough work to earn it."

"I appreciate that, Mr. Mendenhall. Also, I want you to know that standing up for that student today was wonderful. You're the first principal I've worked for that would've done that. I know a little about Eric and his problems since Luta and I are friends. That's all I have to say."

She left and her words made me feel better but still with a decision to make. I sat and thought for another half hour before leaving. I decided to go by and watch football workout. We had another scrimmage this Friday and would play our first game the following week.

I continued to be surprised to see so few boys working out. Today, I counted only fifteen, with two in street clothes watching. I assumed they were either sick or injured. I'd paid little attention to football in my previous school, never attending workouts. I wondered what kind of football player I would've been. I went to a large school and was never around the athletes. I enjoyed the band and made many friends. A voice interrupted my thoughts.

"Mr. Mendenhall, how's it going?"

Startled, I turned and it was Mr. Kelly. "Good. How was your day?"

"Wonderful. I have good classes and they're so respectful. I can't wait to start auditioning for my fall show."

"Have you decided what you're going to do?"

"No, not yet. I need to evaluate my students and see what might fit. I'll have something ready by Thanksgiving though."

"I'm surprised to see you at football workouts."

"My dad was a football coach. I actually played up until my senior year."

"Did you play for your dad?"

"No. He didn't want to coach me or my brother. He took a principal's job before we played."

"Did he put a lot of pressure on you?"

"No. Not at all. He always encouraged us."

"He sounds like the perfect dad."

"Well, actually, the pressure came from a different direction. Our family had always been involved in rodeo and our dad wanted us to follow the tradition. He put a lot of pressure on us in the arena. I resented it at the time and feel that he regrets it now. He hasn't told me, but I believe that one day he will. My parents didn't want me to go into education but that was what I wanted. I think now they understand it was the right decision. I love teaching and wouldn't want to do anything else. One of these days, I'd like to teach in college."

"We're glad you're here, and I mean that." I couldn't have been more sincere.

"Thank you. I'm glad to be here. It's hard to believe I'm getting paid to do something I love."

I needed to concentrate on the good that was happening and hiring Mr. Kelly was one of the best. There was something about youth that was exhilarating and contagious. Unless I was mistaken, his show would be something like this community had never witnessed. Mr. Kelly and I continued to visit the remainder of the practice with him telling me about his college shows. After the workout ended, he left and Coach Duncan came over.

"My ranks are getting thinner by the day. I have two more injuries that aren't serious but they'll not be ready for the scrimmage Friday. I'm thinking about calling it off. We can't afford to lose any more players. I was hoping that Eric would come out, but it looks like that's not going to happen. I know he wouldn't have been much help for the team since he's never played, however, I believe it would've been good for him."

"How're your coaches working out?"

"Steve, the young boy, is great. I couldn't ask for anyone better. Bryson is another matter. He disagrees with everything I say or do. I don't understand why he didn't take the head job. He seems to know everything. I'd be better off to switch him and the girls' basketball coach. I'd rather have her helping me. At least she'd have a positive attitude. I need to have a serious talk with him but have been putting it off. It's obviously not going to get any better if something isn't done."

"Are you still okay with your decision to take this job?" I had asked the same question a number of times and always feared the answer.

"Definitely. I'm happier now than I've been since I came home from being cut by the Cowboys. I know we won't win many games but being involved with football again is great. I can even enjoy my PE classes if the little ones will quit pulling the hair on my legs. They gather all around me and can only reach that far."

I laughed. "It would be great if that was the only problem I had. What about your quarterback situation?"

"Oh me. I've been putting that off. I haven't made the move yet even though Luis has been running second string quarterback. I can't afford not to have him in that position when the season starts. I was thinking it might work to switch them out at first so everyone could see how much better Luis was. Of course, Loughton will never admit it."

I moved the topic to something more positive. "Coach, I heard about you going to see Eric. I appreciate it."

"No problem. The entire school knew about the incident by the end of the day, and it bothered me that one of my coaches was responsible. I better get to the dressing room and treat my injured players. I'm the trainer as well as the coach." He left, jogging toward the field house.

I felt better after visiting with Mr. Kelly and Coach Duncan and could go home with a better attitude about my day, even somewhat positive.

23

ERIC

I left school the second day confused but feeling better, since yesterday's confrontation. The remainder of my classes had been good with no problems. I still couldn't believe Mr. Mendenhall had taken my side against Bryson and sent me back to his class. As I drove through town, on my way to the ranch, I passed a beauty shop with a sign advertising 'walk-ins welcome.' I turned around, went back and found a place to park. There were three ladies with two having customers.

"Would you like a haircut?" The lady with the vacant chair asked.

"Yes."

She motioned me toward her chair.

"How would you like it cut?"

"Off my ears and collar. Blocked in the back."

She was talkative as I'd found most barbers to be, asking one question after another. She knew my grandmother and went on and on about how sweet a lady she was. She had nothing to say about Gavin. I wished she'd stop the talking and just cut my hair. Finishing, she turned the chair toward the mirror and asked me what I thought. She'd cut off more than I would've liked, but it wasn't bad. My face looked thinner without so much hair, and I had to admit the person I saw looked pretty good. I paid her and left, wondering if anyone besides Coach Bryson would notice.

Arriving home, the first thing I needed to do was feed. I went inside and changed into work clothes, unable to resist the temptation to inspect myself again. Looking in the closet door full length mirror, the change in my appearance over the last two months was unbelievable. I wasn't fat anymore. My stomach was gone, and I looked just like any other 17-year-old boy. I'd probably lost at least twenty-five pounds. I was never going to be fat again. I actually had muscles replacing the flab. I put on my smallest pair of work jeans and they were still loose. Just two months ago, I had to unfasten the top button on my jeans to breathe. Of course, that was when I was McDonald's best customer.

My favorite part of the day was honking up the cattle and pulling the lever to disperse range cubes to them. It gave me a feeling of importance to be depended upon. They'd come running to the truck and follow me wherever I went. I returned to the house and spent an hour doing homework that had been assigned. For whatever reason, I didn't resent the time spent completing the work. Dawn and Gavin would be home the day after tomorrow, and I went to bed wondering what they'd think about my haircut.

I must've dreamed most of the night. Riley took up most, always being with me and smiling, hanging onto my arm. Football, with the other guys patting me on the back was also part of the dream. But the strangest and darkest came last—two girls about my age in the distance with white dresses speaking but I couldn't make out the words. I woke up suddenly, shaking. It was the twins. I lay there thinking, after several months being here, why now?

I ARRIVED AT SCHOOL EARLY, hoping to talk with Luis. He and two others were at the flag pole, their usual meeting place. When I walked up, Luis extended a friendly greeting. "Eric, you got your ears lowered. You're looking more like a country boy."

"Thanks. I hope that's good."

The talk was of the upcoming football scrimmage and for the most part, I was left out. Luis realized what was happening and asked me how everything was going at the ranch. For the next several minutes the subject moved away from football. I was occupied and didn't see her until she called my name.

"Eric, I need a favor. Could you help me?" asked Riley.

Surprised, it took me a few seconds to reply. "Sure." I walked away with her, hoping it wasn't a dream.

As we went into the building, she explained. "I can't get my locker open. It's stuck, and I need something from there for my first period class. I finally gave up, and seeing you, thought that you might help me."

Her locker door was stuck but after several attempts it popped open. She thanked me, and I just stood there staring at her. She was a little taller than me but not much. I couldn't think of anything to say, but she came to my rescue.

"Your hair looks nice, Eric. Maybe Coach Bryson will get off your back now. He was awful that first day of class. I don't guess you'd ever come out for football now, the way he treated you."

I was desperate for something to say. "You're nice."

She smiled. "Why thank you, Eric."

The first bell rang, and she thanked me again, turning and leaving. I watched her until she disappeared among the other students coming into the building. I couldn't talk to her, that was all there was to it. Maybe if I rehearsed some lines and saved them until the opportunity came. She could've chosen anyone to open her locker, but she picked me. Maybe she just felt sorry for me. I didn't care. At least I was the one she asked to help her. Instead of going to my first period class, I went to the counselor's office.

"Could I talk to you, Mrs. Fields?"

"Certainly, come in Eric and sit down. What can I do for you?"

"I'd like to change my schedule. I want to enroll in football if it's not too late."

"No, of course not. Coach Duncan will be glad to have another player. Let's look at your schedule." She took out a folder on her desk.

"What would you think about moving your seventh period algebra class to fourth period and dropping physical education?"

"Sounds good."

"Done. Here's a pass to your first period class to explain being late."

I couldn't talk to Riley, but at least she would be pleased with me coming out for football. The remainder of the day I had trouble concentrating on my classes, thinking of my decision. No one said anything to me about football, so I assumed the counselor hadn't told anyone. On my way to the field house seventh period, I kept saying to myself, "You made the right decision, now get on with it." I didn't say anything to Coach Duncan when I handed him the note from Mrs. Fields with the schedule change.

"Eric, that's great. Welcome, we're glad to have you as part of the team. Coach Adams will get you suited up. We'll take it easy for a couple of days, and you can just participate in the drills. We'll need to see what position will be appropriate."

"Coach, I'm nervous. I know nothing about football or the equipment." I was hoping he would see I needed help.

"Don't worry, Eric. You'll learn quickly. Wait here and I'll get Coach Adams to fit you out in a workout uniform."

I got sick waiting for Adams to come get me. What if he laughed at me for not knowing anything about putting on a suit? My stomach was churning with butterflies, and I was afraid of throwing up at any time. I sat down, taking deep breaths, trying to calm myself. Finally, he appeared.

"Sorry you had to wait. I had to tape some ankles. We need to get you suited up. Let's go to the equipment room."

Evidently, Coach Duncan instructed him to help me. He selected shoulder pads, jersey, and shoes for me. He found pants that he thought should fit, placing knee pads and thigh pads in them. He found a pair of hip pads that he said should work. He then selected a helmet that he had me try on.

"That about does it, Eric, except for the most important thing." He handed me a square box with a picture of a jockey strap on it. "Take your stuff into the locker room and get dressed. They're plenty of empty lockers to hang up your street clothes."

Following him into the locker room, most of the boys were still in the process of getting dressed. When I entered, they all stopped and stared.

"Eric! You decided to join us." Luis motioned, "Bring your stuff over here. There's an empty locker next to me."

I put my equipment on the bench and sitting down, took off my shoes. I hesitated, dreading getting undressed. I'd never removed my clothes in front of anyone and most of the boys were still in the dressing room, putting on their workout stuff. Nobody seemed the least bit concerned or embarrassed. Of course, they'd done this a hundred times. I removed my clothes as slowly as possible getting down to my shorts. By the time, I got around to putting on my most important piece of equipment, the dressing room only included a half dozen boys. They didn't seem to be paying any attention to me. I put my hip pads on and then slipped into my pants. So far so good, I thought. I slipped my shoulder pads on next and was about to put on my jersey when one of them came over to me.

"Hi. I'm Bruce. We're glad to have you. Let me give you a hand with your shoulder pads. They can be confusing. We need to move them from the back to the front and they'll fit better."

I had my shoulder pads on backwards. I knew something like this would happen. Embarrassed, I said, "Thanks, I'm new at this."

"No problem." Taking the shoulder pads, he turned them around.

I put them on and then placed my arms and head in the jersey, then Bruce pulled it down for me. He would probably tell everyone, and they'd be laughing.

Bruce sat down on the bench. "Get your shoes on and I'll wait for you."

The two of us were the last to leave the dressing room, and when we reached the practice field everyone was lined up for calisthenics. I was surprised when Bruce took his place out front as the leader. I'd done most of the exercises in PE classes and it was no problem to follow along.

Coach Duncan strolled over to where I was. "Everything fit all right, Eric?"

"I think so. Bruce helped me."

We did several drills after calisthenics, and I was able to keep up. Coach Adams spoke words of encouragement. Digging post holes was paying off. After that, the team ran offensive plays. Bruce was the quarterback and Luis was one of the halfbacks. I wasn't assigned a position, so I spent most of the remainder of the workout as a spectator. My blunder with the shoulder pads was not mentioned by anyone. I was fine with Coach Bryson's avoidance.

The final part of practice was wind sprints that covered half the field. We were divided up into backs and linemen and I was placed in the latter group. There were ten in my group and I won. After that, Coach Duncan told me to run with the backs. We ran seven more sprints, and I was in front in all but one, with Luis racing ahead.

Coach called us all together after the sprints, said a few words about the upcoming scrimmage, and dismissed us. As we were leaving he asked me to stay.

"I was surprised at your speed, Eric. That was impressive."

"Thanks. I've lost weight and that helps."

"We're going to try you at fullback. I'm pleased that you decided to play." He smiled, patting me on my shoulder pads.

"Me too."

I LEFT the field house feeling good about my day. No one laughed at me. I was even able to take a shower with everyone. We were supposed to have our own towels, but Luis loaned me his extra one. Everyone had been friendly, especially Bruce. The guys were different from the group I was around last year. We always made jokes about someone or found ways to criticize. At times we'd even turn on each other. I felt better about myself than at any time in my memory. Would it last? Would Gavin's coming home change everything?

I turned the corner of the building and Gavin's truck came into view. Was I seeing things? Yes! Riley was sitting on the hood.

24

LUTA

On the way out of town, we stopped at Walmart, buying a small baby bottle and powdered milk. Gavin held the puppy the entire trip and said little for the first two hours. The last several miles he became more talkative.

"What do you think about increasing our stock? Maybe going to 400 cows and hiring someone to help me."

He caught me by surprise. "That's a great idea. I can help and with the new hire we can handle it without a problem. Eric will also be available especially after football. I'm glad he decided to play."

"Didn't expect that. Does his dad know he's playing football?" Gavin asked.

"I haven't talked to him since Eric told me. I doubt if he's told his dad yet."

"He can't be very good, since he's never played before."

"Gavin, at least he's going to try. I know it'll be beneficial for him, and he'll make new friends."

I'd noticed a change in Gavin the last several weeks. It was gradual but noticeable. Maybe my prayers were going to be answered. Hopefully, returning happier and more positive. He'd already told me he was naming the puppy Jenny after Jenson, his therapist. So far he hadn't been as negative about Eric, and I prayed that would continue. The suggestion that we increase our livestock was a positive sign. One looking to the future. Something he hadn't done for the past sixteen years.

We didn't get to the ranch until after six o'clock, and Eric wasn't home. The first thing we did was fix a bottle for Jenny and Gavin fed her. It didn't take her long to figure out she liked the bottle. After she finished, we fixed her a better bed in the hat box adding an old pillow to the blanket.

We were eating supper when Eric arrived, and I was surprised to see he had a fresh haircut. I got up and hugged him. "My goodness, Eric. How handsome you look."

"I got my hair cut," he stated nonchalantly, like it wasn't a big deal.

"I see that. It looks great. I imagine you're starving. You can tell us about school while we eat."

He sat down and filled his plate. I waited anxiously for Gavin to comment on his hair. At least he hadn't said anything ugly. I assumed Eric expected him to comment, also and when he didn't he went on eating.

"I've got a new dog." Gavin proudly announced.

"Really? What kind?"

"Probably a lab. She's just a puppy, and we're having to feed her with a bottle."

"That's great." Eric was trying to be positive with Gavin.

"How was football today?" Gavin inquired.

"Good. I'm going to play fullback."

"Fullback? I figured you'd be a guard or tackle."

Here we go again. Eric continued to eat, not looking up at his granddad nor offering any response. I was hoping Gavin would say something positive. Eric looked good, much better than when he arrived the first week in July. His weight loss was amazing. With his haircut and tan, he had converted into a good-looking young man. I would go so far as to say, transformed.

"How do you like your coach?" Gavin asked.

"He's nice. He came out to see me and brought pizza after the first day of school. He's the main reason I returned to school."

"Is he the reason you came out for football?"

"Partially."

"What else?"

"Luis wanted me to come out."

Eric finished eating before we did and left the table, going to his room. I was disappointed. "Gavin, why do you have to be ugly to Eric? I don't understand. I thought after your heart attack and almost dying, you would at least, be thankful, and more positive toward your grandson. I just don't understand."

He looked surprised. "I didn't say anything ugly to Eric. I just gave him my opinion of what position he should play. The coach must be out of his mind to put him in the backfield. I could probably outrun him."

I reminded him. "You said nothing about his hair, which you had nagged him about continuously before going to the hospital."

"It looks better, but it's still not short enough to suit me. I'm not happy about him staying here permanently. He needs to be at his home with his dad and brother."

"How can you say that, Gavin? Look what a change he's made since coming here. He has friends and is going to school. He came out for football, and the coach has taken a special interest in him. He's looked after the ranch while we were away. This is where Eric needs to be. Surely, you can see that and accept it."

Instead of responding, Gavin got up and went to the den. I followed him, and after he turned on the TV and sat down I continued, determined that he would answer me. "Do you disagree with what I've just said?"

"I don't know. Maybe I'll feel different after some time. It's obvious that he's here to stay no matter what I think. Now, I'd like to watch *Hawaii Five-0* if that's okay."

I gave up and went to the kitchen to work on my Sunday school lesson. After a half hour or so Gavin came in and started preparing the puppy's bottle. Finishing, he sat down and started talking. I sat there amazed at how he opened up, beginning when we were young and continuing up until the girls were in high school. He stopped before getting to the tragedy. The way they died was still too difficult to discuss. He hadn't talked to me like this for many years. I just listened, not interrupting him. When he finished he spoke directly to me.

"I'll try to do better, Luta. I know it hasn't been easy putting up with me since we lost the girls. I seem to have lost control. Just can't help being angry. At just about everything. I've been so full of hate. What you said about Eric is right. Maybe it's a step in the right direction to be able to admit it."

Without giving me time to respond, he got up and left. Maybe this is the turning point, I thought. Hopefully, we could move forward from here. I went back to studying my lesson and was interrupted by the phone. It was Cameron. I expected him to ask for Eric, but I sensed, by his tone, that something was wrong. Finally, after a few minutes of small talk he told me the purpose of the call.

"Mother, I have a problem. I need to come out and talk with you. I don't want Dad to know, but it's serious and involves a financial situation. Could I come tomorrow?"

"Why sure, Cameron. Eric will be glad to see you."

"I should be there by noon. Could you meet me in town for lunch at the café?"

"I guess so. Why don't you want your dad involved?"

"He'd just be angry and despise me even more than he does."

I agreed to meet him and after ending the call, sat and thought for a long time wondering what could be the problem. Cameron made good money and was always an excellent financial manager. It wasn't difficult to understand why he didn't want his dad involved. Any weakness that Cameron had would only be exploited to make him look even less. It was hard to imagine he and his dad's relationship being any worse, but I guess it was possible.

IT WASN'T difficult to get away without Gavin the next morning. He was tired from the trip home and was napping on the couch. I told him

I had some things to do in town and there were leftovers in the fridge. I was at the Frontier by eleven-thirty and Cameron was already there. I saw immediately, from the look on his face that whatever he had come for was serious. He was seated in a far corner booth. Sitting across from him, he didn't ask about Eric or his dad but went right to the reason for coming.

"Thank you, Mother, for getting away without Dad. I know you're wondering what this is all about. You're aware that the cattle market has been high. Last year I made good money putting cattle in the feed lot. Everybody's been doing it. I had someone buy a lot of fifty to put on feed. I borrowed the money at the bank with only the cattle as collateral. The bank loaned the money for the feed, so I put no money up front. I only put one lot on feed last year but thought since it was so easy that this year, I would expand to ten lots or 500 head. They've been on feed for five months now, and the market has crashed. If I sell them now my loss will be $50,000 plus another $7000 for the feed bill. I don't have anything close to that much money. I don't know what to do."

I was stunned and couldn't respond for several minutes. "Why would you take such a chance, Cameron?"

"Mother, it'd been easy money. Everyone was doing it. Even people that knew nothing about cattle. With my experience on the ranch, I thought I could make a lot of money in a hurry. It was a golden opportunity. The first year I made $5000 on the one lot I fed out. I thought, why not make ten times that much? It was a dumb move but it's done."

"We don't have that kind of money available, Cameron, unless we sell part of the ranch. We have a savings account with a little over $20,000 in it."

"No. I don't want your money. The only thing positive about this whole episode is that instead of steers, I bought heifers, since they were a little cheaper. My only chance to come out of this is to move them to the ranch, put bulls with them and calve them out. Selling even 300 pair should bring enough to pay off what I owe the bank. I know it's asking a lot, but do you think it might be possible?"

"Calving out 500 heifers! You know better than that, Cameron. You were raised on a ranch. You know how much trouble heifers are. It would be impossible. We would need six hands, at least, working full time."

"We wouldn't need extra help until the heifers were due which would be almost a year. We could cross that bridge when we came to it. I know you have the grass. Most of the ranch hasn't been used for years. Mother, I'm desperate. If something isn't done, I'll be ruined. A sixty per cent calf crop would give us 300 pair, which would get me out of debt and if the market improves might even turn a profit. I've already talked to the bank, and they'll loan me the money needed to buy the bulls and cover other expenses as well if you'll sign the note, also. They know this is their only chance for me to repay the debt. If I sell now they'll never get their money. My annual income is only $18,000. There is no way I can come up with $57,000."

The more he talked, the more frustrated I became. He hadn't even asked about Eric or his dad. Here he was asking me to do the impossible—get him out of a fix that he created. Having to sign his bank note would put Gavin over the edge. He was my son and what could I do but try? I took a deep breath. "I'll talk to your dad and see if he thinks it might be possible."

"Mother! You know what Dad will say. He wouldn't cross the road to help me. He hates me. He'd never agree to co-sign the note."

"Cameron, I can't take this any further without your dad being involved." I couldn't believe even with their poor relationship; he would ask that Gavin be excluded.

"Well, I wasted my trip out here. He'll be irate."

"Cameron, you haven't even asked about Eric. Did you know he's playing football?" I couldn't help but express my anger.

"No. He hasn't told me. It's been several days since I've talked to him. I'm surprised. I can't imagine him in a football suit. He's never had any interest in athletics. I doubt if he stays with it."

"What makes you say that?" I fired back.

"I wouldn't think he would put forth the effort."

I was getting angrier the longer we talked. I decided we needed to end it. "I'll get back with you after I talk to your father. Do you want to see Eric or your dad while you're here?"

"I need to get on the road. It's a long drive. I'll be coming back in a few weeks to stay a day or two. I don't expect to hear from you, if Dad's in the decision. I don't understand why he should have a say. The ranch was passed down from your family and really belongs to you. It was your inheritance."

I didn't respond, only telling him to be safe on the drive back to San Antonio. Hugging and thanking me he walked out to his car, not looking back.

25

FRANK

The next several days were quiet with no major problems. Eric came to school with his hair cut and continued to attend Bryson's class. Riley didn't say anything about the class, so I assumed Bryson accepted him back. Riley was interested in Eric, and I was confused as to the reason. She'd always taken up for the underdog, but it could be more than that this time around. He was the only boy she ever mentioned and was excited about him coming out for football. Aubrey, on the other hand, talked nonstop about the boys, moving from one to another. What was concerning to Julie and me, was the fact they were older, with most of them in high school. We attempted to encourage her to make friends with her classmates, but she insisted they were too childish.

Coach Duncan didn't call off the scrimmage on Friday, which was held at our place. I'm sure he regretted it since we looked terrible, not making a first down and being scored on several times. I felt sorry for him and wondered why he didn't play Luis at quarterback, at least part of the time. Of course, Eric didn't suit up for the scrimmage but was on the sideline with the other four players who weren't on the field. I did notice Loughton, walking the sidelines, shaking his head occasionally, showing everyone who bothered to look at him that he wasn't satisfied with our performance. It was a relief when the scrimmage was over.

I went to the dressing room and waited outside until Coach had a chance to talk with the boys. When he opened the door, I went inside and followed him to his office. I wanted to say something encouraging, but it was a challenge to come up with anything positive.

"We didn't have any more injuries today, did we, Coach?"

"No. That's the only good thing that happened."

"We'll get better after you've had the boys longer." I was hoping to make him feel better.

"I didn't give Luis any playing time at quarterback. Loughton has been at every workout, giving me advice on how to coach Bruce, his son. Bruce can't run the offense. He's just too slow. Of course, the *Wishbone* puts pressure on the offense by having a threat at fullback who can keep them honest inside, a halfback that can reach the corner, and a quarterback that can run if the defense gives him the opportunity. Right now, the only threat we have is Luis at halfback. The defense doesn't have to concentrate on the fullback or quarterback at all. The result is that we have no offense."

"What do you think Loughton will do if you put Luis at quarterback?"

"No telling. Probably raise hell with me, you, the superintendent, and the remainder of the board. He might even pull Bruce out of football. It's a sad situation. I've never been around a finer young man than Bruce. The thing about it, he's smart enough to realize he shouldn't be playing quarterback. Of course, he'd never admit that to his dad. I feel sorry for him. I know what it's like, being unable to live up to the expectations of your dad. The most important aspect of my relationship with my dad was football. During football we had a lot to talk about. When the season ended, most of the conversation did also. I can't explain it. It seemed that his respect for me was based on football and not who I was. When I came home with my career over, I knew that our relationship would never be the same. It turned out—I was correct."

As I listened to Coach Duncan, it was obvious why he was so

devastated at not making the Cowboys and started drinking. He came home to a father who was disappointed in him and the distance between them lengthened even further. He was an All American and played on a National Championship team yet that wasn't enough.

"What about Eric? Is there a chance he would help you?" I asked, changing the subject.

"Maybe. It's too early to tell. I do have a problem in that Eric will be ineligible because he hasn't been in school here for a year. Of course, if the district committee will approve his eligibility he could play this year. We have a district meeting next week, and I'll present the request to them. Since he's never played football, along with the circumstances that caused him to move, they'll probably accept him. After all, they wouldn't expect him to make a contribution. However, I firmly believe there are two kinds of players, those that help football and those that football helps. I think that football will be good for Eric, so I hope he's approved."

"Can I do anything to help?" My admiration for this man continued to grow.

"If you attend the meeting, you can show your support for Eric by making some positive comments, Mr. Mendenhall."

"I would be glad to do that," I said, getting up and leaving. I knew that Coach wanted to get back with his boys. I left the field house, meeting Loughton coming in. "Hello." My greeting received no response. Nothing seemed to be easy with a school board member who was determined to be involved in everyday decisions of the school. And, a superintendent who wasn't strong enough to prevent it from happening.

EVERYONE WENT to the scrimmage so our evening meal was late. Julie had been paid today so she had bought pizza which was a treat. Aubrey was talkative as usual, commenting on how cute some of the boys were on the visiting team.

"Aubrey, are boys all you think about?" Julie asked, while she sliced the pizza.

She giggled. "No, just most of the time. I think about tennis and food, too. Sometimes, I even think about my studies. Riley's interested in a boy. Did y'all know that?"

Julie and I stopped eating and looked at Riley, who didn't seem to hear the comment and continued working on a slice of pizza. I cleared my throat and she looked up.

"What?"

"Did you hear your sister's announcement?"

"Sure. I'm not deaf." She returned to her pizza.

"What about it?" Her attitude annoyed me.

"Maybe. I'll let you know when the time comes." Riley continued to munch.

I knew that was all we would get out of her. She looked so much like her mother when she had an attitude. I assumed the boy was Eric but didn't press the issue.

Julie filled in the silence by telling us about her week at the bank. She liked her job and met some interesting people. She continued to amaze me with her resiliency. No matter what the situation—she made the most of it. After all these years, it remained a puzzle as to how a nerd like me with thick glasses was fortunate enough to marry her.

Out of the blue, Aubrey blurted. "I've been invited to a party tomorrow night."

"Who and where?" Julie asked, already frowning.

"Sammy invited me. It's at his house."

"Who's Sammy?" I interrupted.

"He's in my class. Sammy's nice." Riley volunteered.

"So, it's for high school students?" Her mother was getting the idea.

"I guess so, but he invited me." Aubrey pleaded in her sweetest voice.

Julie looked at me, as if to say, do you tell her or do I? I beat her to the punch.

"Aubrey, we've told you before you need to associate with your classmates. Besides, you still have a few days left to serve on your grounding. It wouldn't be a good idea for you to attend. I'm sorry, but your mother and I feel strongly about this."

"I don't see why. I was invited and it's just going to be snacks and a movie." She knew better than to argue but that didn't stop her.

"Aubrey, you heard your dad. He said you weren't going and that's final."

She got up and left the table, headed toward her room. She would pout now for the rest of the weekend. She had half a piece of pizza left on her plate and Riley reached for it. She could eat more than anyone I knew to remain so thin.

Riley bit into the pizza. "She's going to be mad now."

"She'll get over it." I hoped to be right but knew it wouldn't happen anytime soon.

"Would you let her go with me? Sammy has a new VCR and has the movie *Jaws*. It's supposed to be really good and scary. I could make sure she behaves herself by being chaperone."

Julie looked at me to provide an answer. I trusted Riley and knew she'd be good for her word, however, I didn't trust Aubrey in the least. I hesitated, which prompted Julie to quiz Riley.

"Will you not let her out of your sight?"

"No. I'll stay right with her all night," Riley promised.

"Will this boy's parents be home?" Julie continued.

"I'm sure they will be. He's really a nice boy."

Julie knew we needed to be together on this. "What do you think, Frank?"

"It'd certainly make for a more pleasant weekend." I smiled, thinking about a date night with my beautiful wife.

"It's settled then, Riley. We'll let her go. You can give her the news," Julie said.

I wondered if we were doing the right thing by giving in. Maybe this one time it would work out. After all we could depend on Riley.

JULIE and I had Saturday night to ourselves. I let Riley take the car since the party was less than a mile from our house. We didn't dare leave the house since Riley wouldn't be able to get in touch with us in case we were needed. We watched TV, had a late night snack of popcorn and waited patiently for the girls to come home. We talked about the fact that this would be the first of many nights in the years to come we would spend waiting for them. We'd told Riley to be home by eleven and they came in the door, laughing, at 10:58.

"The movie was awesome! I'm never going swimming in the ocean." Aubrey, wide-eyed, announced.

Riley added. "The music was amazing. It forecast each time the shark was going to appear and eat someone."

"Gross." Julie's face registered disgust. "How many kids came?"

"Probably, at least thirty. We had all kinds of snacks. It was fun," Riley said.

"Riley didn't let me out of her sight. Can you believe she went to the bathroom with me? Every time a boy tried to talk to me, she'd give him that evil eye. It was embarrassing, but I still had fun."

We spent the next half hour listening to a recount of the evening. It was evident they had a great time and maybe it worked out for the best. After all, it was important they made new friends and were accepted into the community by the students as well as parents. After they went to bed, Julie and I congratulated ourselves on making a good decision. Of course, we also talked about how fortunate we were to be able to depend on Riley.

AFTER CHURCH and lunch the next day, I went to my office to sort through my mail. Riley asked if I might open the gym for her so she could shoot baskets. I agreed and when we reached the gym it was already opened. Coach Adams and the girls' basketball coach were already there. Both were single and close to the same age. I'd seen them eating together in the school cafeteria on Friday. Tiffany Kennecott was the girls' coach's name, but she preferred to be addressed as Coach Tiff by the girls. She was an attractive young lady, probably a year or two older than Coach Adams. It appeared the staff might have a blossoming romance.

Coach Tiff came over. "Hi, Riley and Mr. Mendenhall. I'm showing Coach Adams a thing or two about basketball since he knows nothing. Join us Riley, and you can help me demonstrate some of the finer points of the game to this football coach."

"Maybe later, Coach. I'm going to help Dad for awhile. Is Coach Adams a good student?"

She smiled at him. "He's a work in progress."

"Don't I have anything to say about this?" Coach Adams asked.

"Maybe later. Right now, we need to get back to work." Coach Tiff insisted as if addressing one of her girls.

After they were out of hearing distance, I asked Riley. "Don't you want to stay and shoot baskets?"

"No. They're enjoying themselves, and I don't want to interfere. Have you got something for me to do so I won't be guilty of telling a lie?"

"Sure. You can run some more copies of the calendar for this month. By the way, would you like to tell me about Eric?"

"Oh, I don't know, Dad. He seems lonely and in need of someone to care for him. I think he's cute in a certain kind of way. Right now, I just want to help him. He has so little confidence. Maybe with a little attention he'll feel better about himself. I'm glad he came out for football."

Again, I wondered how there could be so much difference in my two girls. "I'm proud of you, Riley." I handed her the calendar.

26

ERIC

W e didn't arrive at church in time for Sunday school. I'd gladly accepted Dawn's invitation to attend church with her, hoping to see Riley. We were one of the first to take our seats toward the back. The pastor came by, asking about Gavin, and saying he was glad to see us. I hoped he wouldn't mention coming fishing again since he'd ask me what happened to the boat.

Riley had waited on me after practice Thursday, to tell me she was glad I'd come out for football. I was actually able to speak to her, even though it was limited. I talked to her again after the scrimmage on Friday and did even better. Of course, I didn't suit up for the scrimmage but did stand on the sidelines. There was a party Saturday night, but I wasn't invited. Since she would've been there, I was disappointed.

I couldn't sit still in church, squirming around in my seat looking back toward the door. The preacher came to the pulpit and started speaking, but I didn't hear a word. Riley and her family came in and took seats across the aisle and two rows in front of us. I tried to concentrate on the sermon, but I kept looking at her, hoping to get her attention. The service ended, and I met her in the aisle on the way out.

"Hello, Eric. You look nice today."

"Thanks. You look beautiful."

We were in line together to greet the pastor. "Eric, I heard you came out for football. That's great. Riley, good to see you today. You're looking good."

"Thank you, Pastor. I enjoyed your message today."

When we were outside, she touched my arm. "I'll see you tomorrow, Eric."

Dawn must have seen the exchange. She commented on the way home she thought Riley liked me and was a pretty girl.

"She's nice." I hoped she was right. "Riley is the first girl to pay any attention to me."

"Eric, about your granddad. I believe he's trying to change. It's going to take time, but please be patient with him. You have to admit he's doing better. Also, I didn't tell you, but your dad came to see me Friday. I haven't even told Gavin yet. I'm trying to decide how to approach him."

My first thought when she told me was that he didn't even come to see me after driving all the way out here. That's about right. He could care less about me. Well, I wasn't going back home. I could put up with Gavin. I had friends here and there was Riley. Dawn, then told me the purpose of his visit, explaining his financial problem. I couldn't believe it. He'd always been conscientious of money and careful about our spending. He must be in deep trouble to come asking for Dawn and Gavin's help. It gave me a good feeling, knowing he made mistakes. In the past it'd always been me that was messing up. "Are you going to help him?" I asked.

"I have no choice, Eric. After all he's my son and is in trouble."

"What do you think Gavin will say?" I already had a pretty good idea.

"I fear the worst. I've been praying about it. I have to tell him today. The heifers need to be moved out here immediately. If we put bulls with them they should calve in the summer and be ready to sell by next winter. We've only been feeding 200 cows. I can't imagine what it'll take to add another 500. I know we'll have to hire additional help. I'm counting on you, too. After football season is over, you'll have more time."

"Gavin's going to be mad." That was the understatement of the year. "He's probably going to explode."

"I know, Eric. God and I have our work cut out for us."

AFTER SUNDAY LUNCH, I asked if it would be all right if I went fishing since it was such a beautiful day. Dawn said it would be fine. She had chicken livers in the freezer I could use for bait. Since I didn't have a boat anymore, my best chance was to fish from the bank for catfish. I loaded my new equipment in the truck with a jug of water. I was glad to get away from the storm that was going to erupt when she told Gavin about my dad. It was five miles to the lake, but I could probably hear the explosion even from there.

The water looked like a mirror. I baited my three prong hook with a piece of liver and cast it as far as possible. The bank was grassy and I lay back, gazing at the white fluffy clouds floating past, thinking of the last three months. *What was different about me? Everything, I thought, answering my own question. I came here as a fat kid disliking everyone, including myself. I expected everyone to make fun of me and was on the defensive. I didn't have one real friend. I looked down on just about everyone, hoping to believe someone was worse off than me. What happened? Dawn accepted and believed in me. She treated me like I was somebody—saying she loved me. The couple that rescued me were nice and the highway patrolman was the first adult to shake my hand. Pastor Jacob took me fishing and invited me to lunch. He actually seemed to like me. Luis wanted to be my friend and encouraged me to play football. Mr. Mendenhall took my side against Coach Bryson. Bruce corrected me when I put my shoulder pads on backwards and didn't tell anyone. And then—there was Riley.*

Suddenly, I heard my reel clicking, grabbed the rod, jerked and set the hook. The rod was bent almost dipping into the water, and I came close to having it pulled from my hands. I tried to reel in the line, but it wouldn't budge. I held on as the line came off my reel making a zinging sound. I finally got it stopped and began slowly winding it in, losing control several times, with the line going out. After at least half an hour, I had the fish close enough to shore to see it. It was huge! I'd never seen a fish that large. Just before I tried to drag it on to shore, it flopped, rolled over, and came loose. I sat down, exhausted and wondered if anyone would believe me.

I continued to fish for another two hours, catching three nice ones that would be plenty for a meal. The three together wouldn't even come close to being as large as the one that got away. The first thing I did at the house was clean the three fish. The catfish were different from the bass but the fillets came out good. When I presented them to Dawn she was impressed.

"I'm going to fry these for supper. Thank you, Eric. They'll be delicious."

I didn't tell her about the one that got away. "How did it go with Gavin?"

"Bad at first but it got a little better. He's down at the barn. I'll tell you about it later."

I was going to make an effort to avoid him as much as possible. "I need to do some homework. I'll get that done while you're cooking."

Going to my room, I washed my hands again with soap to get the fish smell off before starting my homework. I'd just finished my assignment when Dawn called to me that supper was ready. I checked Gavin out before sitting down on the other side of the table, but couldn't tell anything about his mood. Dawn said the blessing, and once we began eating, I decided to tell them about the big one that got away. I didn't exaggerate but expected Gavin not to believe me. I was caught totally off guard by his response.

"There're some big fish in that tank. It's never been dry. These fish you caught are the perfect size to eat. The big one wouldn't have been as good."

I didn't know how to respond. That was the first time he'd ever spoken to me that way. What happened? I decided not to press my fortune, thinking that remaining quiet might be the best thing to do.

"Eric, these fish are delicious and you don't have to bother with bones," Dawn said.

"Pastor Jacob showed me how to fillet fish."

"Did you use the boat today?" Gavin asked, glancing up at me.

I knew things were going too well. "No, I fished from the bank." I looked down at my plate.

"You should've used the boat. I've had it for thirty years and used to take the girls fishing in it."

Suddenly, my mouth full of fish . . . lost its taste.

I THOUGHT of little else Monday except football practice. When my sixth period class ended, I beat it out to the field house hoping to be dressed before most of the guys arrived. Since the majority of players already were there, everyone else must've been as anxious. I undressed and got into my suit as quickly as possible, making sure my shoulder pads were on right. Luis pulled my jersey down over my pads, and I returned the favor.

After calisthenics and drills, we broke off in offensive groups with the backs going with Coach Duncan, line with Coach Bryson, and receivers with Coach Adams. Coach Duncan spent time showing me how to take the ball by forming a pocket, with my arm closest to the ball always being up. I took handoffs from Bruce and Luis. I learned three plays, two of which I carried the ball. The practice went quickly and when it ended, I was pleased, especially with Coach Duncan's compliments. In all the fifty-yard sprints conditioning, I came in first.

Bruce walked with me back to the field house. "You did good today, Eric."

"Thanks. It was fun," I replied, pleased beyond words.

There was a man at practice who stopped Bruce as we were going into the field house. I assumed it must be his dad. I didn't hear what he said to Bruce but it sounded angry.

Bruce's comment gave me confidence. I was more comfortable getting undressed and showering with the rest of the team, and I'd thought to bring my towel today. As I was leaving the dressing room,

Coach Bryson was coming in. He stopped and glared at me. I walked around him, getting away as quickly as possible. A great day and it had to end like this. I hurried to my truck, hoping Riley would be waiting on me again. She wasn't and my spirits sank. Maybe, I could call her tonight and tell her about my day. On the drive home, I made myself a promise. *I wouldn't let Bryson get to me.*

THE NEXT SEVERAL days went by without a hitch. I was enjoying football more each practice and found myself looking forward to it. On Friday, between first and second period, Riley stopped me in the hall, saying her locker was stuck again. This time the door was more difficult and it took me several minutes of pulling on it before it opened. By the time I went to my locker and made it to class, the tardy bell had rung. I expected a problem and wasn't surprised.

"You're late, Sager. I don't tolerate that. You have adequate time between classes. Go to the office and get a tardy permit." Coach Bryson glared at me like I had committed some terrible crime.

I went to the office, explained to Mr. Mendenhall why I was late, and he sent me back to class with an excused tardy. When I presented the tardy to Bryson he blew up. "It figures! You can get by with anything. I told you once before to get out of my class and he sent you back. I'm telling you again. Get out of here. Now!"

Riley spoke up in my defense. "Coach Bryson, he was helping me get my locker door open. I'm the reason he was late."

"You weren't late." He snapped back at Riley.

He turned back to me. "Get out, now."

I left the room, but this time instead of going home, I went to the office. Mrs. Kraal told me to wait while she told Mr. Mendenhall. She came back shortly, telling me I could see him now.

"What's the problem, Eric?"

I explained what had happened when I returned to class with the note. "It would be better if I didn't go back to his class. I know all juniors take American history but maybe it could be worked into my schedule next year. He hates me for some reason." My best chance at avoiding confrontation was not to be around him.

He didn't respond for several minutes as if trying to decide what to do. "Eric, I'm sorry. I've never had anything like this happen. Maybe you're right. Let's go see the counselor and see what we can do."

Mr. Mendenhall told Mrs. Fields what had happened before he left. She agreed that a schedule change would be for the best. "Come with me, Eric."

"Where to?" I asked.

"I want you to meet someone."

We ended up in a building that was still on campus but not connected to the main one. She stopped at the door and knocked. A young man appeared.

"Mr. Puckett, would you like to have another student?"

"I sure would."

"This is Eric and he lives on a ranch. I thought Vocational Agriculture would be appropriate for him," she explained.

He immediately brought his hand forward. "We'll be glad to have him."

I shook his hand and I liked him immediately. He was even shorter than I was, but his grip was firm. The counselor left and I stayed in Mr. Puckett's class. I'd look back many years later at Bryson kicking me out of his class—and be thankful.

27

LUTA

"He owes $50,000! He asks us to co-sign the note to borrow additional money!"

"Gavin, you know what the doctor said about stress. You need to stay calm."

"Stay calm! You're telling me our son owes $50,000 and is asking for our help. What do you expect me to do, just smile and say no problem? He's heard me say many times I'd never invest in feedlot cattle. Of course, he never listened to me."

"He's our son, Gavin, and we're going to help him. We have the grass, and it's the only way he can get out of this."

"Bull! He can get himself out of it. I'm not about to sign any note." He rubbed his chest, becoming quiet, and then he left the table going into the den. I followed him and watched as he sat down in his chair, still rubbing his chest.

"Gavin, are you okay? Do you need a nitroglycerin pill?"

He whispered. "Yeah. I think so."

I went back into the kitchen and opened the bottle of pills that we kept on the counter, taking one out and returning to the den. He took the pill and put it under his tongue, leaning back in his chair. I stayed with him for the next half hour, finally asking if he needed to go to the doctor.

"No. It's better. I need to sit here for a few more minutes. Would you get me a glass of water?"

I brought his water and he took several swallows and started talking. "I want to select the bulls. We'll need to find hay. It's late and not going to be easy. Maybe we can handle the load with one extra hand until they begin calving, and then we'll need at least two more. It's not surprising that they've agreed to give him an additional loan. After all, it's the only way the bank will get their money. You'll need to get in touch with Cameron and tell him to ship the heifers out here as soon as possible. We need to check the windmills. They've been turned off now for a long time. I know they'll need greasing. There hasn't been anything in the back ten sections for years and the grass should run them several months if we cake them occasionally. Can you imagine how much feed we'll need to buy?"

"Yes Gavin, but the additional loan will provide money for all the feed. Are you sure that's the best pasture?" Thank God he had accepted the fact we were going to help Cameron.

"Yeah. It runs into the mountains and they can get shelter if we have some bad weather this winter. It could be one of those years where we get snow and ice. We'll move them down to the East Pasture in the early spring. When they start calving we'll need to have them as close as possible. At least one out of every five or six will probably need help, even with Angus bulls. I'll begin making calls tomorrow about buying round bales. It's been a long time since we've run this amount of stock and never this many heifers."

He leaned back and closed his eyes as if it was too much for him to consider. For an instant I felt sorry for him having all this dumped in his lap. Then I closed my eyes and thanked God for answering my prayers. I didn't expect it to happen this way, but it was a blessing to have Gavin's cooperation. It also showed him, in the future, he couldn't become angry and agitated. Suddenly, falling into my grandmother's maple rocker, I realized the strain of the last two days.

Dreading telling Gavin about Cameron's problem had taken its toll . . . I was tired.

CAMERON WAS surprised when I called and told him the next day he could ship the heifers to our ranch and to send the papers from the bank for us to sign. He thanked me over and over, telling me he'd begin making arrangements immediately. He even asked about Eric. He also surprised me, by saying he might come out this next weekend to help get ready for the delivery of the heifers.

I told Gavin his response. "He was pleased we're going to help him. He thought it would be about a week before the heifers were shipped." I prayed silently he would respond in a positive manner.

"The sooner the better."

"Gavin, we have to do something about Eric's transportation. You need the pickup, and I can't give up my car. We need to get a used car for Eric." Maybe I was pressing my good fortune. "We're going to need him here at the ranch as much as possible to help."

"Can't he ride the bus?"

"No. Not since he came out for football," I reminded him.

"Shouldn't his dad take care of that?"

"I don't imagine he can afford it. We can buy him a second hand car for probably $1000 or so that would be dependable. Maybe we can find something in the Odessa-Midland Thrifty Nickel. It would be better than buying from a dealer."

"See what you can do," he said, "I don't have time to mess with it. I need to find hay and locate some good young Angus bulls."

BY FRIDAY, I'd found a 1966 GMC pickup in Midland. The owner wanted $750 for it, which wasn't a bad price since it only had 60,000 miles. I convinced Gavin we needed to go look at it before someone else bought it. We left in his pickup after Eric had gone to school in my car. I didn't tell him, wanting it to be a surprise. On the drive to Midland, Gavin was in a good mood.

"I got in touch with a breeder who has some outstanding young Angus bulls. They're high but worth it. I'm going to buy thirty and will be surprised if they don't make money when we sell them. I still haven't located enough hay yet. Most of it has been sold or the farmers are keeping it for themselves. If we had a mild winter, we might get by without it, but we can't take a chance. You remember the winter of 1957? We had snow on the ground for over a month."

I listened, thinking that he hadn't looked to the future for the past sixteen years. "This is going to turn out to be a blessing," I mumbled to myself. Of course, we had Jenny with us. She was eating now but still liked her bottle. She was between us in her hat box but had already been trying to crawl out—looking over, paws on the edge.

We were in Midland by noon and found the address. The pickup was even better than we expected. I followed Gavin home in it, excited about Eric's response to his own pickup. He wouldn't be home until late tonight because they had an out-of-town football game. He was traveling with the team but didn't expect to play. I would park it in the garage so he wouldn't see it when he came home.

GAVIN and I had already finished breakfast before Eric came into the kitchen after sleeping late. I asked him what time he got home and how the game came out.

"It was a three-hour trip, and I didn't get home until around two o'clock. We got beat 50-0. Coach was disappointed but the other team was good. We had no offense. It was only 14-0 at half, but our defense gave out in the second half. I didn't play, but Coach told me coming home that next week I'd be in the starting lineup. I'm hungry, could I have some breakfast?"

"Sure, but go look in the garage first. We have a surprise for you."

Coming back within minutes, his face beamed. "Is that really mine?"

"Yes, Eric. You needed something to drive to school." The look on his face was worth the pickup.

"Thank you! It's great," he said, first hugging me and then going to Gavin and squeezing him on the shoulder.

"I can't believe it. My own truck. Can I drive it now?"

"Don't you want some breakfast first?" I reminded him.

"No, I'm not hungry."

"Go ahead. You can eat when you get back." He was gone by the time I got the words out of my mouth. I looked at Gavin and he was smiling. "You better go ahead and fix his breakfast. I need him to help me grease the windmills today. Would you like to go with us? I could put you to work, too. We have several tanks in the Mountain Pasture but we can't always depend on them to have adequate water. We have six windmills that will give the heifers better access to water."

"Sure. I'll go help you, but I'm not climbing any windmills. I'll fix us some dinner to take. It would save time from having to come back to the house to eat."

ERIC WAS BACK within half an hour and even more excited about his pickup. While he ate his breakfast, I told him about our plans to grease the windmills. Of course, after his surprise this morning, he was agreeable.

We left the house with me riding in the middle holding the hatbox containing Jenny. It was a twenty-minute drive to the Mountain Pasture. Gavin had bought a box of grease tubes and a new grease gun earlier in the week. This was one of my favorite locations on the ranch. The pasture ran up to and included the mountains, which had a rugged beauty. There were even some pine trees toward the top of the mountains. There were few trees leading up to the mountain, and without grazing the grass was lush. We came to the first windmill which, like the others, hadn't been turned on in years.

Gavin looked at Eric. "You ready to climb?"

"Sure. Just tell me what to do."

"You'll find some grease sockets on the windmill. There're four. Just attach the gun to the socket and pump the handle till you see grease coming out. Be careful. It would be a long fall." He attached the grease gun to twine which Eric could tie to his belt. "When you get on top, you can pull the gun up. That way you'll have your hands free while you're climbing. This was the way we did it when Stacy climbed the windmills. She used to beg me to do this job."

I was nervous at first, but after watching Eric handle himself, I relaxed and could see that he was going to do fine. After he finished and climbed down, Gavin turned on the windmill and it started turning, the sucker rod moving up and down. Within a few minutes, a stream of water began pouring into the cement trough.

We repeated the process at the second windmill with the same success. By this time, it was noon and we had our sandwiches and tea. It was a beautiful early fall day and a breeze with the 5000 feet altitude, caused it to be cool. I loved this country with its vastness and serenity. I never wanted to live anywhere else. To some it might seem barren and desolate, but to me it was and always would be my home. My thoughts were interrupted by Eric.

"What's that up on the side of that mountain?"

"Aoudad sheep. A whole flock of them." Gavin answered.

"Are they wild?"

"Very. I'm surprised we haven't seen deer yet."

"Does anyone ever hunt here?"

"I used to bring Stacy. She got her first Mule deer in this pasture on a Thanksgiving Day. Do you remember that, Luta?"

It took me a minute to respond. "Yes, he was a big one and you hung him in the barn to cool out. Stacy was excited. I cooked venison all winter at her insistence. Macy wouldn't eat it, and I would fix her something else. They were fourteen that year." I almost choked up before getting it out, as memories came flooding back.

Gavin came to my rescue. "Time to get back to work."

It was amazing, but we had the same success at the other four windmills, leaving them all pumping water. I expected several to be stuck and unable to pump. Gavin told Eric to drive when we headed back toward the house. I know Eric must've been tired but he didn't complain. Gavin gave him directions which would take us by the loading pens. Each pasture contained a set of shipping pens. A fence also enclosed fifty or so acres adjoining the pens. The pens constructed of wood were not in the best of shape.

"We'll hold the heifers here several days, and get them used to the cubes. I wanted to see how much water was in the small stock tank in the fifty-acre trap. It looks like there's enough to last them several days. Now, one more stop and we can get to the house by dark."

The one more stop was the cemetery which Gavin hadn't visited for several years. Eric and I stayed in the pickup while he walked over to the graves of the twins and the area where we'd buried Max.

"Dawn, my dad told me what happened but that was about all he said. It must've been terrible. I know better why Gavin is so angry."

Maybe if he knew more, he would be more understanding. "The girls went to a party. They had a curfew of twelve midnight. When they weren't home by then we didn't worry. We thought they were having so much fun, they lost track of time. By one o'clock we were concerned and went looking for them. We found an abandoned car but it wasn't theirs. From then on it was a nightmare. We hoped. Prayed. Begged and pleaded. Please bring our babies home. A week after they disappeared, our little girls were found in a culvert outside of Santa Fe, New Mexico." I paused, took a deep breath and continued. "We'd expected the outcome but weren't prepared for the grief that struck us." I couldn't go any further.

"Did they ever find out who did it?"

I shook my head, unable to answer. Eric must've understood. He didn't ask another question. I saw Gavin coming back. He wasn't gone long, and I was afraid he'd come back grieving.

"I'm glad you buried Max with the girls," he said, getting into the pickup and reaching inside the hatbox, petting Jenny.

Gavin opened and closed each gate on the way to the house, with me holding Jenny. When we drove up to the front, Eric asked if he could go into town in his new pickup to show Luis. I didn't know what Gavin thought as he remained quiet.

"I don't see why not, Eric. You've done a good day's work." I expected Gavin to object. Eric must've thought so too, because he was out of the pickup and gone in an instance.

"I need to get inside and feed Jenny, she's starving," Gavin commented.

After sixteen years, we had experienced . . . our best day.

28

ERIC

It had been one of those weeks where everything seemed to go right. First, my own truck, then attending the Ag class which was fun, then football practice where I was going to be the starting fullback in this week's game. Coach had gotten permission from the District Committee to declare me eligible. Getting to walk Riley to class beginning on Monday, however, was the most exciting. It was kind of an accident the first time. I happened to meet her in the hall, and she was carrying an armload of books. It gave me an opportunity to offer my help and she accepted, smiling, then thanking me. After that, it just seemed natural to meet at her locker and walk her to class. We had three classes together anyway, so we were going the same direction.

In football, I knew the offense which was simple. On our most basic play, the quarterback would put the ball in the pocket I'd formed, leaving it if there was an opening in the line and pulling it out if not. When he kept the ball, if the defensive end moved to tackle him he'd pitch to the halfback going around end. Bruce and Luis were alternating at quarterback, and it was obvious Luis was much quicker than Bruce. We scrimmaged half line on Wednesday, and with Luis at quarterback everything was smooth. Coach had told me to stay low when taking the ball and hitting the line. Since I was short anyway, it wasn't hard. Seldom was one person able to bring me down. Coach was in a good mood all week and several times I was praised.

We had a home game this Friday with Wink. Coach said they would be tough. After the 50-0 drubbing last week, our fans would be expecting the worst and Wink an easy win. The pep rally on Friday was neat with the band playing and everyone cheering. The players sat in chairs placed on the gym floor. I'd never felt this important. I'd been to pep rallies before but never paid much attention, except to join in with my group to make fun of them. This week Coach Duncan made a speech promising the crowd that we would have a better game.

Coach dismissed us after the pep rally, and I was home by 3:30. Dawn was at the house, but Gavin was feeding the heifers that had been delivered earlier in the week. She asked me about my day and said she was looking forward to the game.

"I had a good day. The pep rally was neat. Is Gavin going to the game?"

"Probably not. When he's not with those heifers, he's worrying about them. I bet he hasn't slept over two hours any night since they were delivered. I'll be there. I know you'll do great. I'm so proud of you, Eric."

"I'm nervous but really excited about playing."

"I baked a chicken for you. You'll have to eat something before you go in for the game. I always cooked the same meal for your dad when he was playing."

It must be a dream I thought, receiving all this attention. Was it only three months ago that no one seemed to know I existed?

I WAS at the field house at 5:15 but several guys were already there, including Luis. We put on our game pants and a t-shirt before lying down on a mat placed there for this purpose. For the next hour we talked in a whisper. At 6:30 we finished dressing to go out for our pre-game warmup. When we took the field and lined up for calisthenics,

Coach Duncan wasn't present. When Coach Adams walked by during a stretching exercise, I asked him about Coach Duncan.

"He's not feeling well, but should be here shortly."

After pre-game warmup, we returned to the dressing room. Coach Duncan was still not there. I asked Luis what he thought, and he just shrugged and said he had no idea what was going on. Just before we took the field, Coach Bryson told us to listen up.

"Coach Duncan's wife came by a few minutes ago and said he was ill and couldn't make the game. I'll be in charge tonight. We'll start the game with the same eleven that played last Friday. Last week was an embarrassment. It would be a shame to repeat that performance in front of a home crowd. Now, let's show everybody what we can do."

I couldn't believe this. I wasn't going to start like Coach Duncan had promised. Maybe Bryson would put me in the game when Luis rotated at quarterback. The game started and I watched from the sidelines. It was a repeat of last week's trouncing. I kept looking at Coach Bryson thinking he might send me in. At the half the score was 20-0, and we hadn't come close to scoring. Bruce had played quarterback the entire half. During the intermission, I got up enough courage to ask Coach if I was going to get to play the second half.

"I'll decide that later," he said, turning away.

We returned for the second half and things didn't get any better, with them scoring twice in the third quarter, making it 33-0. I asked one more time to get in the game at the beginning of the fourth quarter. Instead of answering, he ignored me. I was the only one of the six standing on the sideline that didn't play a down. I felt the stares of the crowd, thinking, they must be laughing at me. The game ended with the score being 41-0.

I ran to the dressing room, leaving my teammates who met with the players from Wink at midfield in a show of sportsmanship. I was out of my uniform and in street clothes within minutes, leaving the dressing room as the other players were coming in. I made it to my truck without talking to anyone and drove away, promising myself that was the last time I'd put on a football uniform. All week, I'd talked to Riley about being in the starting lineup and now she must be thinking I'd lied.

Of course, when I got home, Gavin was watching television. I tried to reach my room without talking to him but it was futile.

"Eric, how was the game?"

"We lost 41-0." I didn't stop, determined to get to my room.

"Did you play good?"

I hesitated, knowing I had to answer. "I didn't get to play at all."

"But you were supposed to start. What happened?"

"Coach Duncan was sick and wasn't there. Coach Bryson was in charge and wouldn't let me play." I made it to my room before he could ask another question.

I shut and locked my door, feeling miserable, hoping not to have to see or talk to anyone. I just wanted to hide and make the world and everything in it go away. I heard Dawn come in, desperately hoping she wouldn't bother me. She and Gavin were talking but I didn't want to hear what they were saying. Lying down on the bed I covered up my head with a pillow. I stayed that way until no sound was coming from the den except the television. I checked the time. It was eleven.

A knock at the door and Dawn asked. "Eric, would you like something to eat?"

"No, I'm not hungry." I hoped she would go away.

"Would you eat a sandwich if I brought it to your room?"

"No, I don't want anything to eat. I just wanta be left alone."

"I made you a chocolate pie. Please come eat one piece and I'll leave you alone. It's your favorite."

It was no use. I might as well go eat a piece of pie and maybe she wouldn't bother me anymore. Her pie was delicious anyway, and thinking about it, I was getting hungry.

"Here you are." She put down a piece of chocolate pie that covered an entire plate. It was a little bit runny with clear drops on the frosting, just the way I liked it. I expected a barrage of questions but none came as she watched me eat.

I ignored her as long as possible. "This pie is delicious. It's the best I've ever eaten. I didn't get to play tonight."

"I know, Eric. I was at the game. It worries me that Coach Duncan wasn't there. He must really be sick. The boys tried but Wink was too good. I know you're disappointed but there'll be other games."

I might as well tell her and get it over with. "No, not for me. I'm changing my schedule first thing Monday morning and quittin' football. I told everyone I was starting tonight, then didn't play a down."

"Eric, you and I both know why you didn't play. If Coach Duncan had been there it would've been different. Coach Bryson has something against you. I'm not the only one who knows that. You liked football up until tonight and you're just terribly disappointed. Please don't make a decision tonight. Think it over, and you'll feel better tomorrow."

"Nope. Don't think so." I left the table, taking my dish to the sink.

Returning to my room, I went straight to bed. There's something about sleep that allows you to escape. That's what I wanted to do. I didn't wake up the next morning until the sun was shining through the window. At least I didn't feel any worse and maybe even a little better. I wasn't going to town for the next two days and wouldn't have to talk with anyone. I might go fishing today if Gavin didn't have something planned. I wasn't here when they delivered my dad's cattle and there might be additional work to do at the windmills or on the fence. I'd actually enjoyed greasing the windmills last Saturday. It made me feel useful and Gavin was actually civil.

Going into the kitchen, Dawn sipped a cup of coffee. "Morning, Eric. Hope you slept well, and feel better today. Are you hungry this morning? How do pancakes sound?"

"Good. I'm hungry. I slept late."

"Just sit down, and I'll get you a glass of juice and start breakfast."

"Do you know if Gavin has any work for me today?"

"You'll have to ask him when he gets back. He left before daylight this morning. I tried to get him to wait but you know how he is."

"Is he checking on Dad's heifers?"

"No. He went into town to talk with Coach Bryson. I made him take his bottle of nitroglycerin pills."

29

FRANK

I kept looking for Coach Duncan to show up on the sidelines and by the end of the first quarter, I was in a panic. I asked Riley at the half if she could find out what happened to him. She came back later and told me the word going around was that he stayed home because he was sick. I didn't buy that for a second. He would've come to the game sick or not. I left immediately, knowing something wasn't right.

His house was within walking distance of the stadium, and I was knocking on his door within ten minutes of leaving the game. I'd about given up on anyone answering when his wife opened the door. She'd been crying.

"I'm sorry, Mr. Mendenhall. Please come in."

I was expecting the worst and wasn't surprised at her explanation after we sat down in the living room.

"I'm so sorry," she repeated. "I went to get my hair fixed and was gone two hours. When I returned he was already drunk. I have no idea where he got the liquor. I didn't think we had any in the house. He was so excited about this game and thinking we were going to play well. I don't know what happened. The thing about it, when he takes one drink, he won't stop until it's all gone. He's been doing great and happier than I can ever remember since coming home. Maybe it was the pressure. I don't know. Please give him another chance."

She broke down and started sobbing. My heart went out to her. When she regained her composure, I asked. "Where is Coach Duncan now?"

"I put him to bed. I sent word to Coach Bryson that he was sick and couldn't come to the game. I'm sorry," she said for the third time.

"Have him come to my office tomorrow afternoon at 4:00. To be truthful, I don't know what to do. He's a good man, however, the kids come first and his conduct is not acceptable."

"Please, please, Mr. Mendenhall, give him another chance. I won't let him out of my sight when he's home. I promise."

"I need to think about it. Have him come to my office tomorrow at 4:00," I repeated, getting up and leaving.

"Thank you, Mr. Mendenhall," she said, as she closed the door.

It was the fourth quarter, when I returned to the game and the score was 34-0. The crowd had already begun to exit the stands. I paid little attention to the game, thinking this was going to happen. I should've expected it. Coach Duncan was doing great, but he was an alcoholic. He was going to need help to overcome it. Help, that me or his wife couldn't provide. If I told Cleburne what happened, he would be fired immediately. The parents would demand it. I couldn't afford to sacrifice the students to try and help him. What was the alternative? Fire Coach Duncan and replace him with Bryson. That wasn't much of a choice. I noticed the scoreboard read 41-0 before leaving the stands.

Julie and I walked home in silence. Once inside the house, she began asking me questions about Coach Duncan's absence. I explained the visit to his house and the pleadings of his wife to give him another chance. She listened intently, without interrupting until I finished.

"Do you know what you're going to do?" she asked.

"No. Do you have any suggestions?"

"Of course not. You'll make the right decision. That's why I love you so much. You're fair and compassionate, yet strong. I know you'll do what's best for the school and for Coach Duncan."

No one deserves that kind of support, I thought. Right now, my high school was in a mess. On the one hand was Coach Duncan, a good man, who was an alcoholic.

On the other hand, was a coach who was negative and not concerned about anything but getting his way, but at least he wasn't a drunk. My thoughts were interrupted by Riley and Aubrey coming in.

"Dad, Coach Bryson didn't let Eric play. Can you believe it? He's terrible. He was supposed to start tonight. Eric left before I could talk with him. He'll be devastated. Is Coach Duncan going to be all right?"

"Coach Duncan should be fine, Riley," I said.

"What're you going to do about Bryson?" Riley asked.

"It's not my job to get involved in the coaches' problems."

"But, Dad, it's not right. Eric was supposed to play tonight. Bryson doesn't like him because you took Eric's side. You have to get involved!"

Evidently Riley didn't have the same confidence in me that her mother did. Of course, she was not objective when it came to Eric. She finally accepted that I was not going to respond to her outbursts and went to her room. That gave Aubrey a chance to talk about her evening. She told us all about Levi, a high school boy, asking her to go out with him tomorrow night. I told her that was not going to happen. She didn't respond, I'm sure anticipating my answer in advance, but still giving it a try. She went to her room slamming her door, leaving Julie and I alone again.

"No use going to bed. I couldn't sleep. We might as well watch *Johnny Carson*."

AFTER A SLEEPLESS NIGHT, I spent Saturday trying to decided how to handle the situation with Coach Duncan. I expected to be contacted by Cleburne but was not disappointed when it didn't happen. I really needed to talk with Coach Duncan before making a decision. He might want to resign and go back to the ranch. I didn't know how he would react to last night. I did develop a plan if he admitted his failure and wanted to stay. I checked my watch every few minutes, thinking time seemed like it was standing still. I was in my office at 3:30 and Coach arrived at 3:45. I stayed behind my desk for this meeting. He sat down and started talking immediately.

"I screwed up, Mr. Mendenhall. I was going to have one drink to calm my nerves. I should've known that would lead to another and another. When I start, I can't stop. I was excited about this game. Our offense had looked so much better with Luis at quarterback and Eric at fullback. I just knew we were going to have a good game."

When he paused, I asked him. "Do you realize how much you let everyone down? I felt sorry for your wife. She was devastated, begging me to give you another chance. Coach Bryson didn't let Eric play. My daughter lit into me when she came home about Bryson. She said that Eric thought he was going to start."

Looking at the floor, he responded, "I know, you're right. I know what a difficult place this puts you in. I want to keep coaching and will do anything you ask. If I stay, something has to be done about Bryson. Eric was supposed to play and Bryson was aware of that. I can't believe he kept him out the whole game. Eric has the potential to change our team, especially, with Luis at quarterback."

"I can't depend on you to keep your word. You've proven that. Right now your drinking problem is larger than you are. I believe it'll happen again and all the assurance you give me, means little. However, I have a proposition. Are you interested?"

"Yes. I'll do anything to stay." He looked up, with hope in his expression.

"Do you attend church?"

"Vicky does, but I don't go with her."

"You have to start going with her every Sunday. Hopefully, you'll gain strength through a stronger faith. I know this is an unusual request but we're facing a difficult situation."

"No problem. I'll start tomorrow."

"Pecos has Alcoholics Anonymous meetings on Monday and Thursday nights at seven in the evening. I want you to attend *every* meeting. You might have to cut practice short but that can be done. You're not to miss a meeting unless you inform me, and it better be for a good reason. Are you willing to do that?"

"Yes, gladly."

"Now, since that's settled—on to the next problem. What're we going to do about Coach Bryson? I'm limited because my daughter, Riley, and Eric have a relationship. What kind? I have no idea but it's there. Because of my daughter, anything I do is going to be viewed as being biased."

He replied with a determined look. "I'm going to talk directly to Bryson for the first time. With him not following our game plan, I have something solid with which to confront him. He can get with the program and follow my leadership or quit. We'll make do without him someway. At the present time, he's doing more harm than good for the team."

"He may bring up last night, asking why you missed the game. I suggest you tell him that you have a sickness and are going to deal with it. That will be my explanation to anyone who asks me. It's the truth and you shouldn't be required to go into detail. If they assume that you were drinking, then that's their prerogative. Let them assume and we'll just move on. I need you to let me know how your talk with Bryson goes."

"Thank you, Mr. Mendenhall. I appreciate it."

"Coach, I hope that this is the right thing to do." I stood and offered my hand across the desk. "I guess we'll have to wait and see."

After he left, I sat down, wondering if I'd lost my mind. This wasn't over by a long shot. People were going to ask me about last night. My explanation would not be accepted by some, while others would appreciate it. Everything depended on the future and Coach Duncan's conduct. I liked him and had no doubt he was a good man. Truthfully, he did have a sickness. One only he could cure.

At home, Julie asked me what I decided to do. I relayed the entire meeting with her. After I finished, she came and hugged me. "See, I told you that you'd make the right decision."

"That remains to be seen," I replied.

"You need to relax after all this stress. I have just the treatment that'll get your mind off all your problems."

THE NEXT MORNING at breakfast Riley asked me if she could call Eric and ask him to take her to church. I had a mouthful of eggs that had to be swallowed before I could respond. She explained before I could answer her.

"I'm worried about Eric. If I know him, he probably isn't planning on coming to church today. Also, he may quit football. I need to talk with him and this would be an opportunity."

"You're being kind of forward, aren't you?" This was an unusual request from Riley.

"With Eric, that's the only way to be. If I waited for him to ask me it would never happen, Dad."

"Sure. It's fine with me. You might ask your mother, though. I'm not sure she will approve."

"Go ahead, Riley, maybe you can cheer him up," Julie said.

"I can't believe this. You won't let me have a date with a boy who asked me and here Riley is inviting boys out. It's totally unfair," complained Aubrey.

Julie reminded her of something she already knew. "You're fourteen and she's nearly seventeen. That's the difference."

Not giving up, she continued to protest. "People think that I'm older than Riley. I hear it all the time."

"Stop arguing with me. You're not going anywhere with a boy until you're fifteen, and I may go with you then," Julie warned.

That ended the dating conversation, with Aubrey going to her room and Riley heading to the phone. From what I heard, Eric accepted her invitation and was going to pick her up at ten o'clock, in time for Sunday school. The excuse she used for calling him was that she wanted to ride in his new truck. Anyway, I guess he accepted it. I really don't think she needed to give him a reason but evidently it made her feel better.

I started getting ready for church and was interrupted by the phone, with Julie saying it was for me. I answered and a woman's voice spoke in an aggressive voice.

"Mr. Mendenhall, this is Gertrude Williams and I'm terribly upset. I don't know what this world is coming to. I'm eighty-two years old and never seen anything like it."

"What's the problem, Mrs. Williams?" I asked, aggravated at being called on Sunday.

"It's Ms. Kennecott, the teacher at your high school. Mr. Adams' car has been parked in front of her house all night. I couldn't sleep last night worried about what was going on. It's a disgrace and something needs to be done."

"I'll take care of it first thing tomorrow," I said.

She continued ranting as if she hadn't heard me. Finally, I told her it was nearly time for church and hung up. Julie came in and asked what was going on and I explained the call.

She laughed. "Welcome to small-town America."

MONDAY, I received my first question about Coach Duncan from Snuff, the custodian and handy man. I was at school early and we arrived at about the same time. I told him Coach had a sickness that came and went. He was going to be treated and hopefully it wouldn't happen again.

"He's a good man, Mr. Mendenhall. I hope it works out. He could be good for our kids."

I wish everyone had that same opinion, I thought. No one else mentioned it that morning. I visited some classes and was impressed with several of our teachers. One that stood out was Mr. Borski, our math teacher. I'd heard how hard his class was and how the students were dreading it. He was a quiet little man who never raised his voice. He was never sitting down, continuously walking around the room. His students seemed comfortable, and if one needed help he raised his hand. I'd looked up his grade sheets from last year when I heard how hard he was. What I found was very few failing grades and lots of A's and B's.

The day went fast with no problems. Coach Duncan showed up at my office at the end of sixth period. This time I sat out from behind my desk as he explained his visit with Coach Bryson.

"I couldn't wait until after football practice and since we both had a sixth period conference, I used that to talk with him. You wouldn't believe how cooperative he was, admitting he should've played Eric and apologizing for not putting Luis at quarterback, at least part of the game. He agreed to do whatever I asked of him and was not the least bit defensive. I was confused until toward the end of the meeting he told me that Eric's granddad had come to see him Saturday morning. I don't imagine you've ever met Gavin Sager, Eric's granddad. He's stayed away from everyone since his twin daughters were killed years ago. His wife, Luta, is friends with my mother so I've kept up somewhat with them through the years. Gavin must've really laid into Coach Bryson. In fact, he would've probably frightened me. It makes sense that Bryson changed his attitude because of his respect and fear of the area ranchers. On the one hand we have Loughton, who is a pain in the butt, and on the other we have Sager, who it seems, has helped us out."

"How was your day?" I asked, hopefully.

"I didn't have one question about missing the game. I'm going to apologize to the team, and afterwards, I expect to have a great workout."

After he was gone, Mrs. Kraal came into my office. "Mr. Mendenhall, did we dodge a bullet?"

"I certainly hope so, Mrs. Kraal. Time will tell."

30

LUTA

Gavin left at midmorning Saturday, taking his trailer and going to Alpine for a meeting with a long time friend who had horses for sale. He'd determined that we needed horses to look after the heifers. After we lost the girls and cut back on our stock, we had no need for them. Gavin and Stacy had ridden almost every day in the summer before the tragedy. I'd always thought that Gavin associated horses with Stacy and was reluctant to keep them. When I first met Gavin, he was good with horses and quite a cowboy. I'd ridden some but not nearly as much as Stacy.

I was pleased beyond words with Gavin's trip into town to talk with Coach Bryson. He'd refused to discuss what he said, but it didn't matter. Gavin had defended his grandson and that was wonderful, a hint of my husband before we lost the twins. Now, if we could just move forward.

Eric moped around the house Saturday, not willing to talk about the game and his disappointment. I tried to get him to go fishing or even to town, but he stayed in his room most of the day. Gavin wasn't home for lunch, and Eric said he wasn't hungry and didn't eat. I was worried but didn't know what to do to cheer him up. Everything had been going so well and then the Friday's game disappointment. He'd improved but was still fragile in many ways, including his self-image. His dad had still not come to see us, despite his indication that he was going to. I wanted, so much, for him to take an interest in Eric, however, I couldn't force that on him. It had to be his decision. I was hoping that football might be what caused it to happen—the catalyst.

GAVIN WASN'T HOME until midafternoon. I'd begun to worry since he'd been gone so long, but he came into the house smiling with a gleam in his eye. He must've found some good horses.

He hung his hat on the wall. "I finally made it home."

"Did you buy a horse?" I asked.

Before answering, he held up two fingers. "Good ones. Worth the money."

"Great. Lefty must've given you a good deal." It was wonderful to see him smile again and have that mischievous look in his eyes.

"Well, there's more to it than that. His granddaughter has come to live with him. Her parents have a world of problems. He asked me to let his granddaughter do some day work for us at the ranch. She loves horses and, according to Lefty, is quite a cowgirl. Of course, grandparents exaggerate, but he's always been truthful with me. I met her and, Luta, she resembles Stacy and Macy so much. Looking at her my heart almost busted."

"Is she still in school?" I asked.

"Yeah. A senior, but she'll have weekends and the summer to work for us. Lefty gave me a great price on the geldings if I agreed to let her work. It was an easy decision."

"Why you, Gavin? He could've asked others closer that would've given her day work?"

"I've known Lefty most of my life. He trusts me. He's not going to let his granddaughter work for just anyone.

"Lefty doesn't look good, Luta. You know he's always been tall and thin but he'd lost more weight. I bet he won't weight a 130 pounds. Being over six feet he's just skin and bones."

I didn't see how any good could come from this deal Gavin had made. There was no way anyone could be a replacement for our girls. It was obvious that Gavin was comparing this girl to Stacy, who loved horses and ranch work. Anyway, Gavin was happy again and that was worth a lot.

"Go with me, Luta, and we'll try the horses out in the Mountain Pasture. I need to check the windmills and make sure they're pumping before turning the heifers out. I rode these horses and they're gentle and as good as they come."

"Sure. Let me tell Eric and then change into my jeans. I won't be long."

WE STOPPED AT THE BARN, saddled the two geldings, loaded them back into the trailer, and drove to the Mountain Pasture. We rode for three hours, going from one windmill to the next. It was a beautiful fall day, and I was glad to have a light-weight jacket, with the breeze coming down off the mountain becoming cooler as the sun went down. We saw deer and Aoudad sheep on our tour. My horse was a twelve-year-old gelding, named Casper because of being white. Gavin's shorter gray horse was named P. J. It had been years since I'd ridden a horse, forgetting how exciting it was. When we loaded the horses back into the trailer to return to the house, I thought—what a wonderful day.

On the return drive, I told Gavin how enjoyable the day had been.

"We're going to have more of these days, Luta. Like we used to do."

Eric was still in his room when we returned. I warmed up stew that was in the freezer and knocking on his door, told him supper was ready. He came into the kitchen, looking like he'd been asleep.

While we were eating, I asked Eric if he'd changed his mind about quitting football.

"Nope. I'm changing my schedule first thing Monday morning."

"I was looking forward to seeing you play on Friday," Gavin said.

Eric stopped eating and looked up, like he couldn't believe what he was hearing. I was surprised Gavin had made that statement. He wouldn't have said that a month ago.

Eric went back to eating. "I'm not going to church tomorrow."

"Why?" I asked.

"Don't want to."

I knew there was no use to argue with him in his present frame of mind.

WE DIDN'T HAVE breakfast until late the next morning. I'd asked Gavin to attend church with me but he'd declined, saying he had too much work to do. After breakfast, while I was washing the dishes, the phone rang. I thought it would be Eric's dad, but answering, a girl asked to speak with Eric.

I heard Eric say, "Sure that'd be great. I'll be there at ten." I'd never seen anyone change so quickly. Suddenly he was smiling and telling me he had to get ready. Riley had asked him for a ride to church and wanted to drive his truck. He asked me to iron his favorite shirt while he shined his shoes. Within twenty minutes he was ready to go even though it was too early to leave.

"I need to clean the front seat of my truck," he said, hurrying out the door.

Thankful for the good fortune, I finished getting ready and left when Eric did. On the drive in, I was beginning to feel better about everything. Maybe it was Eric's improved mood but probably it was realizing that Gavin was right. I'd always been willing to help people. I believe a Christian should be there for people who needed them. Certainly, Lefty's granddaughter would enjoy coming to our ranch. If she reminded Gavin of Stacy, so be it. He was different, talking and smiling without the anger that had been present for so many years.

I always looked forward to my Sunday school class and meeting my friends there. We had a prayer list, and this morning, I was going to ask for my family to be included. We still faced a challenge even though improvement was obvious, but it was a good feeling knowing that I wouldn't face the future alone.

I was already seated when Eric and Riley came in for the eleven o'clock service from their Sunday school class. They selected a pew on the other side of the church from where her family and I were seated. Eric looked nice and Riley was beautiful in her white dress. I was hoping they'd sit with me but knew that was only wishful thinking.

After church Eric informed me he wouldn't be home for dinner. He and Riley were going to eat in town. As they walked away, I noticed for the first time that Riley was taller than Eric. That explained the reason for Eric being excited about the cowboy boots I gave him on his birthday.

I was home by twelve thirty and started lunch which was fried chicken. This was the first time to have Gavin's favorite since coming home from the hospital. I'd cut back on fried foods and opted for a healthier menu. This would be a treat for Gavin, and I would remind him that it was payment for yesterday spent on horseback with him. I paid the price for the pleasure though. I was so sore it was difficult to get out of bed this morning. It took me an hour before I was able to move around without pain in my legs and backside. Gavin was sitting in his easy chair when I called him to the table. I noticed he was having some difficulty getting around also, even though he probably wouldn't admit it.

"What's the occasion? Fried chicken, finally."

"You deserve a treat today. You've been good to Eric. The horse-back ride yesterday was wonderful and worth my soreness."

"I'm starved after smelling that chicken for an hour. Nothing smells as good as chicken in the frying pan. Where's the gravy?"

I smiled, anticipating the question. "My violation of your diet can only go so far. No gravy or fried potatoes. You'll have to be satisfied with the salad, red beans, and rolls."

I said the blessing, and we enjoyed our Sunday dinner, with Gavin eating too much of the fried chicken. We'd just finished when we heard a car drive up. I went to the door and saw a pickup pulling a trailer. A man and girl exited the pickup. Opening the door before they knocked, I recognized Lefty and a girl I'd never seen.

"I apologize, Luta, for barging in. Feather, my granddaughter, nagged me until I agreed to bring her out here. I tried to call earlier but couldn't reach you."

"That's no problem, Lefty. We're always glad to see you."

Feather was smaller than me, wearing an old hat with jeans tucked into her boots. I gasped, thinking how much she *did* resemble the twins, especially Stacy, with her cowboy attire. It took me a minute to gain control. "Come in, we just finished dinner. Gavin will be glad to see you."

Gavin responded just as I expected. "Welcome, Lefty and Feather. It's great to see you again. Have you had lunch? I destroyed most of the chicken, but we do have some leftovers."

"Much obliged, Gavin, but we stopped in town and ate. At least we had sense enough not to impose any further by eating with you. Feather kept after me, until I agreed to bring her out here. She wanted to see where she would be working. We brought a couple of horses, and if it's okay we'll go for a ride."

"Sure. Feather, this is my wife, Luta," Gavin said.

"Hi, Mrs. Sager. It's good to meet you," she said, smiling. "I'm sorry for intruding on your Sunday, but I was excited about working on a ranch and couldn't wait to see it."

"That's fine. I was anxious to meet you. Gavin had told me you were going to be helping us."

She removed her old hat, reveling short blonde hair. "Yes, and the good news is that I'll graduate in January and be able to start immediately after that."

Gavin rose from the table. "I'll ride with you this afternoon. We'll drive back to the Mountain Pasture and unload the horses there. It's five miles from the house. I want you to see the heifers. Luta, would you like to go with us? I can saddle your horse."

"No thanks, I haven't recovered from yesterday's ride."

They didn't stay but a few more minutes before leaving. I could tell that Feather was anxious to get started. I was ashamed of myself for questioning Gavin. It was evident that she was a nice girl and had probably been through a difficult time whatever it was, having to live with her granddad. She would be a big help for us until we could hire additional hands.

Lying down on the couch, and dozing off, I woke up to the sound of a door shutting. It turned out to be Eric. I'd slept for over an hour, which was unusual for me. Eric was in a good mood.

"Hi, Dawn. I had a great time. After church we had lunch at the Frontier Cafe and then she drove my truck all over the country. I'm not quitting football. Riley wants me to play. Where's Gavin?"

I told him about our visitors. He didn't know about Gavin buying the horses and making arrangements for Lefty's granddaughter to work for us. Probably still thinking about his day with Riley, he was only halfway listening. In a dream-like-state he wandered off toward his room.

It was late afternoon before Gavin and his visitors returned to the house. He brought them into the den, introducing them to Eric. Eric was polite but didn't seem interested enough to make conversation.

"Do you ride?" Feather asked.

Eric looked surprised at the question. "No."

Gavin broke the awkward silence that followed. "That's going to change. The white horse that Luta rode yesterday will be a great beginner horse."

"I love Casper. He's wonderful, but he can't go very fast," Feather said.

"We need to be going. I apologize again for showing up unannounced. We'll be in touch," Lefty said.

"Would you have some work for me next Saturday?" Feather asked.

"Sure. Just plan on every weekend. We haven't agreed on a salary yet."

Lefty didn't give Feather a chance to respond. "You decide. She'd probably work for nothing. I know you'll be fair."

Lefty and Feather left, and for supper I heated up leftovers. We listened to Gavin tell us what a good rider Feather was and how she was going to be a big asset. Eric toyed with his food, eating little and obviously not hungry or interested

31

ERIC

It was Friday and game day. Less than a week ago, I was through with football for good. That all changed last Sunday when Riley called and asked me to take her to church. Ever since then, I was floating somewhere in the clouds, not wanting to come down. We were a couple now or at least it looked that way. I walked her to every class, and we'd been eating lunch together. Tonight, in a home game against Tornillo, I was going to be in the starting lineup. Workouts had gone well, and Luis had been playing quarterback, with Bruce taking over at a tight end position. I'd seen Bruce's dad talking to Coach Duncan several times this week and he didn't look happy.

Besides football, I was enjoying my Vocational Agriculture class. I was trying to decide what kind of animal to select for a project. At the present time, I was leaning toward a pig. Mr. Puckett had said they were the easiest to take care of and not expensive. Most of the students either had a sheep, pig, or steer. I'd asked Gavin and his only comment was, "There's never been a pig set foot on this place." He'd been so involved with the heifers that I don't believe it made him any difference what animal I selected.

I seldom had contact with him since he left early and came in late. We generally had supper together but after that I would do homework in my room. The good thing was Gavin's mood. He didn't pay much attention to me, but when he did his manner was polite and the anger was gone.

EVEN THOUGH IT was a home game, the crowd was less than last week, which wasn't surprising, due to our past two performances. After our pre-game warmup and back in the dressing room, Coach Duncan addressed the team.

"We have disappointed our fans, but tonight is an opportunity to change that. I feel good about our preparation and game plan. We have made some changes in our lineup which I believe will make a difference. Without doubt, Tornillo, will not take us seriously. Let's get after them from the start and show them we're not the same team!"

I had butterflies in my stomach while standing on the sidelines watching the coin toss. They won the toss and chose to receive, which meant I would remain on the sidelines since I wasn't playing defense. We kicked off and they made two first downs then had to punt, giving us the ball. I was so nervous, going onto the field, that it was difficult to breathe. Luis was starting at quarterback and Bruce at end. In the huddle, Luis told us the play, which was a handoff to me over right guard. The play started and I took the ball, staying low, moving into the line. I felt someone hit me, but I kept my legs moving before a swarm of defenders brought me down. I got up and saw the referee motioning first down. I'd made over 10 yards on my first carry. Luis called the next play which was the same except to the left. I took the ball, gaining another first down after dragging a host of defenders an additional 5 yards. On the next play, Luis faked the handoff to me and kept the ball going around left end and out ran the defenders 50 yards for the touchdown. Everyone was celebrating! We met him coming back, offering our congratulations. We missed the extra point, and the score was 6-0.

After that, our confidence grew, and we scored the next two times we had the ball. I wasn't the least bit nervous anymore and was only stopped for no gain one time when I almost fumbled. Just before the half, on a 20 yard run I scored. Receiving congratulations from my teammates was an awesome feeling. At half the scoreboard showed 20-0, and we left the field to our fans' applause.

Coach couldn't contain his excitement at the half, moving around the room, congratulating everyone. He realized his mistake and immediately began warning us that we had another half to play. I was anxious to get back on the field and was glad when an official came to the dressing room, telling us it was our choice whether to get the ball or not to begin the second half. Of course, we took the ball.

On the first play after the half, Luis called trap right. A down defensive lineman was released and our guard pulled, blocking him, and I took the ball up the middle and moved to the right. I was hit once, then twice, as I broke tackles and suddenly was in the open, going the 80 yards for the touchdown. I'd never felt such excitement as when our guys were pounding me on my back, congratulating me. Luis completed a pass to Bruce for the two-point conversion, and we were ahead 28-0.

Tornillo finally scored in the fourth quarter, but we also added two more touchdowns, with the final outcome of 40-6. Celebrations started on the field. But the best part of everything was Riley meeting me and taking my arm squeezing it, walking me off the field, saying, "You played great."

The festivities continued in the dressing room with laughter and high-fives. Of everyone, I believe that Coach Duncan was the most excited, going around and hugging everyone, including me.

"You were awesome, Eric. I'm so proud of you."

"Thank you, Coach. It was fun."

"We're just getting started," he replied, moving on.

"What do you think now?" Luis asked.

"I never realized football would be like this. Amazing."

"It's not always this way. When you lose, it's totally different. I saw Riley walking you off the field. I told you girls liked football players."

"Yeah, you did. You played great tonight. Where was your girl?" I asked.

"Remember what I told you? She's white. We can't be seen in public. Her dad would come unwound. She's waiting for me outside. We'll have a few minutes together and then we'll go our separate ways. Maybe someone will have a party tomorrow night, and we can spend time together."

"I'm sorry, Luis. It doesn't seem fair."

He shrugged. "That's just the way it is here."

After showering and dressing, on the way out, I noticed Bruce sitting on the bench with his head down. I asked him if he was all right.

"Yeah. I just dread going home. My dad will be upset that I didn't play quarterback even though we won. By the way you were great."

"Thanks. You were, too." It must be terrible not to be able to enjoy winning.

I walked out of the dressing room right into the arms of Riley who hugged me. "Can we go for a coke at The Drug Store? It's open late tonight."

"Sure."

Holding on to me like I might get away, we walked to my truck. Gavin and Dawn were parked beside it and getting out of her car, she hugged me.

"Oh, Eric. I'm so proud of you. I wish your dad could've been here."

Gavin, smiling, shook my hand. "Well, one things for sure, I can't outrun you. You did really good, Eric."

"Thank you. I'm glad we won. Me and Riley are going for a coke. I'll be home later."

Dawn hugged me again. "Okay. Be careful. Don't be too long. I'm going to wait up for you. I want to hear all about the game."

IT WAS two hours before I left town. On the twenty-minute drive, I couldn't believe this was all happening to me. I thought the football game and making several touchdowns was the best it could get but kissing Riley goodnight topped everything. She was my girl. The first one I'd ever kissed. I couldn't be happier and wouldn't trade places with anyone in the world.

Dawn was waiting up for me, as she had said she would, and we spent half an hour talking about the game. I tried to be modest, but she kept saying how wonderful I was. I could've stayed up all night, but she ended our talk.

"We better get to bed. Gavin has plans for you tomorrow, and it's going to be an early start. Y'all are going to drive our cows to the Mountain Pasture to mix with the heifers. The more he thought about it the more he realized that would be the thing to do. It would have a calming effect on the heifers and they would follow the older cows to the pickup horn when we fed. I'm going to tell you one more time, Eric. I'm so proud of you. Please remember that."

I went to bed, thinking of the game and, of course, Riley. I didn't expect to sleep good, but suddenly someone was shaking me, saying it was time to get up. My head was foggy, and I couldn't remember where I was. In several seconds, it came to me. I was at Gavin and Dawn's. I was a football star and Riley was my girl. I smiled thinking how good everything was. I took a deep breath, stretched, and got out of bed.

Breakfast was ready, and I was starved. Dawn had eggs, potatoes, gravy, and biscuits. I sat down and after the blessing began filling my plate.

Gavin laid out the plans that were to begin after breakfast. "Busy day. Five-mile cattle drive. Your job will be to drive the pickup, honking to get the cows to follow. They'll get impatient when they realize no feed is coming out. Me and Feather will be on our horses to encourage them to follow the pickup. You might put out a few cubes. Hopefully, we can get them the five miles to the Mountain Pasture without them scattering. It's not going to be easy."

I was finishing my last biscuit with jelly when someone drove up. It was just getting daylight when Luta opened the door and Feather came in. She was dressed the same as Saturday except she had on a jacket.

Her excitement was obvious. "Morning, everybody. We have a north wind and it's cold."

"Would you like some breakfast?" Dawn asked.

"No, thank you." She brushed her hands together trying to stay warm. "Pops cooked me eggs before I left. While I ate, he saddled and loaded Glo, my appaloosa, in the trailer. He was glad to stay home since it turned colder."

I hadn't paid much attention to her Saturday. She was much smaller than Riley and not nearly as pretty. I couldn't tell that much about her. She had her old hat pulled down and I couldn't see any hair. I finished my biscuit and went to my room to get my coat. Of course, I didn't have a hat but put on one of my several caps.

Returning to the kitchen, Gavin was ready to go.

"Eric, you take the pickup, and I'll load my horse with Feather's and follow you to the pasture with the cows. You start out toward the Mountain Pasture, honking, and we'll unload our horses and follow, encouraging the stragglers. After you see the cows begin to lose interest, put out a few cubes. Hopefully, once we get them moving in the right direction, they'll follow right along."

EVERYTHING WENT AS PLANNED, and by noon we had the cows going through the gate into the Mountain Pasture. They stopped and milled around the area that held the heifers. Gavin told me to put out more cubes, and we would go back for lunch.

On the drive back to the house Feather sat between me and Gavin. Watching her ride this morning, she was actually good. Dawn had a great cold weather lunch for us, consisting of stew and cornbread with cherry cobbler for dessert.

Gavin talked throughout the meal. "Feather is an amazing rider, Luta. Lefty wasn't exaggerating about her being a cowboy. She was worth at least two hands this morning. It went smooth as silk, and we didn't have any problems moving the cows."

We finished our meal, with Gavin continuing to praise Feather, but not mentioning me. I wasn't disappointed, only glad I wasn't criticized.

We left after the meal, returning to the cattle. We opened the gate and drove the heifers out to mix with the cows, and I thought our work was done for the day, but Gavin had other ideas.

"Eric, I'd like you to ride my horse and go with Feather to move the cattle out into the pasture. I rode Casper today, with that in mind. He's a great beginner horse. You're going to need to learn to ride. Now's a good time to start. Y'all can just mosey along with the cattle, and it'll at least get you started. Feather can give you some basic instructions."

This was unexpected. I came close to saying no. Taking orders from a strange girl would be humiliating. I knew nothing about riding a horse. I'd never been on one or even around one. Instead of refusing, I remained silent, hoping Gavin would get the message—he didn't.

"I'll wait here for you to return. Might take a nap in my warm pickup. Let's get started. Come over here and mount this good horse."

I couldn't refuse, now that Gavin's attitude toward me had improved. I didn't want to give him any reason to bad-mouth me again. I did as he asked and followed his instructions on mounting the horse. Once in the saddle, it seemed awkward.

"Just relax now. Keep your heels down in the stirrups and nudge him when you want to move forward. Don't jerk on him. Just pull back lightly on the reins when you want to stop. It's like driving a car with power steering. Same with turning. Pull the reins against his neck when you need to turn. You'll do fine. Now listen to Feather and do what she says."

I nudged the horse with my heels, bouncing forward, and we started off at a walk. It was uncomfortable and I must've looked stupid. We were out of hearing distance before Feather said anything. "Don't worry, Eric. You're going to do fine. I fell off, my first time. Casper will take care of you."

For the next several hours, we rode along with the cattle never getting in a hurry. I became more at ease and unlike what I'd expected, didn't receive any coaching from Feather. From time to time, she'd make a positive comment. We finally left the cattle and turned back toward the pens and Gavin. We rode side-by-side on the return trip. I kept looking at my watch, worrying about getting back in time for my date.

"What time is it?" she asked.

"A little before four."

"You keep looking at your watch, like you're worried. Do you need to get back for something?"

"Yeah. I need to be in town by six."

"That shouldn't be a problem. We're not that far from the pens. Maybe another half hour. You have a date?"

"Yeah." I didn't know her well enough to tell her about Riley. Maybe later.

"You did good today. You'll like riding in no time. Sitting on a horse will make you feel like a king on a throne." She wasn't so bad after all, I thought. I expected her to be a know-it-all and give me a lot of instructions. On the contrary, she'd been nothing but positive.

We arrived back at the pens and Gavin met us. "How'd it go?" he asked, looking at Feather.

"Great. Eric's going to be a good rider. He just needs a lot of hours in the saddle. The cattle seemed to be getting along fine and had begun grazing when we left."

"It's been a good day. Let's get back to the house. That wind is getting colder by the minute."

I hadn't noticed it until now, but Gavin was right. The inside of the pickup felt good on the drive to the house. *It's been a good day and is going to get better. The riding was more tolerable than I thought it would be, and Gavin was still in a good mood. Feather was more positive than I expected and didn't put me down one time. Now, I was going to see Riley and my good day would have a perfect ending.*

32

FRANK

I t was Monday morning, October 4 and Mrs. Kraal came into my office and informed me Loughton was waiting to see me. I halfway expected this to happen. Our three game winning streak had been broken Friday night by Iraan, a power house team that was ranked fifth in the state. The game came down to the wire with them winning 21-20. We probably played our best game to date. I'd been aware that he was upset and doing a lot of talking since Coach Duncan had moved Luis to quarterback and his son, Bruce, to end. The sad thing about it, he was an arrogant bully and no one disagreed with him. Naturally, he thought everyone agreed with his dissatisfaction. I detested bullies. He was one of the worst I'd encountered.

"Show him in." I stayed behind my desk.

He came in, without a greeting. "I guess you know why I'm here?"

Before, he could get started, I said, "It's good to see you. Your daughter, Becky and my daughter have become good friends."

"I'm not here about my daughter. I've been to Duncan and didn't get anywhere. I went to Cleburne and he told me to see you. So, here I am. My son is a senior, playing his last year of football. The Mexican boy who replaced him is only a sophomore and has two more years to play. Bruce played quarterback last year, and he shouldn't have been moved. I'm pissed at the whole thing, and I want something done about it. I've talked to a number of people, and they all agree. We start district this week, and he better start at quarterback or else." He stopped and stared at me, waiting for a response.

I had to be careful not to say something that would be unprofessional. That would move the issue to me. It wasn't going to be easy. I waited too long to respond.

"Well, I'm waiting." He moved to the edge of his chair and glared.

"I'm sorry, you're talking to the wrong man. Where your son plays on the football team is not my decision. Coach Duncan is the one who determines that."

He came right back at me. "But Duncan answers to you."

"Not about decisions on the football field," I replied.

"I should've known you wouldn't have the guts to do anything. You didn't even play football. You know nothing about the game. Everyone can see that Bruce should be playing quarterback. That's why we lost Friday night. That Mexican boy got us beat."

Stay calm—I kept repeating in my mind. When I didn't reply, he continued.

"It's not the end of this. I'm not through with you or Duncan. I may just have to pull Bruce out of football until after this is settled.

By this time, he was loud enough to be heard in the hall. I said as quietly as possible. "Mr. Loughton, you can proceed with whatever you want to do, but I'm not going to change my mind." It took all my willpower to stay calm.

"So that's the way it's going to be, huh? I'll tell you right here to your face. You're going to be sorry!" He got up, pushed his chair back, and stormed out.

Mrs. Kraal came to my door. "Would you like some coffee, with a shot of bourbon instead of cream and sugar?"

I laughed. "That sounds like something I could use right now, but I'd better pass on the bourbon. Coffee sounds good though."

After my dose of caffeine, I walked out to the field house. Coach Duncan had a PE class playing soccer since it was a nice day. He was watching from the sideline. I told him about the visit from Loughton.

He responded by telling me Loughton had been to talk with him several times and threatened to take Bruce out of football and also to have him fired.

"The sad thing about it, Mr. Mendenhall, Bruce is fine with the move. He apologized to me for his dad, saying he'd told him he liked playing end, and it was best for the team. Loughton's a nut case. It's ironic isn't it. We've already won more games than I thought we would. It looks like everyone would be happy. Moving Luis to quarterback and Eric joining the team has been the difference. Eric is something else, and he just gets better every game. The other coaches in the district will think I lied to them about Eric never playing. If they had it to do over again, there's no way the district committee would approve his eligibility.

"Coach, I told Loughton it was your decision who to play and I'll support you. It's doubtful if we'll receive any backing from Cleburne."

"I appreciate it. If Bruce is taken out of football he'll be devastated. Nothing we can do about that, though.

"While you're here, I need to thank you again for giving me a second chance. The AA Meetings have been great. I never realized other people had the same problem. It's been an eye-opening experience. Vicky and I haven't missed a Sunday going to church, either."

"That's good news, which I need at the moment. I better get back to my office in case another problem comes up. I'm looking forward to our district opener this week."

ANOTHER ISSUE WAITED for me upon my return. Two freshman girls were sitting in the outside office, with Mrs. Kraal. She followed me into my office, closed the door and told me what the teacher who brought them had said.

"They got into it in their PE class. Coach Tiff said she separated them but not before the fight started."

"It looks like one of those days. Have them come in, and remain here with us, if you will." I'd learned years ago not to be left alone with this kind of problem. A witness is good insurance.

Seated in front of me, I asked them what the problem was. Both started talking at once. I stopped them and asked their names. One was Elaina. The other Wanda. I pointed at Wanda to go first.

"I didn't do nuthin'. In the gym, she kept lookin' at me. I warned her to stop but she kept on. We've had problems before today."

"What do you mean, 'she kept looking at me?'"

"She kept lookin' at me. I told her to stop and she didn't. My momma told me not to take nuthin' off nobody."

"I still don't understand what you mean by 'she kept looking at me.'" I was confused.

"You know, giving me the eye, lookin' at me like she had something to say."

I then asked Elaina to tell her side of the story.

"She started it. She knows about Javier and me. She's always hanging around him. She was talking to him between classes," she accused.

"So, it's all about a boy?"

Wanda stared at her. "It's a free country. I can talk to anyone I want to. It doesn't seem to bother Javier."

"You better stay away from him," Elaina threatened.

It was evident that we were getting nowhere. I'd seen enough of these conflicts to know it wasn't going to end today. More than likely it would break out again, probably in the hallway and prevent us from having a productive school day. Based on my experience, I made my decision.

"Both of you need to call your parents to come get you. You can return to school tomorrow, but bring at least one parent with you. We'll meet here in the morning and see if we can solve this problem before you're allowed back in class. Mrs. Kraal will let you use the phone. Wait in the outer office with her until they come get you."

I thought it was over—wrong. Fifteen minutes later Wanda's mother was in my office giving me the third degree. Of course, it was not her daughter's fault. The girls had been having problems for years, always started by Elaina, and she didn't appreciate me sending her home. She threatened me a number of times, saying her husband would be up here to talk to me. It was kind of like the mother telling the child, "Wait until your daddy gets home."

I tried to be as polite as possible telling her that fighting was unacceptable, and it would be a pleasure to meet her husband. Failing to get an argument started, she left.

I went out to the Vocational Agriculture building looking for something positive. Mr. Puckett was teaching a shop class, and the students were learning to weld. I couldn't have visited a better place to improve my morning. They were getting instructions on how to use a cutting torch.

I watched in awe as they stood around Mr. Puckett, giving him their undivided attention. I could only hope that students would be that eager to learn in their other classes. After he finished, two cutting torches were available and each had a few minutes, putting to use what they had been instructed. Some did good, others not so good, but he corrected them without being critical or discouraging.

Unlike other classes I visited, the students paid little attention to me, because they were so intent on what they were doing. I left without some of them even knowing of my presence.

Thus far, most everything had gone well this year. I had a good faculty with only a couple of exceptions. I had experienced more serious discipline problems with students in my last job. Rural students were much better behaved, and thus far there had been a minimum of problems sent to my office. The fight between the two girls was the first of its kind this year.

Loughton, was another matter. This type of situation was new to me. My last position, I didn't have any contact with board members. Now, with the superintendent passing a board member's anger down to me that had changed. I handled the situation correctly but the problem hadn't gone away.

THE NEXT MORNING Mrs. Kraal informed me the girls and their mothers were in my office. I'd already added two more chairs in front of my desk. Coming in, I invited them to have a seat. I knew better than to try and solve the existing problem. Instead, I needed to concentrate on the future.

"The reason I asked you to bring your daughters this morning was to ask for your help. Fighting is unacceptable in school. First, it's dangerous and somebody could be injured. Second, a confrontation such as occurred yesterday disrupts the entire school day. I'd like to ask you to encourage your daughters to get along and for this not to happen again." I looked from one to the other parent.

"She started it yesterday. Wanda told me what happened and . . . "

I held up my hand stopping her in mid-sentence. "We're not going to talk about what happened yesterday. I'm concerned about what will happen today and the remainder of the school year. I'm asking for your help in preventing further problems." I waited for a response.

"We've already told Elaina, it better not happen again," said her mother.

I looked directly at Wanda's mother. "My husband's pretty upset about this whole thing and wants to come see you. We feel that Wanda hasn't done anything wrong. We've always told her to take up for herself."

"Are you not going to help me with this problem involving your daughter?" I asked.

"I'll tell Wanda not to start anything, but I won't make her walk away from trouble started by her." She pointed at Elaina.

I looked at Elaina's mother. "Elaina can go to class. Thanks for coming in this morning. I appreciate your cooperation. That's all."

After she left, I directed my attention to the other mother. "You can take Wanda back home with you. She's not going to come to school until I receive assurance that you're trying to stop this conduct."

"Fine! You can expect to see my husband." She left with Wanda.

Mrs. Kraal came into my office after they left. "What did you think about *Mean* Jean?"

"Is that her name? She never introduced herself."

"Her name's Jean. She's well deserving of the nickname. The entire community avoids her."

. . .

IT WAS FRIDAY, October 15 and we were getting ready for the game. Julie had taken off work at three o'clock. We'd dismissed school early for the trip to Dell City which was about a three-hour drive. It was our first district game, and everyone was excited.

We left at 3:30 to give us plenty of time to make the seven o'clock kickoff. It was an opportunity for us to catch up on the day-to-day events of the girls. As usual, Aubrey did her share and more of the talking.

"The pep rally was great today. I'm going to try out for high school cheerleader next year. I've been talking to Denny at lunch. He's only a sophomore, but he's the starting halfback, since Luis has moved to quarterback. I was thinking about walking him off the field tonight."

"What have we told you about high school boys?" Julie reminded her.

"Becky has been worried sick that her dad is going to take Bruce out of football." Being the peacemaker, Riley changed the subject.

"Why would he do that?" asked Aubrey.

"He believes that Bruce should be playing quarterback."

"That's stupid. Even I know Luis is better," said Aubrey.

"Becky is the nicest girl I know," Riley confided. "Her dad is consumed with Bruce and seldom pays attention to her. Bruce tries to make up for his dad's treatment of his sister. Eric says he's nice to everyone and the most respected player on the team."

"Are you and Eric going steady?" asked Aubrey, out of the blue.

"I don't know. Maybe. Eric is a different person than when I met him. He's happier and has more confidence. I hope, at least, part of the improvement is due to me. I like to help people. It gives me a good feeling. What could be better than making a difference in someone's life?"

"Someone got us off the original subject. Aubrey, what've we told you about high school boys?" resumed Julie.

She spoke as if she was a recording. "Stay with people my own age."

"You can walk the high school boys off the field when you're in high school," her mother affirmed.

. . .

IT WAS an exciting game with us winning, 27-12. We played good and it was going to be difficult for Loughton to find fault with our effort. I don't know why that thought even entered my mind. Coming out of the stands he stopped me. "I'll be in to see you first thing Monday morning."

33

LUTA

Jenny was almost two months old and chewed up everything she could find lying around, especially shoes. Gavin took her with him when he had outside work to do, hoping she would run down, but she had boundless energy. It had been sixteen years since Max had been a pup, and we'd forgotten that they could be so destructive. She was smart and when scolded, you'd receive that, *I'm sorry look*, and then she'd go right back to her misbehavior.

Eric had decided on a pig for his FFA project, which he named Arnold. Mr. Puckett told us he was a "fresh" pig. I didn't know what that meant but evidently it was a pig that had plenty of energy. Arnold was never still except when his back was scratched. He would stop moving and finally lie down on his side, not moving a muscle as long as you continued to scratch him. It was a strange sight, with the only explanation being that it felt so good, he was afraid you'd stop if he moved. It took Gavin awhile to adjust to Arnold, but it was impossible not to get attached to him. I'd always heard how smart pigs were and it was true. Gavin said they'd probably starve if you tried to use a self-feeder for horses or cows before they figured it out. It took Arnold about two minutes to master the feeder.

It was October and Feather had returned the past two weekends to work. I felt guilty about her missing church, but she assured me she was attending the Sunday evening and Wednesday prayer meeting services. She was a sweet girl and mannerly. She ate her noon meal Saturday and Sunday with us and always offered to help with the dishes.

After she left last Sunday, Gavin surprised me by his suggestion. "Luta, it seems we should offer to let Feather stay over on Saturday night. That way she wouldn't have to make the fifty-mile round trip. I could move back into the bedroom with you, and she could have my room. It's just an idea but would save her drive time. What do you think?"

I tried to contain my enthusiasm. "That's a wonderful idea, Gavin. I know she would appreciate it." He actually asked my opinion about something. More important, we'd be sharing the same bedroom for the first time in many years. My prayers which I'd almost given up on . . . were being answered.

"I'll call Lefty tomorrow and have him ask her about it. If she does stay over, it'll give her the opportunity to bring additional clothes next weekend."

"I should've already thought about it. It will be much more convenient." No doubt about it, Gavin was better. I didn't know where to place the credit, which was probably due to several factors. The challenge that the extra cattle brought was one, I'm sure. Eric's success in football had to be a part of it. We'd made the last four games and Gavin couldn't hide his pride in Eric's performance. When people congratulated us, Gavin's reaction was like any other granddad's would've been. And then Feather was part of it also. At first, I thought it might have an adverse effect on Gavin to have someone around who reminded him of the twins but the truth was the opposite.

What hadn't shown improvement, was Gavin and Cameron's relationship. They talked each week on the phone about the heifers, but you'd have never known it was a father talking to his son. A conversation between two business associates was a better description. There wasn't an ounce of personal feelings expressed by either. Maybe it was the confidence from Gavin's change, or it could be I was tired of waiting for one of them to acknowledge some affection for the other. I was going to do something about it, starting with Cameron. I was already put out with him for not coming to any of Eric's games.

When Gavin left the house on the Wednesday following Eric's big game against Dell City, I called Cameron at work. "Do you have a few minutes to talk?"

"Sure. Is there a problem at the ranch?"

"You could say that, Cameron. I want to know why you haven't been out here to see one of Eric's games."

There were several seconds of silence. "I've been really busy and had trouble getting away, plus there's not anyone to keep Ethan. I might be able to get off this next weekend."

"Why don't you bring Ethan with you? He'd be proud of Eric, and we'd like to spend time with our other grandson." I was doing my best to control my frustration.

"I'll try. Maybe it'll work out, but I'm not making any promises."

That did it, I was fuming. "Cameron, you listen to me and listen good! You have a son we agreed to take because *you* had given up. He's a different young man than when you left him. He's told me several times his dad doesn't care about him. How can I disagree with him? You don't come see him and seldom call. It's like he's not part of your life anymore. You're at a crossroads, and if you don't begin showing some interest in him, he'll be lost forever. This amazes me after the lack of a relationship you and your dad have. Do you want the same for you and Eric?"

Silence. I continued, "I'm sorry for having to be this blunt, but I don't know of any other way. Can't you see what's happening?"

More silence. "You make whatever arrangements are necessary and come for this week's home game." I didn't give him a choice.

"Okay," he said, in a whisper.

"Good. I'll cook some of your favorite foods for Saturday. You're going to be surprised at Eric and Gavin."

We said goodbye, with me telling him I loved him. I didn't confront him about his and Gavin's relationship, having already said enough. I hadn't talked to him that way since he was a child, but he needed it. I was only a mother telling her son the right thing to do and didn't regret a word of it.

THE MONTHS of September and October on the ranch were my favorite. The mornings were cold and the afternoons cool with little wind most days. We'd had some good rains in the middle of September and the temperature was even cooler than usual. When Gavin and I left the house on Thursday morning, October 21, there was a heavy frost on the ground. We had Jenny sitting between us—moving between us would be a better description. We drove the five miles through the ranch to the Mountain Pasture. The grass had been good enough that Gavin had only been putting out range cubes a couple of times a week. We drove through the pasture, with Gavin honking, and Jenny barking. Cows began coming up along with several of the bulls Gavin had chosen.

"Luta, those are really good young bulls. Their calves will be outstanding. We'll drive a little further, but the roads have become so bad it'll be difficult. I need to get a dozier in here and do some work. These heifers aren't the best I've ever seen, but the bulls will make up for it. If we can have 350 pairs ready to sell in a year or so, Cameron should easily be able to pay off the loan and have money left over."

Since he'd mentioned Cameron, I thought it would be a good time to bring up his visit. "Speaking of Cameron, I talked with him yesterday, and he plans on coming for Eric's game tomorrow night."

"'Bout time. I'd begun to think he wouldn't see Eric play this year. He's going to be surprised."

"Do you think y'all might get along better?" I asked.

"Who knows? Up to him. The only interest he's shown in me is dropping Eric and 500 heifers on us."

"Are you sorry he brought Eric out here for us to look after?"

"No. Eric has been a help to us on the ranch, especially after my heart attack and he's changed. School and football have made a difference. I imagine this young lady he's fond of has played a role in his improvement. Where's Cameron going to sleep? Remember, Feather will be here this weekend."

Oh, me. I'd been caught up in getting Cameron out here and had forgotten Feather. This could be a problem. Cameron would see his dad taking on over her and rekindle memories of his sisters and how partial Gavin was to them. I attempted to help one situation and another was created.

Gavin eliminated any chance of her not coming. "I need her this weekend to ride the pasture. There're some heifers that I haven't seen in a week. Maybe Cameron could share Eric's room, and sleep on the other bed."

That could work, I thought. I'd neglected to speak much of Feather, but now, I had no choice. "I realize that Feather reminds you of Stacy. That's not bad, but I'm afraid that Cameron will be upset."

"Why should he be?" he asked.

"You know the reason as well as I do, Gavin."

"Yeah. I guess so. Feather won't be around much and when she is, I'll keep in mind what you said."

I sighed with relief. "Thank you."

"Luta, it's been over two years since we heard anything from law enforcement. Do you think they've given up on finding *him*? Up until then, they were good to stay in touch with us and keep us informed about the investigation."

Talking about Feather, had rekindled the memories that always brought grief and anger. Gavin was handling it better this time. "I don't know. They probably just don't have any new information. I can't believe they'll ever give up."

ERIC WAS at school when Cameron arrived the next afternoon. I hadn't told Eric his dad was coming—afraid he might not show up. I halfway expected Cameron to be upset with me for the way I'd spoken to him, but that didn't seem to be the case. He hugged me and shook hands with his dad, which he didn't usually do, "What time's the game?" he asked.

"It's at seven o'clock so we have time to eat a bite. I have liver and onions, one of your favorites."

"Sounds good," he replied.

We had supper, with most of the talk being about the heifers. Both Gavin and Cameron's exchange was civil. I kept thinking *so far, so good.* If it could only last.

We left for the game shortly after eating and arrived half an hour early. I suggested that Cameron go to the field house before the game and speak with Eric, which he did. Returning, he commented on how much weight Eric had lost. Before the game several of Cameron's high school classmates came by and visited. He seemed to enjoy seeing them, with several praising Eric and what he'd done for the team.

When the game started, Gavin leaned over. "Bruce Loughton's not playing tonight. I guess Loughton made him quit after all."

Eric had told us about him being upset that Bruce wasn't playing quarterback, but I'd never have thought he would've made him quit the team. Bruce not playing didn't affect the outcome, however. Cameron being at the game must've brought out the best in Eric, and for Garden City was bad news. He was unstoppable. Scoring four times with us winning 32-13. When the defense shored up the middle to stop him, Luis would keep the ball around end for big gains. From time to time, I would glace at Cameron who remained quiet throughout the game.

At the end of the game a crowd gathered around Cameron with many of them expressing their amazement. It was evident that he didn't know how to respond. At first, he offered a simple, "Thank you" and when that didn't seem to be enough, he countered with a modest remark such as, "It was a team effort." Finally, he downplayed Eric's performance by responding with, "Garden City wasn't very good."

One of his best high school friends from the past, said, "Come on, Cameron, why don't you just admit your son's a stud and better than you ever were." That comment brought laughter from everyone, including Cameron.

We went to the dressing room, with Gavin and me waiting outside. Cameron was gone longer than I expected before returning. "Sorry, it took so long, but I was talking to Coach Duncan."

On the ride home, I asked him what Coach Duncan had said about Eric, knowing the answer but wanting to hear it from Cameron.

"He said that Eric was the difference in a winning and losing season. Coach's offense is built around the fullback just like it was at Texas when he played. Eric changed the whole offense when he came out for football. He was surprised at Eric's talent, especially his speed. I wasn't because when he was in elementary school, he could outrun everyone before he gained so much weight. How did he lose that much?"

Gavin laughed. "Digging post holes."

"I'll admit it surprised me that he stayed with the work or football. I figured he'd quit," Cameron said.

I bit my tongue and stayed silent. Gavin didn't. "Maybe if you'd have ever made him work a little and paid attention to him, you'd not have been surprised."

"You mean, work hell out of him from the time he was a small boy, like you did me? Only thing is, that's the only attention I ever received from you. All your other time was reserved for my sisters, who you never asked to do anything they objected to."

"That's enough! Both of you are dwelling in the past. We're not going there. Just stop it. Both of you should be proud of Eric at least for the moment and that should give you common ground."

Silence and tension rode the remainder of the way home with us. When we arrived, I asked if they wanted me to make coffee for them.

"Naw. It's too late for coffee. Where's that bottle of Jim Beam you keep hidden from me? Me and Cameron are gonna have a drink to his son and my grandson."

34

ERIC

I was shocked when my dad walked into the dressing room before the game. Not knowing how to react when he came over to me, I waited to see what he would do. He gave me a brief hug. "I came to see you play."

"I hope you're not disappointed."

"I better get out of here. We'll be rooting for you."

I couldn't believe it. I'd been a part of the team for the last five weeks, and he finally makes a game. Why did he show up now? "One thing for sure, he wasn't going to be disappointed. I'd show him what he'd been missing," I mumbled to myself.

The whole team was devastated at Bruce quitting this week. His dad was something else. Bruce had spoken to the team before practice on Monday, with tears, telling us how sorry he was to be quitting. Coach had tried to be upbeat and positive throughout the week. Workouts had gone as usual, but Bruce was going to be missed tonight. I wondered if he'd even be allowed to attend the game.

Luis and I talked briefly before leaving the dressing room, agreeing that we were going to take the fight to Garden City. I told him to get me the ball as much as possible. We'd won the toss and chose to receive. Luis was the deep man on the receiver team and had a good return to the 38-yard line. The first play was the option and he left the ball in the pocket I'd formed, and breaking several tackles, suddenly it was open field between me and the goal line. Scoring on the first play of the game, gave us the momentum which we never lost. By halftime, we were leading 19-7, and I'd scored again on a 25-yard run.

Coach reminded us at half-time not to let up and we didn't, with Luis going 70 yards for a score, our first possession of the second half. By the end of the game, I'd carried the ball over thirty times, scoring four touchdowns. I was on the sidelines when the game ended, but Riley found me, which made everything worthwhile.

My dad came to the dressing room again, this time giving me a longer hug. "Great game, Eric. I'm proud of you."

"Thanks. I'm glad you could make the game. Are you staying the weekend?"

"Sure. I'll stay until Sunday afternoon."

"It'll be awhile before I get home. Riley's waiting on me, and we'll go for a coke."

"Sure. I'll probably wait up if you're not too late," he said.

When I left the dressing room, my dad was still there talking to Coach Duncan. I wondered what they had so much to talk about.

RILEY WAS WAITING for me but wasn't her usual self. In the truck, I asked her if something was wrong.

"Becky is worried about Bruce. Their dad wouldn't let him come tonight. She thinks he's close to the breaking point. I can't believe how unreasonable their dad is. She came to the game by herself. Her dad doesn't care what she does and never has. It's a sad situation."

"What about their mother?" I asked.

"She's afraid of their dad. He's a bully and runs over everyone. That's what my dad says. He's had several run-ins with him. I feel so sorry for Bruce. Becky said he was crushed by having to quit football. He'll be eighteen in January, and she thinks he might leave home then. They're so close it'd devastate her if he did. I wish there was something that could be done."

It worried me that she wasn't taking on over me and how great I'd played tonight. This was altogether different from the previous games. I was sorry for Bruce too, but it wasn't the end of the world. I changed the subject, asking her if she enjoyed the game.

"Sure. You played great. Your grandmother introduced me to your dad. He's nice. Is this the first time he's seen you play?"

"Yeah. I was surprised he came. I have a younger brother who lives with him instead of my mother. She doesn't want anything to do with us. My dad's never had time for me, with most of his attention directed to my brother." Maybe if she knew what I'd been through, she'd show me some sympathy.

"I'm sorry. At least he came to see you play tonight."

After all, Becky and Bruce weren't the only ones with problems. It didn't work the way I expected. The remainder of the night she kept feeling sorry for Bruce and Becky, wanting to do something about it. Maybe it was just me, but there didn't seem to be as much feeling in the goodbye kiss when I took her home.

Everybody was still up when I arrived. There were more congratulations, especially from Dawn. I answered questions from my dad about the game and some of the other players, especially Luis. I was impressed with my dad's knowledge of football. It was more extensive than Gavin's or Dawn's as he had an understanding of the Wishbone Offense and what made it work. I tried to concentrate on what was being said, but my mind kept returning to Riley and her strange conduct. I was relieved when Dawn announced it was late and time for bed.

I SLEPT LATE the next morning and arriving at the breakfast table, everyone was already there, including Feather. Dawn had a huge breakfast with sausage, eggs, biscuits, gravy, and pancakes. They'd already started when I sat down.

"Morning, sleepyhead. I imagine you're hungry. I made your dad's favorite breakfast."

"Looks good," I replied sitting down at my regular place which was next to my dad.

"Are you sore?" asked my dad.

"Little, not much. A bruise on my side hurts a little when I turn a certain way."

Gavin laughed. "I imagine those guys that tried to tackle you are in a lot more pain than you this morning."

I felt a nudge on my leg and knew it was Jenny wanting a piece of table food. When no one was watching, I'd been giving her treats. It was going to be hard to do, with this many people at the table. She might just have to wait. After a few minutes, she gave up, but then I noticed Feather drop her hand below the table. Good, someone else was breaking the rules.

"Feather, you need to be horseback now, checking out those heifers," Gavin said.

"Yes sir. I'm ready. Glo's already saddled, waiting in the trailer. Are you going to ride with me today?"

Gavin issued an invitation to Cameron. "What about it, Cameron? Think you can still sit on a horse? It would give you a chance to get a good look at your stock."

"It's been a long time, but I'll give it a try. Do you have something gentle?"

"I'll give you Casper. He's the best. I'll ride the other horse. He's gentle also, but not like Casper."

"Will you be back for lunch?" Dawn asked.

"You bet. We're not that serious," Gavin said.

"Eric, you want to show your dad Arnold while I saddle and load our horses?" Gavin asked.

"Sure. I need to fill up his feed trough and check his water this morning."

Arnold was feeling good and put on a show for my dad, running around his pen. After filling up his feeder and running water for him, I showed my dad how he would lay down when his back was scratched. That was the first time I'd ever done anything to cause my dad to laugh out loud.

"Eric, that's unbelievable. He's a show pig in the truest sense of the word. When's your county show?"

"The second week in February. He's a crossbreed and will show in that group. Mr. Puckett likes him and thinks he'll do good."

"You like Puckett?" he asked.

"It's my favorite class, and Mr. Puckett's my favorite teacher. He was a bull rider in college. He treats everybody the same. It makes no difference who you are."

"If I'd taken Ag in high school maybe I would've been more interested in the ranch. Have you ridden any?" my dad asked.

"Not much but I enjoyed riding Casper. He's a neat horse and takes care of you. I plan on riding more when football is over."

"I see my dad has the trailer hooked on. I'll help him saddle the horses," he said, heading in that direction to help Gavin.

I went back to the house thinking; *a nap would be nice after being up late last night.*

THEY WERE BACK at the house for lunch. Dawn spent the morning cooking, and the enchiladas, rice, refried beans, and tortillas were delicious. Dessert was apple pie with ice cream.

My dad leaned back in his chair with his hands on his stomach. "Mom, this is one of my favorite meals. I haven't eaten this good in years."

"Mrs. Sager, you're a wonderful cook. Those are the best enchiladas I've ever eaten. I'm going to have trouble getting on my horse this afternoon." Feather responded with another compliment.

Gavin changed our plans for the afternoon. "Cameron, if you'll ride my horse, maybe Eric can take my place. You ride well enough to have a little more horse under you. I need to rest a bit after this morning."

"Fine with me. What about it, Eric?" asked my dad.

"Sure, as long as we're back by six o'clock. That'll give me time to clean up and get into town to see Riley."

We left immediately after that and were riding within the hour. I was more comfortable today than on my first experience. I was surprised at my dad's riding ability but shouldn't have been since he'd grown up on the ranch. We found several bunches of cattle far from the pens that hadn't been coming to feed. Everything we saw appeared to be healthy. Dad remarked several times about how good the heifers were doing and the high quality of the bulls that Gavin had purchased.

I could tell that dad was impressed with Feather, saying several times how well she rode. I wondered if she had any clothes besides the jeans, shirt, boots, and old hat. Her shirt and jeans were too large for her, and she always had them tucked into her boots. Maybe she wanted them large to allow more comfort in the saddle.

We rode for four hours before making the round-trip back to the pens where we left our truck. My dad commented that he estimated we'd ridden at least fifteen miles. That added to what they had ridden this morning would probably be about thirty-five miles.

Dismounting, my dad groaned. "Oh, me. I over did it. I may not be able to get out of bed tomorrow."

We loaded the horses, and I rode back with Dad but Feather took her own truck.

On the drive back to the house, I asked my dad how long it'd been since he'd ridden.

"This is the first time since the death of my sisters. I seldom came home after that and then I only stayed a short while. My dad and I didn't see eye-to-eye on anything, and it was best to stay away."

"Do you miss your sisters?" I asked.

"Yes. I think of them often and what they'd be doing now if they were living. For a long time after they were gone, I felt guilty. I was jealous because my dad loved them more than me. At times, my anger spilled over to them. It wasn't their fault. They were sweet girls and looked up to me. We didn't have much of a relationship because my dad stood between it. He never included me in his and the twins' activities. If he took them fishing when they were eight and I was fourteen, I wasn't invited. From the time I was in high school, he kept me working at every opportunity. He and the girls would come by in the pickup to check on me. It was like we were two separate families. My mother saw what was happening and tried to intervene but was not successful."

Listening to him, I could understand his feelings toward Gavin. I didn't understand why he was doing the same thing to me. Maybe my treatment was more deserved because of my attitude when living at home. He answered my question without having to ask him.

"I haven't been fair to you. I had a great many anger issues with my dad and your mother. I regret it and am going to make an effort to do better. I finally did one thing right, by bringing you out here to live with Mom and Dad. You've made an amazing change in a short time."

"I hated it at first. After Gavin started treating me like a human being it got better. Now, I like going to school here and playing football."

We arrived at the house and he told me to go on and get ready for my date, he would put the horses up. That was fine with me. It was already after six.

I went directly to my room and started running bath water. I didn't hear the knock on my door, but Dawn yelled. "Eric, you have a call!" *Who could that be*, I thought, making my way to the phone.

I answered and it was Riley.

"Eric, Becky is here at my house and I can't see you tonight. I'm sorry for the last-minute change, but she needs me. Are you going to church tomorrow?"

"I could come in later this evening after Becky leaves."

"She's spending the night. Are you going to church tomorrow?" she asked again.

"I don't know. My dad's here."

"Well, if you don't, I'll see you Monday."

I hesitated.

"Eric are you still there?"

"Yeah."

"I have to go now. Bye." She hung up.

35

FRANK

It was Monday morning, October 25, and I was thinking about my year thus far. We had finished nine weeks of school, and for the most part, I was pleased with my faculty. I'd been to several of Mr. Kelly's rehearsals, coming away even more impressed than I'd expected. His fall show was going to be outstanding. It was amazing how he was able to bring out the talent in our students. I was looking forward to the community being introduced to our theater program.

No more fights had occurred at school. The threats that *Mean* Jean, Wanda's mother made about her husband coming to see me turned out to be comical. He did show up the day after I sent Wanda home the second time with her mother. I've never met a nicer man who like me was frustrated with Wanda and her mother. We had a nice visit, and I promised myself that Jean would never know how well we hit it off.

The girls had started basketball and were now practicing after school. Riley was excited and impressed with Coach Tiff. I assumed she and Coach Adams still were a thing. After the call from Coach Tiff's neighbor about his car being parked in front of her house all night, I visited with him about the disadvantages of living in a small town. Of course, he should've known about it already, being a local boy, however, his mind probably wasn't on proper etiquette. I ended up telling him that it wasn't my job to chaperone his love life but not to leave his car parked in front of Coach Tiff's house all night.

My most disappointing challenge thus far had been my failure to prevent Loughton from taking his son, Bruce, out of the football program. I tried to reason with him, but it was hopeless. He'd always gotten his way and wasn't going to accept this outcome. Bruce had played one more week after our conference before he left the program. I assumed Loughton believed that after we thought about it for a week, either myself or coach would give in. When that didn't happen, he made Bruce quit. Bruce's sister, Becky, had confided in Riley about how devastated Bruce was. She played basketball and had become Riley's best friend, staying overnight with her several times.

I was pleased and surprised at how well my family had adjusted to their new home. Of course, Julie had gotten along well at the bank, being rewarded with a raise after completing her first month. She'd accepted the smaller house, arranging it to better suit our family, and even setting up a morning bathroom schedule for us. Riley was doing great and looking forward to their first basketball game. She'd been dating Eric which seemed to be working out for both. Aubrey continued to be the challenge, and not the fact she wasn't adjusting. She attracted boys like bees to honey. What concerned me and her mother was that the boys were always older, sometimes by as much as four or five years. Try as we might, it wasn't possible to keep them away. Aubrey did nothing to help us either—probably the opposite.

As usual, I hadn't made any friends out of school. I spent my time at work or with my family. Recently I joined the local Lion's Club, which would be an opportunity for outside fellowship. I did enjoy visiting with Coach Duncan, Mr. Kelly, and Mr. Puckett at every opportunity which presented itself. I'd also come to depend on Snuff the custodian to answer many of my questions about the school. I tried to avoid Mr. Cleburne as much as possible.

Interrupting my thoughts, Mrs. Kraal came to my door saying that a Mr. Walker was here to see me. When he came in, I moved from behind my desk and introduced myself.

"Sherman Walker," he responded.

I sat down in one of the two chairs at the front of my office. I took a chance that this was going to be a positive meeting and not a problem. It's discouraging to be wrong on a Monday morning.

"Mr. Mendenhall, I have a problem that you need to help me with. My daughter is seeing a Mexican boy behind my back. She knows I disapprove. But she's doing it anyway. I don't believe in mixing races. Understand, I have nothing against Mexicans. She's too young and doesn't understand. I need your help."

"What do you mean?" I dreaded the answer.

"Call him in and tell him you want it stopped. I don't want him around my daughter at school."

"Mr. Walker, I can't get involved in your daughter's social life at school or anywhere else, for that matter."

"She's not obeying me by seeing him at school. Why can't you help me stop it?"

"That's not my job. He's not breaking any school rules, and I have no right to interfere."

"Can you do anything?" he asked.

"You can visit with the counselor and explain how you feel. She, in turn, can talk to the boy and convey your feelings to him. Of course, he's probably already aware that you don't approve."

"Maybe, I'm overreacting, but this is something that me and my wife feel strongly about. You have a daughter. What would you think if she was dating a Mexican?"

"Who's the boy your daughter is seeing?"

"Luis Ortiz."

"Luis is a good student and seems to be a very nice boy. It wouldn't bother me if he was dating my daughter. I know we disagree. It would be more unacceptable if she was interested in a student with a bad attitude that caused trouble. The student's race is not an issue with me. However, I respect your opinion and certainly I'm not saying you're wrong. My job is to ensure that your daughter has access to the best education possible—it ends there. I will confide in you a problem we have with our youngest daughter. Older boys are attracted to her because she's mature for her age. My wife and I strongly oppose her being around boys four or five years older. It might be fine for your daughter to date older boys. You see, we all have problems at home, but I don't expect the school to be involved in their solutions."

"I appreciate your honesty, Mr. Mendenhall, and understand where you're coming from. It's just something that we can't accept. I'll talk with the counselor and maybe she can help."

"These things usually work themselves out. Thank you for coming in, and it was good to meet you." I stood and offered my hand, which he accepted.

As he was leaving, he turned around. "I've heard good things about the way you run the school and how fair you are. By the way, Luis is a much better quarterback than Bruce. It took guts to stand up to Loughton."

I sat motionless. *This doesn't happen very often. A parent comes in with a problem and leaves complimenting my performance.*

RILEY HAD a basketball scrimmage Tuesday night with a neighboring school. Becky came home with her and joined us for an early dinner to allow time for their food to digest. She was a pretty girl with blonde hair and blue eyes. I always enjoyed our family mealtime conversations.

"Are you excited about basketball starting, Becky?" asked Julie.

"Yes. Coach Tiff is neat. She's an amazing player herself. I think we're going to be good. I'm feeling better about Bruce since our dad is going to allow him to play basketball. Bruce is not as upset and is looking forward to basketball, since we only have two football games left, unless we make the playoffs. He's even better at basketball than football."

"We're going to be good. I can't wait for the first real game," Riley said.

Aubrey added her opinion. "I don't like basketball. The uniforms they gave us are yucky. They're faded and mine is too large. I bet the high school wore them for years before handing them down to us. I'd quit if y'all would let me."

"You're going to play this year. When you get into high school, we'll talk about it again." I had told her this more than one time.

"Theater is my favorite class. Mr. Kelly is awesome and can sing and dance like no one I've ever seen. I have a part in the play that'll be performed next month."

I wasn't surprised about Becky's statement about liking theater.

"I can't wait to see it. Dad, how did you get Mr. Kelly to come way out here to nowhere?" asked Riley.

"He wanted to start his career in a small school, and had lived in remote areas growing up. Both of his parents were educators. Outside of that, I was just fortunate beyond belief that he saw my announcement of a vacancy and called me."

"We have our first dance in November. I can't decide if it's even worth attending." Aubrey moved the topic back to herself.

"Why?" asked Riley.

"The boys in my class are so immature. I don't care to dance with any of them. I'll probably stay home and wait until next year when boys that interest me are there. I'll probably get asked to go to the high school dances this year. Of course, they probably won't let me go."

"You're right. It's nice that you realize it, so don't bother asking." Julie settled it before it was even an issue.

It was a pleasure to have Becky eat with us. She was an attractive girl with a radiant personality. Riley had chosen her best friend well, which wasn't surprising since they were alike in many ways. Finishing our meal, Riley and Becky left for the gym to get ready for the scrimmage, and Aubrey went to her room.

"Frank, how in the world does someone like Loughton raise a child as sweet as Becky?"

"Julie, I've asked myself that question more than once. According to everyone, Bruce is one of the nicest students in school, too. I can't answer it. From what I hear, Loughton has nothing to do with Becky, giving all his attention to Bruce. I'm sure Bruce would be more than happy to share some of that attention."

"Frank, I'm glad she's Riley's best friend. If only Aubrey could find a friend like Becky."

"Not much chance of that. The girls in her class are jealous of her, and the junior high boys are intimidated by her. You know who that leaves . . . older boys."

A strange thought came to mind, but I didn't express it to Julie. *I imagine people were wondering how we raised a child that looked and acted like Aubrey.*

I WALKED TO SCHOOL FRIDAY, in a cold drizzle. We had a home game tonight with Fort Hancock, with a miserable outlook for fans, according to the weather forecasts. I usually was one of the first to arrive at school, but several students were already in the hallway. I noticed one had on a sweat shirt with 'BAND' on the back of it. It was the first one like it I'd seen. As students began coming in, several other students had on the same sweat shirt. I complimented one and asked where they bought their shirt.

"We didn't buy them. The band boosters gave them to us. Aren't they cool?"

Nothing like discovering we were violating UIL rules to start a Friday, I thought. By the first bell, there were band shirts up and down the hall. I guess everyone had worn theirs today. After the halls were cleared, I went out to the band hall to talk with Mr. Wister, who didn't have a class first period. I found him in his office eating a donut, with three more lying on a paper towel beside him. He was dressed in his usual attire—red coveralls.

"Morning, Mr. Wister. Having your breakfast?"

He must've had half a donut in his mouth and couldn't answer for several seconds. "Yeah. Stopped at the donut shop on the way to school. Watcha need?"

"I need to ask you about the shirts your band students are wearing today."

"What about 'em?" He took another large bite out of the donut.

"One of the students said the Band Booster Club gave him the shirt. If that's the case, it's a UIL violation."

"Been doing it for twenty years. Didn't bother other principals."

"Surely you realize it's a rule violation to give special consideration to a group participating in activities."

"We're way out here in West Texas. Nobody cares what we do."

"Mr. Wister, we're still a part of the University Interscholastic League, and we are going to abide by the rules. I can't send the band students home, but the shirts are to be returned to the booster club as soon as possible."

"It's going to be raining tonight. We wear shirts to keep our band uniforms from being damaged."

"You inform your students when they come to class today, not to wear them tonight. They can bring them to school Monday and turn them in to you."

He didn't respond.

"Do you understand?"

"Yeah. I understand."

I left as he was reaching for another donut. On the way back to my office in the rain, I remembered my previous superintendent, who was in his seventies, saying, "Frank, if it wasn't for the band, cheerleaders, and flat roofs, my job would be much easier." I guess if it continued to rain today, I might experience two out of the three.

36

ERIC

I t was cold and raining when I left. This game would probably decide the district championship since both of us were undefeated. After tonight, we only had one more game. The pep rally had been great with the entire school attending. The little ones could make a lot of noise. According to Riley, all week the game had been the talk of the town. Things were back to normal with her which was a huge relief. I didn't attend church Sunday after she broke our date Saturday night, but when I went to school Monday, she was her old-self and was glad to see me, apologizing.

My dad wasn't coming back for tonight's game but planned on making the last one. He treated me better on this visit than he ever had, actually seeming to care about what was going on in my life. The horseback ride with him and Feather had been the best time we'd ever spent together that I could remember. Maybe it was him seeing me play football, or it could've been the fact that he and Gavin had gotten along so well. It didn't matter the reason—I had seemed to be important.

Arriving at the field house, it was raining even harder, and by the time I was inside my clothes were soaked. Changing into my game pants and a t-shirt I lay down on the mat that covered the floor. Luis and I talked in a whisper until it was time for our pre-game warmup.

Coach came in, telling us to listen up, he had something to say. "We're not going out for pre-game. It's raining, and all we'll accomplish is getting wet and cold. We'll warmup in the gym and wait until game time to take the field. You know how important this game is without me telling you. More than likely it'll decide the district championship. We haven't won a title for the past ten years, and it'd be a life-time memory for you if we're successful. I've always believed that in adverse conditions such as we have tonight, the team with the most desire to win has a big advantage. We're the underdog, but the field is going to be an equalizer which will help us. Regardless of how the game comes out, this year for me has been a great experience. I want to thank you for giving me a new beginning." He ended his talk with, "Give it your best!"

We moved into the gym, which joined the field house, and did our pre-game warmup. Throughout the twenty minutes of calisthenics and drills, it was quiet. I couldn't decide whether that was good or bad.

When we took the field, the rain was coming down in sheets. I looked in the stands at the few present, who were holding umbrellas. Dawn had told me before I left that Gavin couldn't afford to sit out in the cold rain. They'd park as close to the field as possible and see the best they could. We lost the toss and were on defense first. Fort Hancock ran two series and fumbled at midfield with us recovering. Our field had never been in good shape and tonight it reminded me of Arnold's pig pen.

Throughout the first half, neither team scored. After last week's effort, motivated by my dad being there, I couldn't seem to get going. I blamed it on the field conditions but realized that the intensity wasn't there either.

When we went in at the half, Luis asked, "Eric, are you all right?"

"I don't know, Luis. Something's not right. I can't seem to get into it tonight."

"We depend on you, Eric. The way you go, our team goes. It's been that way since the first game you played. I don't think you realize how important you are."

"I never thought about it that way."

"The field is terrible. And with the rain it's almost impossible to throw. You're going to have to carry us with our straight-ahead running game."

We received the second half, and I carried the ball six times in a row, moving the ball down the field, until we were on the 10-yard line with first and goal. Three plays later, we were on the two. With a fourth and goal, Coach called time out. Luis went to the sideline to talk with him. When he came back, he had the play Coach had given him.

Luis spoke quietly. "This could be the ballgame. Power right."

I would get the ball on an off-tackle play with our tackle and end doubling down and the halfback kicking out on the defensive end. Luis took the snap, turned and gave me the ball. The halfback missed his block and the defensive end was waiting on me. Staying low and keeping my balance after contact, I spun off him and fell across the goal line. We missed the extra point and took the lead 6-0.

The remainder of the game was a defensive battle, and the one score was enough to win. The game ended with our fans swarming the field, ignoring the rain. Riley was there, hugging me, in my muddy uniform and telling me how wonderful I was. I couldn't believe this was happening to me. It was like a dream. In the dressing room Coach was ecstatic. Congratulating everyone and heaping praise on me. Fans came into the dressing room that I didn't know, shaking my hand. Luis came over, giving me a hug.

"You did it, Eric! You carried us. I knew you could do it."

It was at least thirty minutes before I left the dressing room. Dawn was standing in the rain waiting for me alongside Riley. She hugged me. "Eric, you were wonderful. I wouldn't let Gavin get out of the car, but he said to tell you that he was proud of you."

I kept thinking. *This can't be real. I'm a hero. Everyone likes me.*

THE NEXT WEEK the praise and recognition continued, with students' and teachers' congratulations. Riley and I were spending more time together. I'd started going to the gym after football and waiting for her to finish practice. Most of the time we finished before the girls. I'd take her home and we'd sit in my truck and talk, sometimes for an hour.

The week passed quickly and it was Friday and game day. Workouts had gone well, with everyone being excited. If we won this game, it would mean a district championship. The pep rally was even better than last week's. As I sat with other team members in chairs placed on the gym floor with everyone cheering and clapping, I felt like a king.

Thoughts surrounding me, I found myself comparing my life here with what I'd left behind in San Antonio. Why didn't at least a few good things happen to me there? *Because I didn't allow anything positive in my life*, answering my own question. I associated with negative people and attempted to fit in, trying to feel better about myself by belittling others. Continuing to live on junk food, I hated being fat but did nothing to change my appearance. I came out here to live with my grandparents, bringing anger and rebellion. Losing weight was a result of Gavin almost working me to death. My grandmother was the first person who showed me a genuine concern and love. I found a friend in Luis who was an athlete with a positive outlook. I felt useful for the first time in my life and was given responsibility. I came close to dying twice but asked GOD to help me and survived. Maybe there was something to this GOD thing after all.

I'd never thought it possible to have a girlfriend. Now, this beautiful girl who was with me constantly at school, shared my life. Hearing my name called brought me back to the present. The team was being introduced individually. I stood up. The applause was deafening —continuing longer than for anyone else.

THE NIGHT, unlike last week, was beautiful. It was clear and cold with no wind—perfect football weather. The game was away, but the hometown stands were full. Our fans were excited, and we could do nothing wrong. Our offense was the best it had been, and our defense shut them down. We were ahead 19-0 at the half and went on to score two more times in the second half. The scoreboard read, 33-0 when the game ended.

Our fans stormed onto the field, congratulating us. It took at least fifteen minutes to reach the dressing room, with people stopping me every few steps. Of course, Riley was hanging on to me, tighter than some of the opposing players tackling me. In the dressing room, with tears in his eyes coach praised our performance. My dad had kept his word and was at the game. He came to the dressing room and hugged me like he meant it.

The celebration continued on the ride home with country music. Several of my teammates knew the words to "Good Hearted Woman" which was sung by Willie and Waylon and "If You've Got the Money I've Got the Time," sung by Willie. It didn't take long for everyone to be singing along. The two-hour ride went quickly, and when I got off the bus, Riley was waiting on me, capping the best day of my life.

WE LOST our bi-district football game, basketball started, and I made all of Riley's home games. She was something else on the court, and I watched with pride as she was the high-point scorer in most contests. The attention was now shifted to Riley, which didn't bother me. Even having to share Riley with her best friend, Becky, was okay. Everyone was nice to me, even Coach Bryson.

The weather had turned colder and we'd had some freezing rain. I worked on the ranch weekends, feeding and looking after the cattle. Feather came every Friday and stayed until Sunday. I kept trying to get up enough nerve to ask her if she had any other clothes. The only addition to her wardrobe was an old coat that was at least three sizes too big. Gavin didn't venture out in bad weather; hence she and I spent many days by ourselves, either feeding or horseback. My riding had improved and I was even enjoying it. I'd never noticed the beauty of nature until moving out here. The rugged mountains, covered in ice were beautiful. For the first time I also became aware of wildlife. I was amazed at the huge mule deer that we jumped while riding one morning. We nearly always saw a herd of Aoudad when we rode. Late one afternoon, we'd even seen a mountain lion.

After spending days at a time with her, she'd become more like a sister. She listened as I told her about Riley and my experiences at school, occasionally giving me advice on issues. She surprised me one afternoon with her questioning.

"Eric, do you love Riley?"

"I guess so."

"Does she love you?" she asked.

"I hope so." That was a scary question. What if she didn't?

"Is she your first girlfriend?"

"Yeah." I wasn't comfortable with the personal questions. What brought this about? She must've realized I didn't like the questions because she changed the subject.

"How long have your parents been divorced?"

"It's been about four years, but they never did get along. All I remember is them arguing. What about yours?"

"My parents got into drugs during the sixties and never quit. As far as I know, they're still not divorced. Neither of them could keep a job and we lived on welfare. I hated living at home. I stayed with Pops at every opportunity, finally moving in with him. He's not well now and can do very little. He depends on me to bring in enough income to live on. I appreciate your granddad hiring me."

I hadn't realized he was sick. "What's wrong with your granddad?"

"He's diabetic. He's on a strict diet and has trouble controlling his blood sugar. He's passed out several times when it became too low. I worry about leaving him but have no other option. I enjoy the ranch work but didn't have a choice. Pops is too proud to admit that he's not able to work."

Now I understood why she wore the same clothes. Money wasn't available to buy new ones. Everything went to basic necessities. Surely, she didn't wear these clothes to school.

"When I graduate in January, it'll be necessary to get a full-time job."

Surprised at her confession, it'd never occurred to me that she had to work. All along I'd thought it was because she was doing it for her enjoyment. The first time we were alone, I'd share with Dawn what Feather had told me.

. . .

OUR THANKSGIVING HOLIDAYS started when school let out on Wednesday, the twenty-fourth. I wasn't looking forward to the four-day vacation since Riley was going with her mom and dad to visit family in Abilene. I couldn't imagine going that long without seeing her. My dad and brother were coming in late this afternoon to spend Thanksgiving Day and Friday with us. Dawn had already started cooking for the big meal. At Dawn's suggestion, Gavin had invited Feather and her granddad to eat lunch with us on Thanksgiving. She'd take him home that afternoon and return early Friday to work during the weekend.

I wanted the four days to pass quickly and sitting around watching TV wouldn't make that happen. The best solution would be to stay as busy as possible. Dawn had told me this morning before I left for school that the weather was supposed to turn bad late tonight. It was going to be colder for the next several days with a chance of freezing rain and sleet. That would mean putting out more feed. Spending the holidays with Feather would be a poor substitute for Riley.

37

LUTA

For the first time since we lost our daughters, we were having a family Thanksgiving Dinner. My prayers had been answered. Therefore, I was determined to have a meal that was perfect. I started baking on Wednesday morning and by noon had two apple pies and a pumpkin pie done. That afternoon I cooked the dressing, since I'd need the oven the next day for the turkey. I made a fruit salad which had been Cameron's favorite since he was a small boy. I planned to cook homemade rolls because that was a favorite of Gavin's. The few times that Ethan had been here, I discovered how much he liked candy so fudge was on the menu, too. I didn't have to cook anything special for Eric since he liked food, period. When Gavin came in for lunch on Wednesday, smelling and seeing the food he expressed amazement.

"Goodness, Luta, we're going to have enough food to feed the whole county. What about me sampling that apple pie?" Gavin suggested. "It may not be any good."

"I made several fried apple pies for us. Your doctor wouldn't approve, but since it's Thanksgiving we'll make an exception."

Gavin had been good to stay on his diet which was hard. He'd always eaten a lot of meat and fried foods. He'd kept his weight off and cut back on his cigars. I knew when the doctor told him he couldn't smoke that wouldn't work. He drank very little liquor so that wasn't a problem. Jenny hadn't taken up with him like Max. She preferred to stay with me.

"What time did you tell Lefty and Feather to be here tomorrow?" I asked.

"Around one o'clock. I told him we'd eat later, so they'd better have a good breakfast. I was wondering, Luta, just how much did you spend on the clothes that you bought Feather? Y'all were gone to town for half a day, Saturday."

"Not too much. The store had some good sales."

He frowned. "I bet you spent at least a $100."

"Goodness, Gavin, the poor thing didn't have any clothes. We found her several cute dresses that she can wear to church. It broke my heart when Eric told me about them having to live on what we paid her. I have several pairs of boots that I kept of Stacy's and if it's okay with you, she can have them. Also, I'd like to increase her salary."

"That's fine with me. Do you think she can wear the boots?"

"You know, Gavin, her clothes size is about the same as Stacy's. I also gave her the money to get her hair done and buy some make-up. She needs to have what other girls do. She's pretty."

"I can't argue with you about that. She's really good help, and we're going to need her this winter. What do you think about offering her full-time work after she graduates in January?"

"I think that's a great idea. We'll pay her a good salary. The additional loan we co-signed should take care of that." I was pleased that Gavin came up with the suggestion. He was slowly but surely moving back to the man I married. My prayers were being answered.

"It looks as if we're going to have a rough winter, the way it's starting. With this kind of cold at Thanksgiving, by January we could be in for some rough times. I hope we have enough hay."

"Gavin, moving to another subject, do you realize this will be the first Thanksgiving we've been together in sixteen years?"

"I thought about it this morning. Eric or Ethan have never sat down with us for a holiday meal," he replied.

"I hope the weather doesn't become bad before they arrive. Cameron said they were going to try to be here by dark. The weather forecast predicated the cold front would be here late this afternoon. It's not supposed to get out of the thirties tomorrow."

Gavin was already making plans. "We'll put out hay in the morning. Maybe Cameron can go with me and do the outside work while I drive. I've already attached the hay fork to my pickup."

"I'll get out the Monopoly and cards. That should keep the boys entertained." I kept telling myself over and over, *I may be expecting too much for this being the first time we've been together.*

THE TWO DAYS that Cameron and Ethan spent with us were wonderful, even better than I expected. After a big breakfast Thanksgiving morning, Cameron went with Gavin to feed. Eric took Ethan with him to feed his pig and after I had the turkey in the oven, me and the boys played Monopoly.

Ethan kept asking Eric about football. "Did you really make four touchdowns in a game?"

"Yep. I carried the ball at least thirty times."

"Wow! I would've liked to have been there," Ethan said.

"Ethan, maybe you can come to see Eric play several games next year." There shouldn't be any reason for that not to happen.

"I hope so!" he exclaimed.

I had to leave the Monopoly game to finish dinner. Eric took Ethan back to the barn to show him Arnold's trick of laying down when you scratched his back. Later, they came back in laughing. It was wonderful to have them spending time together.

Promptly at one o'clock Feather and her granddad arrived. Opening the door, I was stunned to see Feather wearing her new full length church coat and one of her bargain dresses, with her pixie haircut, and makeup. She was absolutely beautiful. She looked like a picture in a magazine.

"Are we early, Mrs. Sager?" No doubt wondering why I didn't speak.

"Oh, my, Feather. You look gorgeous. Please come in out of the cold. Hello, Lefty. Gavin and Cameron are feeding. They'll be back shortly."

Feather twirled around. "I love my new clothes."

"You look so nice. Eric and his brother are watching the Dallas Cowboy game. You might want to join them. Lefty, I have a pot of coffee on. We can visit in the kitchen."

I didn't follow Feather into the den. I doubt if Eric even noticed how pretty she was. He was so enthralled with Riley. I could hear them talking but not what they were saying.

I poured Lefty a cup of coffee. "How's everything going?"

"It could be better. I appreciate you buying the clothes for Feather. I'd like to do more for her."

He looked sad.

"You give her a good home, Lefty. That means a lot."

"At one time, I had some savings but spent it bailing Feather's mother and daddy out of trouble. I gave up on them and Feather came to live with me. I should've done it long ago, but it's hard to stop trying to save your daughter and son-in-law."

I felt sorry for him, knowing how it feels to almost give up on someone you love. I came close several times to doing that. Now, everything was looking up. We visited for the next half hour, moving away from family, to the ranch and a time when we were both younger.

When Gavin and Cameron came in from feeding, Gavin's reaction to Feather was even greater than mine. "Feather! What've you done to yourself? You look like a movie star or one of them models. The cattle may stampede if they see you like that."

She blushed. "I don't plan on coming to work tomorrow dressed like this. I look this way because of Mrs. Sager."

"Well, I'll tell you this; I've never seen anything prettier."

Cameron was impressed also. "It makes me wish I was twenty years younger."

"I have dinner ready. All I need to do is set the table. You can help me if you like, Feather."

It only took us a few minutes and we were ready to eat. We sat down and I said the blessing. The meal turned out good, even if I do say so myself. We ate until we were stuffed and the kids went back to the ballgame. Gavin, Cameron, Lefty, and I stayed at the table and visited over coffee for another hour. Most of the topic concerned the heifers and the cattle market with the weather also discussed. Politics were brought up with some opinions about our newly elected President, Jimmy Carter. Not enough interest was present to generate an argument.

"Luta, that meal was something else. I appreciate you having us over and thank you again for what you did for Feather. She's the most important thing in my life. Knowing she has you to look after her gives me a lot of comfort. We need to be going now. It's time for my afternoon nap," Lefty stated.

"Thank you for coming, Lefty. I'm going to fix some of this food to take home with you. It'll just go to waste if you don't take it."

"I'm not going to argue with you, Luta."

Within fifteen minutes they were gone, but we stayed at the table, talking. All this time and not a cross word between Cameron and his dad. I prayed silently it would continue.

"Eric has made an unbelievable change since coming to live with you. He doesn't act or even look the same. He'd be a good influence on Ethan now if he wanted to return home. He could play football at his high school in San Antonio. He's that good. What do you think?" Cameron looked at me for an answer.

"I don't know, Cameron. He's smitten by this girl he's seeing. You would just have to ask him." I didn't think this was a good idea.

"What about me?" Gavin piped up. "Is anyone going to ask me what I think?"

"Sure, what do you think, Dad?"

"I need Eric here this winter to help me with the ranch. All I have so far is him and Feather. I'm concerned that you didn't want him when he was a problem. Now that he's more to your liking, we're supposed to ask him if he wants to go home. It doesn't hardly seem right," Gavin protested.

I had to intervene before it got out of hand. "Let me make a suggestion and see what both of you think. What if we just leave things the way they are for now? Eric can stay here and help Gavin through the winter. Cameron, when school is out you can ask Eric if he wants to return to San Antonio. I wouldn't force Eric to make a decision now, but would work toward a compromise. With his girlfriend, I have no doubt what his decision would be now, anyway. Is that reasonable?"

"Suits me." Gavin had calmed down.

"I agree as long as we can ask him when school is out if he wants to return home," Cameron responded.

Maybe we had avoided a confrontation. I changed the subject, asking Gavin if he was going to take his afternoon nap. He didn't reply, getting up and going to our room.

"I guess things were going too good," announced Cameron.

"I've taken your side and defended you all your life, Cameron, but not this time. You shouldn't have mentioned taking Eric home with you. He's doing well here and Gavin is better than he's been in years. We're trying to get you out of a bind that you got yourself in. Now, your dad is upset. We've had a wonderful Thanksgiving so please don't mention Eric leaving again. I don't think you understand how much help Eric is to us. He's done a man's work after the first month he was here. We couldn't have done without him when Gavin was in the hospital."

He wouldn't look at me. "I shouldn't have said anything. Eric has changed so much I wanted him to be at home with me and his brother. I won't mention it again."

"Why don't you take your sons and show them the ranch. Gavin will sleep for a couple of hours and y'all can spend some time together. I need to get off my feet, too."

"Sure. That's a good idea." He rose and coming over, gave me a hug.

After they left, I checked on Gavin. He was not asleep, lying on his back, looking at the ceiling. "Are you okay?"

"Yeah. It was a fine day, wasn't it?"

Sitting down on the bed, I took his hand. "Yes, it was, Gavin. A wonderful day. What made it special to me was having our little family together."

"Cameron has a way of getting to me," he admitted.

"I know," I agreed continuing to hold his hand. "This time it's different though. You and I are on the same side."

38

FRANK

"How'd he do it, Julie? How in the world did he put something together that fast which is awesome? There were kids on that stage who I had no idea possessed any talent. Some of them had never been involved in even one activity."

"I don't know, Frank. He's young, full of energy, and talented. Maybe, even more important, he has no pre-conceived notion about the students. To him, they all have ability. I know that doesn't answer the question but for now that's the best answer. Maybe later we'll understand better as we get to know Mr. Kelly.

"Pinocchio was the perfect play and the casting was right on. You were fortunate to find such a talented young man to come out here to nowhere. He could've gone to a larger school with a better salary," she said.

"I know. On the negative side, Julie, did you notice that Mr. Cleburne wasn't present? I guess theater isn't his thing."

"No, but that's not a big deal. Several of the board members and almost all the faculty were present. It was obvious they were as impressed as I was. How could you not be?"

"I've never worked with anyone like Cleburne and maybe he'll be the last. He's not going to support me. He's demonstrated that more than once, the worst being when he took Wister's side over mine with the violation of UIL rules. He took money out of the school budget and paid the Band Booster Club for the shirts. That money could've gone to buy supplies for the teachers. It all comes down to one thing—Wister has more influence in the community than I do."

"Well, anyway, it was a wonderful show. Let's move to another subject. Are we leaving for Abilene tomorrow?" she asked.

I was looking forward to a four-day holiday. "I think so. The traffic will be light since it's Thanksgiving Day. It's only about a five-hour drive and we'll make it in time for the big meal. I know you're anxious to see your parents. Will you have time to pack this afternoon after you get off work? Since we get out of school at 2:30 today for the holidays, I'll get home early."

"I think so. We're not going to be gone but two nights and it'll not require much packing. Frank, Aubrey is not happy about Becky going. I wish it was just us but Riley had already asked her before she told me. I can't blame Aubrey since she'll be left out of whatever the other two are doing. On the other hand, Riley was doing something nice by inviting her."

"We can't worry about that now. Maybe on our next trip Aubrey can take a friend." I can't remember many times when Aubrey was happy about our decisions.

Riley and Becky had become almost inseparable, especially since basketball started. Becky never mentioned her dad around me. I feel sure he spoke negatively of me to her frequently. She and her brother, Bruce, were both courteous and nice. Bruce was playing basketball, and like his sister had said, was actually better than in football. He was one of the most popular students in school and was president of his class. It was hard to believe that Loughton wasn't satisfied because he didn't play quarterback.

Our football season had been unbelievable, after starting out the way it did. Coach Duncan had been selected "Coach of the Year" in our district. He'd continued to attend his AA meetings, and to my knowledge, had remained sober. It was obvious, even to someone like me who knew next to nothing about football that Eric had made the difference in our team. Of course, moving Luis to quarterback was a big part of our success as well.

Now, basketball was in full swing with two games a week. I made all the home games and the out-of-town games on Friday. Coach Duncan would go to the away games that fell on Tuesday, which I appreciated. A hundred-mile out-of-town game was actually considered a short trip.

I hadn't realized the change in weather would be this drastic from Fort Worth. The mornings were much colder due to the high altitude with freezing temperatures. It would warm up as much as thirty degrees during the day. The remoteness contributed to a feeling of isolation, but the breathtaking beauty of this part of the state was difficult to put into words. I never tired of the awesome sunsets.

I WAS HOPING for a quiet day at school before we began our Thanksgiving break. Everything was fine until I returned from lunch. A man and Mrs. Parton were waiting for me in the outside office. He introduced himself as Trent Ballard and asked if he could talk with me. Both followed me into my office.

He got right to the point. "I'm concerned about a book my son is reading in Mrs. Parton's English class. It's required reading for all the class. It's filled with profanity and has no place in a classroom. I've talked with Mrs. Parton, and she refuses to select another book to replace it."

"What is the book?" I asked.

"The name of it is *Of Mice and Men*. It's filthy and you should have her replace it with another book. I would've thought you'd be aware of what the students were reading."

"It's a classic, Mr. Ballard, written by John Steinbeck. I've read the book and it does have some profanity in it, however, that has little if anything to do with the main theme of the book. It's about compassion, caring, and friendship."

"I don't care about any of that. It has cussing, and being a Christian, I find that disgusting."

"Mrs. Parton, can you find another book for his son to read. One of which he approves?" I looked in her direction.

"Sure. That won't be a problem."

"Mr. Ballard, we will continue to teach, *Of Mice and Men*."

"Is that your final answer?" He still seemed annoyed.

"Yes, it is."

"I'll pray for you and Mrs. Parton," he said, getting up and leaving.

Mrs. Parton's face registered confusion. "You said 'we' would continue to teach, *Of Mice and Men*. Why did you put it that way?"

"I wanted to make sure he understood that I was taking responsibility, too, for the book being taught."

"I appreciate that very much." She nodded her head.

"No problem. I hope you have a nice holiday."

After she left, I took a few deep breaths, congratulating myself for staying calm, and hoping he didn't go to the superintendent with his problem. If he did, Steinbeck, might be taken out of the library. How could anyone be that narrow minded?

EVERYONE EXCEPT AUBREY enjoyed our trip to Abilene to visit Julie's mom and dad. It was Julie's hometown and her parents still lived there. Of course, Julie, her mother, and the girls wanted to go shopping Friday to take advantage of Black Friday sales. Aubrey went with them but Julie said she found something to complain about the entire time. Worse than the complaining, they became separated in the mall and couldn't find Aubrey. After searching for an hour and in panic mode, they located her talking to a boy. She left Riley and Becky with her mother at the mall and brought Aubrey back to the house for me to deal with. Julie was embarrassed that the episode had happened in the presence of her mother and was as mad as I'd ever seen her.

She asked quietly. "Is my dad here?"

"No. He went to visit a friend in the hospital." My answer allowed her to immediately let loose.

"She's out in the car, Frank. I could just pinch her head off! I don't know what to do with her! If we hadn't found her when we did, Lord knows what would've happened. They were huddled up in the corner of a shoe store. Riley happened to see them as we walked by. I guess it may be necessary to attach a leash to her when we go out. I've already chewed on her until I'm exhausted. It's your turn now."

"She's too big to spank, Julie. We've grounded her and that doesn't do any good. I'll talk to her but so far that's been useless. First thing Monday, I'll talk to the counselor and ask her if she might be able to work in some sessions with Aubrey. Maybe she can make her understand how dangerous her conduct is and where she's headed if it continues."

"I'm ready to try anything. I never thought we'd raise a child that acted the way she does. I'm going back to the mall and join them. I've never been so embarrassed in my life than having this happen in front of my mother."

Aubrey came in, I'm sure, glad to get away from her mother. I lectured and questioned her for half an hour but didn't feel like anything was accomplished. She'd heard it before and probably knew every word that was about to come out of my mouth. The only emotion she showed was boredom. I finished and sent her to the room where the girls were staying.

I was glad Julie was getting to shop in a larger town. We'd been able to sell our house last month and extra money was available. She deserved to splurge on this trip. She was in a better mood when they returned from the mall. I'd learned a long time ago, living with three girls, that nothing does more for their disposition than shopping. We had leftovers for dinner and spent a quiet evening visiting with Julie's mom and dad.

We left early the next morning to get home for an afternoon basketball practice. Riley had insisted that she and Becky be there when the practice started at two o'clock. I didn't understand why a practice was necessary over the holidays. In my opinion the time with family was more important. Maybe not being an athlete had something to do with the way I felt. The girls were in the back seat with Aubrey sitting by the window and not saying a word for two hours. Julie and the other two girls talked excitedly about the clothes they'd purchased and then moved to basketball season.

Riley was determined to include Aubrey and was finally successful by asking her if she was going to try out for cheerleader this spring. That led to a discussion of tryouts and if she'd thought about a routine. By the time we stopped for lunch in Pecos, she was talking as much as anybody. Leave it to Riley to be the peacemaker.

I'D DISCOVERED that between Thanksgiving and Christmas was usually a quiet time with few problems. Usually, most everyone was in a good mood, maybe because of the holiday spirit. I was surprised when the superintendent asked me to be at the December 6, board meeting. I couldn't imagine what my presence would add. When the agenda was posted, my name wasn't listed but there was an executive session with personnel identified as a topic.

Tuesday evening arrived, and the meeting was a repeat of the one in August, with Cleburne asking for a vote on every purchase, sometimes accompanied by a lengthy discussion. All members were present at this meeting. I sat there for three hours until the board went into closed session.

Loughton opened the meeting. "We have a personnel issue that needs to be discussed. There's a lot of talk around that Duncan missed one of our football games because he was drunk. If that proves to be true, we cannot tolerate that type of behavior. We all knew he had a drinking problem when we hired him. Mr. Cleburne has asked that the high school principal be here and provide information about the incident. We're waiting, Mr. Mendenhall."

Caught completely off guard, I hesitated. "Coach Duncan missed the third game which was three months ago. He was sick and has been receiving treatments for his illness since that time. I can't say enough positive things about Coach Duncan and the job he's done, both in his classes and football."

"You said he has an illness. What you mean is he's an alcoholic and missed a game because he was drunk," Loughton countered.

"Alcoholism is an illness that requires treatment, and since that time three months ago, he has been an exemplary model for our students." I knew Loughton wouldn't accept my answer but hoped the other board members would be reasonable.

"None the less, he missed a football game because he was drunk, and everybody in the community knows that." Now, I understood where Loughton was going with this and the purpose of the board meeting.

I kept looking at Cleburne, hoping for support from him, but he was looking down and shuffling some papers. Four other board members were not making eye contact either, however, two were looking directly at me.

I concentrated on them. "I've had no complaints from anyone about Coach Duncan. He has exceeded my expectations, and I support him 100 percent. He's been a positive influence on all of our students."

"I've talked with the school attorney and he informed me we had every right to terminate his contract immediately if the accusation was true. You've just admitted that he was drunk and missed a football game. If there's not any more business we can reconvene in open session," Loughton announced.

With the board conducting business in open session, Loughton spoke. "Is there a motion to terminate Duncan's contract?"

When no one responded he demanded. "I want a motion to terminate this drunk's contract, now!"

A board member said, "I move to terminate his contract."

Another said, "I second it."

"I have a motion and a second to terminate Coach Duncan's contract. All in favor raise your hand." Loughton was both angry and demanding.

When two hands went up, I prayed silently that would be it.

"Listen to me! He's a bad influence on our kids. We can't tolerate a drunk. Everyone I've talked with in the community agrees with me."

I cringed as another hand went up.

"I vote in favor of the motion to terminate Coach Duncan's contract immediately. Coach Duncan's contract will be terminated by a vote of

4-3. Mr. Mendenhall, you will inform him of our decision. He's to be out of school housing immediately, and you'll need to find a replacement for him. Do I have a motion to adjourn?"

I left immediately, angry and frustrated, thinking this had to be the low point in my career. How could one man with no ethics bully others into following his leadership?

39

ERIC

I'd settled into a routine, rising early to feed my pig, going to school, spending as much time as possible with Riley, and helping feed the cattle whenever available. Arnold was growing and had weighed 172 pounds when Mr. Puckett came out last week with his scales. He was still a 'fresh pig' with plenty of energy.

The seventh of December was a normal morning until I arrived at school and heard the news everyone was talking about. Rumor was going around that Coach Duncan had been fired by the school board at last night's meeting. Riley's dad hadn't told her anything about it, so she couldn't provide any additional information. That was all the students were talking about prior to the first bell. Arriving in my first period class, the teacher was asked if the rumor was true. He denied knowing anything about it.

Throughout the day the rumor gained momentum until it appeared to be a certainty. When we arrived at the field house seventh period Coach Duncan told us to meet in the gym. The remainder of the football team that had come out for basketball were present also. There was silence when he began speaking.

"I know you're aware of the rumors that are circulating. They're true. I will no longer be coaching and teaching here. I made a mistake earlier in the year. I've had a drinking problem in the past and prior to the third game of the season this year, it returned. I was absent from the game because I wasn't fit to attend. I apologize to you for my weakness. After that, with the help of Mr. Mendenhall, I was able to get help that has proven to be successful.

"I've experienced the best year of my football career, including playing on a National Championship Team. I owe that to each of you who performed above expectations. Now, I encourage you to move on, remaining proud of what you've accomplished. When something like this occurs, the reaction is to strike back with anger. Don't do this. This situation occurred because of my mistake, and I deserved the outcome. Thank each of you for your efforts and for responding in a positive manner to my leadership."

After he left, we sat stunned at learning the rumors were true. Coach Bryson came in and told the football players to sit in the stands until school was out and for those playing basketball to get dressed for practice.

Luis didn't leave but came over to where I was. "You know what happened don't you?"

"They fired Coach last night."

It was obvious Luis was upset. "No, that's not what I mean. Do you know the reason he was fired?"

"I guess he got drunk and couldn't come to the game."

"No that's not the reason. Bruce's dad got him fired because Coach Duncan moved me to quarterback. I guarantee you that's why he lost his job. We'll never have a coach that's as good as him."

"Would he actually do that? Was Bruce playing quarterback that important to him?" I asked.

"Yes, if you add in the fact that I'm a Mexican. That's plenty of reason for him to get Coach fired. I need to be going. I'll talk to you later."

When the bell rang for school to dismiss, I met Riley at her locker before she left for practice. They had a game tonight so workout would be short. Becky was with her and was crying.

I asked Riley what was going on. "She knows about Coach

Duncan. Her dad told her about the meeting last night when he got home. Word has already gotten out about what happened at the meeting. In her last class someone said something ugly to her. Don't wait on me today. She's coming home with me until time for the game. I'll see you tonight."

They were gone before I could respond. That's just great, I thought. I'd planned to stay with Riley and not go home before the game. Now, I had over two hours to kill before the game at six, if I didn't go home. I decided that was too long to wait.

Gavin wasn't there but Dawn was and questioned my coming home since I'd told her my plans before leaving this morning. I explained what had happened including Coach Duncan being fired. I told her about Coach's speech and also what Luis had said.

"Eric, that's not right. That young man was a good influence on you and is the main reason you came out for football. The team did much better than expected. That is just not right."

"Coach said he didn't want us to be angry."

"He didn't tell *me* that. I'm going to check into this and get to the bottom of it. We can't just sit by and let these things happen without trying to do something."

When I left the house to check on the feed and water for my pig, Dawn was on the phone expressing what she'd told me to someone else. Arnold was a mess. He'd been in his water trough and rolled around in the dirt and was covered with mud. He met me grunting, as if to say, *Get me some clean drinking water.* I didn't want to clean him up now since I'd be as dirty as him after finishing. Emptying his water trough and refilling it, I returned to the house. Dawn was still on the phone, and you could tell she wasn't happy.

"I don't care how the board voted that doesn't make it right. I don't understand what you mean when you say, 'It was out of my control.' You're the superintendent and should've done something about the injustice. You need to understand, Mr. Cleburne, you have not heard the last of this."

I'd never heard her talk like this even when I stole her car and ran away. Her face was red. It was obvious that she was outright angry. In a few minutes she was back to her old-self—speaking softly and calm.

"Eric, I'm not usually like that. Sometimes you have to take a stand against wrong. I've known Slade Loughton virtually all my life. Using his money and aggressive behavior to get his way, he's always been a bully. People are afraid to stand up to him. He was given everything he has. It was inherited. If he had to work for a living he would've probably starved. He should've never even gotten on the school board in the first place."

"What can be done?" I asked.

"I don't know. I'm going to contact some other parents and see how they feel about Coach Duncan being fired. Maybe they'll have some ideas. Mr. Mendenhall will also be on my contact list."

Dawn's reaction caught me by surprise. I'd have never thought she would've been this upset over Coach being fired for drinking and missing a game. Of course, according to Luis that wasn't the cause.

I WAS BACK at the gym in time for the start of the girl's game. Watching the action on the court was difficult, since my eyes were on Riley most of the time. Becky, who usually played well, was terrible tonight, missing even the easy shots. She was short but quick and usually scored on fast breaks. Tonight, she missed a number of layups. According to Riley, she didn't date anyone, even though she was attractive. We ended up winning the game against a much weaker team.

I waited on Riley, planning to sit with her during the boys' game. When she and Becky came out of the dressing room, she told me they weren't staying.

"Eric, Becky wants to get away from everyone. We're going to my house and she's spending the night."

"I thought we were going to watch the boys' game?"

"I need to stay with Becky. She's still upset over Coach Duncan being fired. Several students have been mean, saying her dad was responsible. They don't tell her directly but make the comments within hearing distance. You can watch the boys play, and I'll see you tomorrow."

Confused and angry, I didn't know what to say. She sensed that I was upset, walking away without saying anything else. I went back into the stands and tried to get interested in the boys' game. Luis was good as was Bruce. I wondered if anyone had said anything to Bruce about Coach being fired. We were ahead by twenty points at the half so I left. I thought about stopping at Riley's house but at the last minute decided against it.

Gavin and Dawn were still up when I got home. Dawn must've given the entire account of Coach Duncan to Gavin. He started quizzing me immediately. "Eric, was Coach Duncan ever drinking at practice or during a game? You could've smelled it on his breath or told by his actions."

"No way."

"Was the team aware of the reason he was absent at the third game, prior to him telling you today?"

"I wasn't aware of it. All we were told was that he was sick."

"Do you believe that the boys still respect him after he told you he missed the game because he was drinking?"

"Sure. Maybe even more than ever. We all make mistakes. He's a great coach, and we'll never find anyone as good."

"I assume that Bruce and Becky know their dad was responsible?" He stated, in the form of a question.

"Yeah. Becky was crying when I saw her and Riley after seventh period."

Gavin shook his head. "Poor things. They're both good kids and will suffer the consequences of their dad's action."

Before he could continue the questioning, I went to my room. I was depressed and frightened at Riley's treatment. She'd chosen to be with Becky rather than me. I didn't understand why she tried to help everybody with a problem, especially when it meant ignoring me.

THE NEXT SEVERAL days brought no mention of Coach Duncan from either Gavin or Dawn. I thought they must've accepted the decision and moved on. It hadn't quieted down at school, with much of the talk being about how terrible it was for Coach Duncan to lose his job. Not one student defended the action of the school board.

Riley stayed with Becky most of the time, and I found myself following along after them like a puppy. It made me angry but was better than not being around her at all.

By Friday, frustration got the best of me. Finding myself alone with Riley for the first time, I couldn't hold it in. "How long is this going to last?"

"What do you mean?"

"Spending all your time with Becky rather than me."

"Please understand, Eric. Becky is going through a terrible time at school and home. She's my best friend, and I need to be there for her. She needs me, at least for the time being. She's going to stay with me this weekend since we have a tournament in Van Horn. She'll go home Sunday morning, and I can meet you at church. Things will be back to normal with us soon."

I didn't know what to say. Maybe I should apologize. I took so long to respond she continued. "Are you going to be at church Sunday?"

"I guess."

"Good. I'll see you then." She left with Becky and I went to my truck feeling rejected.

WHEN I DROVE up to the house, Feather's truck and trailer was already parked at the barn. She came out of the house just as I got out of my truck. "I left school early today. Let's ride a couple of hours and check on as many cattle as possible. We have a good two hours of daylight left."

"Where's Gavin?" I wasn't in the mood to spend two hours with Feather.

"In the house. He's not feeling well. We need to get a move on."

"I need to change clothes." I guess, it'd beat sitting around thinking about Riley.

"I'll get your horse saddled and loaded. Hurry up." She was good at giving orders. I give her credit for that.

I was dressed and at the barn in ten minutes, and she already had Casper loaded. She was behind the wheel of her truck when I got in.

"We can cover a lot of ground in two hours and then we'll start early in the morning. How was your week?" She drove too fast over the rough road.

"Could've been better." I told her about Coach Duncan.

"How's your love life?" she continued.

"The pits. Riley has a tournament this weekend. She's been spending all her time with Becky. Said she needed her."

"That's the way it goes when you put all your eggs in one basket. You need to be scouting around for another squeeze. Give Riley some competition."

"I don't want anyone but Riley."

"Your decision. By the way, I looked your pig over today. His tail doesn't curl. Pigs with a straight tail don't show good."

"What can I do to make his tail curl?" I asked.

"Put a gob of Vaseline on your finger and stick it up his rear. That'll do it."

"Gross! I'd never do that."

"Never say never. It'll get you every time."

We made it to the windmill in time to make a big circle to the west before returning right at dark. We counted seventy-five cows and several bulls. One of the bulls was limping badly, and Feather announced that tomorrow we'd need to get him to the pen for doctoring.

For some reason by the time we returned to the house, ate supper, and watched TV for a couple of hours, I felt better.

40

LUTA

I called a dozen or so parents Friday evening and Saturday, and all felt the same way I did about Coach Duncan being fired. The difference was, many didn't believe anything could be done about it. I finally convinced most of them that we should meet and try to get something done about the injustice. I'd made a calling list and two of them agreed to help me in contacting other parents and relatives. I volunteered to visit with the principal to see if he would attend the meeting, which we had set for the following Monday evening at the community center.

I caught Mr. Mendenhall, Sunday after church, asking him if he had a few minutes to visit. After explaining my position and the plans for the meeting, he explained his feelings. "I can't attend the meeting. It wouldn't be professional without the presence of Mr. Cleburne and the board. I'd like to see Coach Duncan stay as the coach. I'd recommend that your group ask for a special board meeting and present your case. I'll be glad to support Coach Duncan at that meeting."

"Do you think we have a chance to have him reinstated?"

"I don't know. The more people you have, the better your chance. I hope you're successful."

"Thank you, Mr. Mendenhall. I appreciate it."

. . .

I'D THOUGHT of little else, after learning about Coach Duncan. I felt we owed him so much for the support and encouragement he gave to our kids, especially Eric. I would've never thought it possible for Eric to make such a dramatic change in a few months. Coach Duncan played a large part in turning Eric around. Now, I worried about Eric's involvement with his girlfriend. Not that she wasn't a sweet girl but Eric's mood changes reflected how well they were getting along on a day-to-day basis. I was worried about what would happen in the event that the relationship came to an end. Eric, no doubt, would be devastated and suffer a major setback.

With the additional responsibility of looking after Cameron's heifers, Gavin was gradually moving toward his old self. He wasn't nearly there yet, but the change was welcomed. I continued to pray daily that it would continue. His attitude toward Eric was positive for the most part. Jenny was growing and continued to chew up anything left lying around. We'd learned the hard way that footwear was her favorite and irresistible.

Feather had become part of the family, arriving on Friday evening and staying until Sunday afternoon. I enjoyed her company, looking forward to the weekends, trying not to compare her to the twins but not being successful. She reminded me so much of Stacy with her love for horses and the outdoors. Gavin had become as attached to her as I was, freely admitting it. She continued to wear her old clothes, saying she saved the others for school and church. The better I got to know her, the prettier she became. Gavin had spoken to her about the possibility of working for us full time after she graduated in January.

Cameron called more often and the communication between him and Gavin was civil but still didn't resemble a father-son visit. I also included that request in my daily prayers, hoping someday it would change. Cameron seldom asked to speak with Eric, which was disappointing. When football ended, it seemed that his interest in Eric did as well. It was hard to understand how a father could treat his son that way, however, Gavin had been even worse to his son. I know that Eric wanted his dad's approval, but thus far, Cameron was either unaware or didn't care.

Eric was in a sour mood Saturday morning at breakfast, but I didn't question him about it. Feather was in her usual good mood but it didn't have any effect on Eric.

They left early to locate the crippled bull and drive it to the pens to be doctored.

I had lunch for them when they came in at noon. Gavin was tired and went to our room, saying he would eat later. I was determined to find out what was bothering Eric and asked directly. He mumbled something I couldn't understand.

"Problems with his lady," Feather volunteered.

He responded angrily. "That's none of your business."

"Well, it's the truth." It didn't seem to bother Feather to upset Eric.

"It might make you feel better to talk about it." Maybe I could say something that would improve his disposition.

"I offered my advice, but he wouldn't take it," Feather slipped a potato chip to Jenny under the table.

Eric continued to eat. "She's at a tournament in Van Horn today. Becky's staying with her so she doesn't have time for me."

"You'll see her at church tomorrow, won't you?" I asked.

"Probably, if I go."

That was all I got out of him. It wasn't surprising that he was jealous, this being his first girlfriend. "Did you get the bull penned?"

"Finally. It took awhile. We had to go slow. He's really lame. We're going to doctor him this afternoon. He may have a thorn in his foot." Feather was never at a loss for words.

"Did Gavin help you?"

"No. He stayed in his pickup. I'm worried about him," Feather continued, leaving Eric out of the conversation.

"It's cold today. He probably decided to stay out of the weather." I hoped my analysis was correct.

They finished eating and left. I checked on Gavin and he was asleep so I didn't wake him. He could eat when he was rested. I cleaned off the table, and put up the leftovers, after saving a plate for Gavin. Then I made some more calls about our Monday night meeting.

Gavin slept an hour and then was ready for his dinner. While eating, he suggested that I go with him to help doctor the bull. I made it a point not to refuse an invitation from him, since we'd gone for years without him asking for my companionship. Of course, Jenny had to go with us, crawling all over me on the trip to the pens. She'd outgrown her hat box. Arriving, they had the bull loaded in the working chute. Walking over to the pens, Gavin asked Feather if they had a plan.

"That's what we're discussing. He's lame in his right front foot. We can't see any type of injury that would have caused it. The problem is how to lift the foot to inspect it. What do you think?"

"Get your rope. Maybe we can lift up his foot, using it."

Taking the rope from her saddle, she gave it to Gavin. He reached through the chute and looped it around the bull's ankle, then draped it over the top railing. "Eric, pull the bull's foot up, and we'll take a look at it."

Eric did as he was instructed and lifting the foot, the problem was visible. A rock was wedged in the bottom of his hoof. With a screwdriver, Gavin pried it out. "He'll be as good as new in a few days. Keep holding his foot up, Eric, and I'll get some turpentine from my pickup to pour over the sore spot."

After finishing, Gavin and I started back to the house but detoured by the pasture with the lake. Gavin mentioned that he wanted to check the water level. It had been some time since he'd visited the area. I cringed as he drove up to the lake and asked the feared question. "The boat's gone. What could have happened to it? The wind couldn't have blown it away. Surely, someone didn't come in and steal a worthless boat with no motor. That's strange."

I had no choice but to tell him about Eric sinking the boat, dreading his response. He remained silent for a full minute. "Well, we can always get another boat. He could've drowned and maybe he learned something. The boat held special memories but that's in the past."

Breathing a sigh of relief, I said, silently. "Thank you, Jesus."

. . .

GAVIN REFUSED to accompany me to the meeting Monday night. I arrived at the Community Center half an hour early and was disappointed to find only a few parents were present. With fifteen minutes before the meeting was to start, we only had a handful of people. I was beginning to wonder if this was a good idea to begin with. With ten minutes left, they began arriving and by the time to start, we had at least two dozen there.

At seven o'clock, I started the meeting. "Could I have your attention please? Y'all know the purpose of the meeting. I felt we needed to do something about Coach Duncan losing his job. We're all aware that he made a mistake, but he's been a positive influence on our students and the board's decision was unfair. Would someone like to express their opinion?"

Luis's dad was the first to speak. "We all know Slade Loughton is behind this. Everyone in the community is aware of it. We need to stand up for Coach Duncan. He was fired for personal reasons which involved my son. I've lived here all my life and won't stand idly by while this happens."

A murmur of agreement spread through the crowd. Another parent spoke up. "What can we do? The board voted to terminate his contract for a good reason. He was drunk and missed a game. I agree, it was a bad deal for Coach Duncan, but he brought it on himself."

"Let me ask you something. Do you trust Coach Duncan with your kids? I mean, do you believe he's a bad influence on them? Sure, he made a mistake, but my understanding is he's getting help with his problem. I believe it's our boys who will suffer the punishment for his mistake if he leaves. I have no doubt but what he has been a positive influence on my grandson and no one can replace him."

The one board member who was present, spoke next. "I didn't vote to terminate Coach Duncan. I agree with what Luta has said. I'd suggest that she go to Cleburne and ask for a special board meeting to consider this issue. Y'all would need to show up at the board meeting and express your concern. Maybe enough pressure can be put on the board to reverse their decision."

After another half hour of individuals speaking their opinion, with the vast majority in agreement, the meeting came to an end. The original suggestion that I talk with the superintendent about calling a special board meeting was agreed upon by the group.

At home, Gavin was less than enthusiastic about me speaking with the superintendent. "Why you? Couldn't someone else have done it? A parent would've been a better choice."

"For all practical purposes, Gavin, we are Eric's parents. We feed, clothe, and care for him, plus he lives with us. I feel strongly about this issue, maybe even more so than anyone else. You've seen what a change Eric has made. We owe it to Coach Duncan to stand up for him. No one should stand idly by and do nothing while an injustice occurs."

"You're pretty fired up about this, aren't you?" he asked, smiling.

"Yes, you could say that."

"If you're able to get the board meeting called, I'll go with you. I'm not going to say anything, though. You'll have to do all the talking."

I MET with the superintendent the following afternoon, taking with me a list of the parents at the meeting who had signed a petition asking for a board meeting. Mr. Cleburne was anything but receptive to the idea of a special meeting.

"Mrs. Sager, I don't want any trouble. I like for everything to run smoothly. The board made a tough decision and will, more than likely, stand behind it. We can hire another coach to replace Duncan."

"No, Mr. Cleburne. You can't find anyone who can replace Coach Duncan. This is not going away. The parents have a right to be heard."

"Duncan missed a football game because he was drunk. We talked with our school attorney, and he said we were within our rights to terminate his contract immediately."

"You're missing the point, Mr. Cleburne. What we're talking about is right and wrong. The board fired Carter Duncan because of an issue Slade Loughton had with him that had nothing to do with drinking or missing a game. You know that and so does everyone in the community."

Fidgeting in his chair he refused to look at me. "I need to talk with Slade about this. I'll get back with you."

It was unbelievable that he had to talk to Slade to make a decision. "The Christmas holidays start Friday. I expect to hear from you by then or you can expect to see me again." I left before he could respond.

On the drive home, I thought about my visit with Cleburne. Our school needed new leadership. That was obvious from his response to a decision that should've been easy to make, one way or the other. He pushed the problem to Loughton who no doubt would not approve the meeting. I wasn't about to give up on this. I smiled, thinking it was refreshing to have a problem that could be solved if enough people would stand up for what was right. For the past sixteen years, I'd dealt with problems that had no solution.

FRIDAY MORNING, I received a call from Cleburne saying that a special board meeting would not be called to discuss Coach Duncan. He refused to answer questions or go into detail, telling me that he appreciated my interest, but the board's decision was final.

41

FRANK

It was Friday morning, December 17, and the Christmas holiday started today at 2:30. Trying to get paper work done, my office door was shut, but the loud voice carried through it easily. A knock and Mrs. Kraal put her head in the door.

"Sorry, but you have a visitor. I could tell him you were busy but that probably wouldn't work."

"Who is it?"

"Loughton."

"Not surprised. Give me a minute and then I'll see him."

I knew about the meeting Monday night and Cleburne's decision not to comply with Mrs. Sager's request. Loughton got his way, but evidently still wasn't satisfied. After several minutes, the door opened, and he came in. The expression on his face was proof that it wasn't going to be pleasant.

"How're you today, Mr. Loughton." I already knew the answer. It was not going to be a good way to start the holidays.

"I'll get right to the point, Mendenhall. Are you behind this meeting that was called Monday?"

"No. I was aware of it, though. Mrs. Sager told me about it Sunday after church. She asked me to attend, but it wouldn't have been professional so I refused. I did inform her that if a special board meeting was called, I would attend and speak on Coach Duncan's behalf."

"You don't approve of the board's decision then?" He stated as a question.

"No. I assumed that was evident at the board meeting where he was terminated."

"So, you know what's best for our students, which would be allowing a drunk to teach and coach them?" He asked another question, but knew the answer before I responded.

"I don't know where this is going, Mr. Loughton, but Coach Duncan is a positive influence on our students. He made a mistake but since then has been an exemplary employee of this school district. I support him and will do so in front of you and the board."

He glared at me. "It doesn't matter though, does it. There's not going to be a called board meeting. I saw to that." It was obvious now the point of the meeting was to let me know he was the ultimate authority in the district.

"So, I understand," I said.

"I run this board and they follow me. They just work for a living. I'm my own boss and answer to no one. It's called entrepreneurship. A few people in this community believe in it and have become involved in *Amway*. I'm helping them get started. I take my hat off to anyone who has the courage to go out on their own. It's the American way. You might want to try it."

This man was something else, I thought. "I love my job. It doesn't bother me to work for someone else. You might want to try it sometime."

"If you want to keep this job you love so much then you'd better stop disagreeing with board decisions. Your contract comes up in February." The reminder was a threat.

That was it! "I was never a tough football player, Mr. Loughton, but standing up for what is right will never be a problem for me, even in the face of threats. If you're finished, I have work to do."

"You better listen to me and take my advice," he growled, getting up and stomping out the door.

I was shaking, not from fear, but anger. A bully making threats and bragging about not having to work for someone. How could anyone be that full of himself?

Mrs. Kraal came in with a cup of coffee. "You ready to get on the *Amway* bandwagon?" She grinned, setting my coffee mug down.

"Unreal," I said, shaking my head.

"It's really kind of sad that a man is given everything from birth and grows up believing he earned it. Just think about his family who has to put up with it every day," she said.

"His kids are wonderful. Becky is my daughter's best friend. She may be the sweetest girl in school. Bruce is an outstanding young man and the leader of the senior class. They couldn't have been influenced by Loughton."

"On the contrary, Mr. Mendenhall, they probably try to think and do the opposite of him."

"Just how big is his ranch, anyway?" I asked.

"It's this way. You can enter his gate a few miles out of town and drive to Mexico, which is seventy miles. You ready for another problem?" she asked.

"Already?" It looked like it was going to be one of those days.

"Mrs. Parton has turned in her grades and half of the freshmen are failing English. She's outdone herself this semester. This is not the first time. The same thing happened under the previous principal. Evidently it makes her feel good to show the students she's smarter than they are.

"She does it every semester. You can expect to hear from parents when report cards go out. It happens every time."

"I thought it was Christmas, Mrs. Kraal. You know 'good cheer' and all that. Has anyone else seen the grade sheets?"

"Just Fields. She brought them in to give to you. It's all right to cuss, Mr. Mendenhall. I won't be offended. The other principal did nothing, hoping it would solve itself, so here we are again."

"Let me see the grade sheets. What a way to start the Christmas holidays."

. . .

I MET with Mrs. Parton immediately after school, and if there was a whining contest, I'd bet everything on her. I reminded her that a high number of failures meant she was also failing. She came back with her students failed to complete homework which was half the grade. Furthermore, she only had two students that passed the semester exam in her freshman class. She complained that the junior high English teacher was not teaching grammar, and they couldn't diagram a sentence when they arrived in her class. She ended her defense by stating that the students received no encouragement from home, which meant their parents didn't really love them.

Throughout the ordeal, I kept asking myself, *Is this real? Can a teacher really believe what she's telling me that parents don't love their children because they don't help them with homework?* I realized that we were beyond reasoning, so there was only one option left.

"Mrs. Parton, a failure rate of 50 percent is unacceptable. I will not defend it. You're going to be on your own when parents begin protesting. Fix it. Do it quickly and never, I mean never, turn in grade sheets like this again while I'm your principal. One other thing, please understand, grades are a poor motivator for low achieving students. They respond much better to interest and excitement in the subject matter, plus success. High-achieving students are motivated by grades. Please don't judge all students by them." She left crying, and I felt like the Grinch who stole Christmas.

I asked Mrs. Kraal to bring me Mr. Borsky's math grade sheets. Sure enough, this teacher the students considered so hard and dreaded had twenty students who made A's, thirty-two students who made B's, and seventeen students who made C's. Two students didn't pass, who upon checking, had excessive absences.

Mrs. Parton and Mr. Borsky had virtually the same students. The conclusion is evident—Mr. Borsky had high expectations and set his students up to succeed, and Mrs. Parton's students didn't respond to her emphasis on grades as a motivating factor.

WHAT A DAY, I thought, entering my house and wondering if this one was going to improve. We had a ballgame tonight that was in Fort Hancock, but we'd decided not to go. It was a tough decision. But, a four-hour drive was not my idea of a good way to start the holidays. Riley was fine with it, saying she understood and not to feel bad.

Julie arrived home at five o'clock, and I told her all about my day. She was a good listener and sympathetic, making me feel better that someone understood my tough job. For the better part of an hour, I wallowed in self-pity.

"Let's talk about what we're going to do during the holidays," she suggested.

I took the hint and we discussed our schedule for the next two weeks, beginning tomorrow, with a shopping expedition to Midland. Aubrey had gone to bed early, pouting because we didn't go to the game. We watched an old movie and went to bed later than usual. I woke up at two o'clock when Riley came in. We spent a few minutes discussing the games, which both teams had won. She was upset that Becky was not allowed to stay the night. Her dad had informed her at the game after getting back to school on the bus, that she was to come home with Bruce in his truck.

She was almost in tears. "I don't understand. She'd planned to stay tonight and go shopping with us tomorrow."

I didn't have the courage to tell her the reason for the change of plans for Becky.

We said goodnight, with Riley giving me a peck on the cheek, and went to bed. I went to sleep immediately and didn't wake up until after seven o'clock since it wasn't necessary to set the alarm. I made coffee and had just sat down at the kitchen table when someone knocked on the door. Who could that be, this early in the morning? Going to the door and opening it, Coach Tiff, the girls' basketball coach, was standing there crying.

"Come in, Coach. What's wrong?"

She tried to speak but was not able. I guided her to the couch, where she sat down. Once again, I asked her what was wrong.

"Ba-d wr-eck. Be-c-ky."

By this time, Julie had joined us. She immediately went to Coach

Tiff, putting her arms around her. "Everything's going to be all right. Just tell us what happened. We're here for you."

"The-re was a wr-eck. Br-uce a-nd B-ecky on w-ay hom-e. Br-uce is hurt b-ad. Fl-own to Mid-land. B-eck-y d-id-n't make it," she murmured, breaking down and sobbing.

I didn't know what to do or say. Julie took over, holding Coach Tiff. "You better get Riley up," she said, looking at me.

Before reaching her room, she came out. "What is it?"

"Come with me to the kitchen, and I'll tell you."

Seated at the table, I told her what we had learned from Coach Tiff. At first, she just stared at me in disbelief then put her head down and started crying. I moved over to hold her and finally the sobbing turned to a whimper.

"Why, wh-y, wh-y w-oul-d God let some-th-ing like th-is happen?"

I didn't attempt to answer, continuing to hold her. Eventually, I took her into the living room. Coach Tiff rose, and hugged her with the grief escalating. I motioned for Julie to come with me and we returned to the kitchen, leaving them to console one another.

Alone, I asked Julie, "How did Coach Tiff find out about the accident?"

"Snuff, the custodian came to her house and told her. A student had called and told him. For Riley, it's going to be devastating. Becky was a special friend."

"What can we do to make it easier for her?" I asked.

"Be there for her. That's all I know. At least for the time being, the team and Coach Tiff will be the best means of support. I just thought of something. If her dad had let her stay the night here, she would be alive."

By noon, with the arrival of several of the girls, the mourning resumed. Julie made sandwiches and some were able to eat. Coach Tiff regaining her composure—like a mother hen with her players— comforted them individually and as a group. Eric showed up but discovered an awkward situation and left. Coach Adams tracked

Coach Tiff down, arriving and sitting down beside her, saying nothing.

By 2:30 in the afternoon, all the girls had left, leaving us alone. We received the encouraging news that Bruce was going to survive but would be hospitalized for some time. Riley couldn't sit still, getting up, and moving from one room to another. I asked her if there was anything we could do.

She was quick to answer. "I want to go to Midland. I know we might not be able to see him but that doesn't matter."

I looked at Julie and she was probably thinking the same thing. Anything, to be doing something, instead of sitting around the house. Aubrey had learned of the tragedy early this morning and had returned to her room, not coming out until the girls were gone. She showed little emotion, looking afraid and confused. It disappointed me that she didn't reach out to her sister to provide comfort. It was proof that even though she was ahead of her years in physical maturity, the same could not be said for the mental development.

WE CAME BACK HOME from Midland on Monday, after doing some shopping Sunday afternoon. Both, Julie and I felt that the two nights spent away from home were helpful in dealing with the pain. Riley had recovered to some extent but would occasionally break down and start crying. She'd been allowed to see Bruce Sunday morning for a few minutes. He was conscious but sedated because of the pain, however, he did recognize her. We did see Bruce's mother but not his dad.

The funeral was set for Tuesday morning at ten o'clock and was to be held in the high school gymnasium. None of the churches could seat the crowd that was expected. They attended the Baptist Church so their minister would do the service but would be assisted by Pastor Jacob from our church, who was an avid supporter of athletics and seldom missed a home game.

Nothing compares to a funeral for a teenager in a small town. The gym was full and the mourning touched everyone present. The minister broke down several times and had to stop. When a soloist, sang, "How

Great Thou Art," there was not a dry eye. At the conclusion of the service, the viewing took what seemed like hours. The line barely moved as one of her friends after another paused looking at her . . . crying. As my turn came, I was overwhelmed at her appearance. Wearing a white dress, Becky looked like the angel that she most surely was.

42

ERIC

I left school Tuesday after the funeral, depressed and feeling rejected. Sitting with her friends, Riley had barely acknowledged my presence. I'd taken a seat as close to her as possible. I was anxious for the service to be over, and uncomfortable watching the grieving. When it finally ended, I approached her outside the gym, but she had little to say, still surrounded by her friends. Her friend had been killed in an accident but that was no reason for me to be ignored. After all, she was communicating with her teammates and coach. I became angrier, on the drive to the ranch—arriving in a foul mood.

Feather had come in last night, planning to stay until the day before Christmas and then return the day after. She, Dawn, and Gavin were eating lunch.

"Would you like to eat?" Dawn asked.

"No. I'm not hungry." In my mood I had no appetite.

Dawn stopped eating. "I imagine Riley was devastated."

"Yeah. She didn't say much to me. Everyone was upset."

"Such a terrible tragedy to lose someone so young," Dawn said.

"Eric, I need you to go with Feather this afternoon. One of the windmills isn't pumping. I couldn't tell what the problem was from my pickup. You may need to climb it to figure out what's wrong. Also, we

have weather coming in tonight with moisture and freezing temperatures. We've been fortunate thus far but this could be a bad spell. Y'all
need to put out hay after you check on the windmill." Gavin had
finished eating and taken out a cigar preparing it.

"Let me change clothes. I'll be ready by the time you're finished
eating." I went to my room anxious to be alone in my frustration over
Riley.

Just great, I thought, while getting into my work clothes. Spend all
afternoon working with know-it-all. I got tired of her being right all the
time. Anyway, it would beat sitting around worrying about Riley who
wouldn't give me the time of day.

Little was said on the drive to the windmill, which we were able to
reach in the truck. The problem was easy to fix, only requiring the cord
that turned the windmill off and on, to be untangled. Using Gavin's
truck with the hay pick attached to it, moving the round bales was not
difficult. We moved fifteen bales to locations that were accessible in
the truck, spreading them out as much as possible.

By the time we were moving the last few bales, it'd turned much
colder. When we reached our destination, both of us would get out and
take the string off the hay, enabling a quick entry back into the truck.
We finished, just as it was getting dark.

Feather was quiet, especially for her. Usually, she was quick to give
advice about everything we did. "Is something wrong?"

"I'm worried about Pops. I shouldn't have left him. He's not eating
and won't go to the doctor. It's almost like he's given up." She was
fighting back tears. "I don't know what to do."

"If you want to go back and check on him, I'm sure Gavin
wouldn't mind."

"I'll go back and spend the day with him tomorrow. We put out hay
today, so we shouldn't have much to do until Thursday. You probably
had a bad day. Funerals are sad . . . especially for someone so young.
Was there a big crowd?"

"The gym was full. People were having to stand up. I didn't sit
with Riley. She didn't seem to want me with her anyway."

"Why?"

"She was with her friends. She didn't want anything to do with me," I explained.

"I imagine she and her friends found comfort in one another."

"I thought she'd look to me for comfort, instead I was ignored." I attempted to hide my anger.

"You need to consider her feelings, Eric. Imagine how devastated she was at losing her best friend."

"I still don't understand why she ignored me." Feather or no one else could understand my disappointment.

THE NEXT DAY, by midmorning, I was desperate to see and talk with Riley. I decided to go into town and show up, unannounced. That way she would be forced to talk with me and explain what was going on.

Arriving at her house, I knocked and her dad answered the door. "Could I speak with Riley?"

"I'm sorry, Eric, but she's gone to Midland with Coach Tiff and several other girls to visit Bruce. I don't expect her back until late."

I felt stupid, standing there like a child asking for a cookie. I said a feeble thank you and went back to my truck. Sitting behind the wheel, I thought, *now what?* Nothing to do but go back home. Then an idea hit me! Maybe I should go to Midland. After all, Bruce had been a teammate of mine for awhile. Riley could ride back home with me, and we'd be together for three hours. I'd do it.

Feeling better immediately, I left town, heading north.

I drove fast, exceeding the speed limit but didn't see a highway patrolman. Two hours and forty minutes later, I drove into Midland. I found the hospital easily, since it was the same one Gavin was taken to. My heart pounding, I asked for Bruce's room number. Within minutes, I knocked on his door, and opened it slightly to look in. There were several girls in the room, but the first thing I saw was Riley sitting on the edge of the bed, holding Bruce's hand. Backing up and closing the door, I stood there, not knowing what to do.

The door opened and Coach Tiff came out. "Eric, it was so good of you to come. We have a room full at the moment. If you'll wait a few minutes, I'll clear some of the visitors out, and you can see Bruce."

I didn't respond and she continued. "Thank you for coming. Bruce will be glad to see you."

"I'll wait in the lounge."

"It shouldn't be but a few minutes," she said.

Going to the waiting area, I found a fishing magazine to thumb through, not really even looking at the pictures. I didn't drive 175 miles to see Bruce. Maybe the way things turned out was deserving. Now, I had to at least pretend an interest in him.

A few minutes later, Coach Tiff appeared, telling me the room was clear. Bruce was sitting up in bed when I entered. "Eric. Good to see you. Thanks for coming."

"No problem." He didn't look as bad as I expected.

He attempted a smile. "I've surprised the doctors, doing better than they predicted."

You seemed to being doing pretty good, sitting there, holding my girl's hand, I thought but instead said, "You look good. How long will you be in the hospital?"

"Probably another week, at least. I have some broken ribs and a concussion. Did you hear what happened?" He continued before I could respond. "There was a bunch of javelinas in the road. I didn't try to miss them. There was no way. I hit several, causing my pickup to go into the ditch and turn over several times. I've replayed it a thousand times, thinking what I could've done differently." Tears streamed down his face.

I didn't know what to say. Maybe just listening would be the best thing. "We were close and there for one another. You know how our dad is. She always took my side and me hers. I can't imagine my life without her," he said, closing his eyes.

I had to say something. "Have you had many visitors?"

"Not really. You're the first of my teammates. Of course, several of the girls' basketball team are here, now. Coach Duncan came by earlier. I know about him losing his job because of my dad. He's a great coach and I'm sorry for what happened, however, he's already accepted an assistant coaching job at Sul Ross. I guess it would be a promotion."

We talked for another fifteen minutes, with him always returning to the accident and crying. I finally told him it was a long drive back home, and I wanted to get there by dark.

The girls and Coach Tiff were waiting in the lounge. Riley met me, reaching out and touching my arm. "Eric, it was sweet of you to come see Bruce. I think you're the first of his teammates to visit him."

"Would you like to ride home with me?" I asked.

"I can't. The other girls and Coach Tiff are returning, but I'm staying the night. Bruce needs someone besides his parents here. My mom and dad are coming after me, and I'll be home late tomorrow. Bruce is suffering, and maybe I can be of some help."

"Couldn't you ride home with me and come back with your parents tomorrow?" I was desperate to spend time alone with her.

"No, Eric. Bruce needs me here tonight. He can't help but blame himself for the accident, and his parents aren't much help."

I had no choice but to accept her decision and leave. She said nothing about seeing me later. She thanked me again for coming and trying to hide my disappointment, I left.

I DIDN'T GET to the ranch until after dark and Dawn assumed I'd spent the entire day with Riley. I didn't tell her any difference, going directly to my room. I wasn't hungry and didn't feel like talking to anyone. Then I remembered my pig and wondered if Gavin had watered and fed him. I went back to the den, where they were watching TV.

"Did you feed my pig?" I asked Gavin.

"No. I thought you'd get home in time."

I left the house immediately, going to his pen and being greeted with a series of grunts. I filled up his water and his feeder. It didn't matter how cold it was, he still got in his water trough and most of the time, turned it over. He actually knew his name and responded with grunts when I spoke it. I scratched his back before leaving and he immediately lay down on his side.

"I'm not going to stay out here in the cold and scratch you." He responded with a series of grunts, which I assumed were protests. By this time, I was hungry and stopped in the kitchen.

I was in the process of making a sandwich when Dawn came in. "Feather went back home to check on her granddad. She's worried about him. I told her to stay with him until Christmas and then bring him for dinner. Your dad called to inform me that he and Ethan will be here late tomorrow night. I've bought gifts for you to give your dad and brother. When are you going to give Riley her gift?"

I shrugged. "Christmas Eve, I guess. If I get to see her then. She may still be with Bruce."

"It's a beautiful sweater. I know she'll love it," Dawn said.

I'd bought the sweater several weeks ago and was pleased at the time. Now she didn't seem to want anything to do with me.

"Eric, we haven't put up a Christmas tree since we lost the twins. Gavin wouldn't allow it. Today, he shocked me by saying that we should have a tree this year because of you and Ethan. Would you go into town in the morning and see what you can find? There won't be much to select from but that doesn't matter. Just find the best one that you can."

"Sure. I can do that. We never get a real tree at home. We have this ugly artificial one."

"Eric, you've been a blessing. There were some rough spots, but Gavin has changed and continues to be more like he was before we lost the girls. Of course, it's been hard for you at times. I want you to know that I couldn't have gotten by without your help," she said, coming over and hugging me.

I was embarrassed, but pleased at her words and affection.

43

LUTA

After the horrible event that took our girls away from us, we dreaded holidays, especially Christmas. Both of us would enter into depression that was indescribable. Memories of decorations, excitement, visiting Santa Claus, and opening gifts Christmas morning were ever present. We tried ignoring Christmas, but that didn't work either. It was a relief for it to be over and return to normal activity. During these times, Cameron was no help. He stayed away even during the holidays, leaving us in our grief.

Christmas was by far the best one we'd had since losing our girls. Eric found a decent tree, and with Ethan's help, we decorated it Christmas Eve. For the past several years, there were a number of times that Gavin didn't get me a present. I'd bought one for myself and put his name on it. I decided to take a chance this year, not buying myself anything, and was rewarded with a beautiful turquoise bracelet. I'd talked with Cameron and we went in together and bought Eric a set of weights. He purchased them in San Antonio since they wouldn't have been available here. I also received permission from Cameron to get Ethan a BB gun.

Eric continued to mope around the house, looking miserable. No doubt, it was because of the way his relationship with Riley was regressing. I'd asked him several times, but he refused to comment. Feather had called Christmas Eve and said that her granddad wasn't able to make the trip. Gavin and I were disappointed but told her she would have a gift waiting when she came. Gavin had surprised me again, suggesting that we buy her a new saddle. The one she rode was old and falling apart. Both of us were looking forward to her reaction upon receiving her gift.

All that kept it from being perfect was Eric's depression. I was hoping after he exchanged gifts with Riley on Christmas Day, he would feel better. However, he returned home even worse. He went directly to his room without saying a word.

I waited half an hour for him to return, before going to his room and knocking. He didn't answer, so I opened the door and peeped in. He was lying face down across the bed. "Eric, aren't you going to join us?"

Without lifting his head, he replied. "No, please leave me alone."

I went in and sat down on the side of the bed, putting my hand on his shoulder and squeezing it. "I'm sorry, Eric. Is there anything I can do to make you feel better?"

Without moving he started talking. "She doesn't want to see me anymore during the holidays. She's spending the time in Midland with Bruce. I don't understand why she's being this way. She kept saying, 'he needs me,' but I need her. I don't know what to do."

"Come back and join us. Your dad and brother are going home tomorrow. Ethan wants to go hunting with his new BB gun. Maybe you can go with him. He admires you, Eric, and it would be good to spend some time with him."

"I don't know what to do, Dawn," he repeated, his shoulders beginning to shake.

I knew it was time for me to leave. I felt so sorry for him. There was nothing anyone could do. For the first time, his heart was broken.

Eric, eventually joined us in the late afternoon. He and Ethan spent several hours at the barn shooting at birds. When they came in Ethan was talking about how smart Eric's pig was and the tricks he could do. "Eric can make him lay down and even roll over. He let him out of his pen and he followed us everywhere, not running off. He's the smartest pig in the world."

Eric might be losing a girlfriend, I thought, but he's gaining a brother who will adore him.

CAMERON AND ETHAN left the day after Christmas. Ethan didn't want to leave, and his dad had to promise to bring him back the first school holiday. It warmed my heart to see Eric hug him as we were saying goodbye. How wonderful it was, to have the family together during the holiday without a cross word being spoken by anyone.

Another pleasant surprise was a visit from Coach Duncan and his wife, Vicky, two days after Christmas. Gavin and Eric were gone to check on the cattle, and I was alone.

Coach Duncan presented me with a beautiful poinsettia. "I appreciate your effort to have me rehired. Everything worked out, and I'll be on the coaching staff at Sul Ross beginning in January. I'm not looking forward to being gone from home on recruiting trips, but we're going to buy a house in town. Now for the good news. Vicky will tell you."

"I'm pregnant! My baby is due in July. We're excited to say the least. Our prayers have been answered." She was glowing.

"That's wonderful." I hugged her and Coach Duncan.

"I'd have liked to visit with Eric. Being on the staff at Sul Ross will allow me to tout his ability. With his strength and speed, if he has a good senior year, Eric would be a prospect for a football scholarship. He probably hasn't even considered that, but it's possible. He was the best fullback in the area last year, and the opposing coaches realized it."

I was surprised at Coach Duncan's statement. "I'll convey that message to him. He's having problems now with his girlfriend but that should perk him up."

They stayed and visited for an hour, and I couldn't help but think how amazing everything usually worked out for the best. Gavin and Eric returned to the house soon after they left. I relayed Coach Duncan's message to him and he seemed as surprised as me.

"That's impressive." Gavin was as surprised as we were.

"Are you sure that's what he said? You're just not trying to make me feel better?" Eric couldn't believe it.

"No. That was exactly what Coach Duncan said."

"That set of weights should be just what you need," Gavin said.

"Yeah. I'm going to start working out right now." He left headed to the barn.

He and Gavin had turned the tack room at the barn into a workout facility, placing his weights there. "Gavin, is the tack room going to be a good place for him to exercise?"

"Since we have electricity out there, I put a small heater in the room. It'll be comfortable even when it's cold. There's plenty of space and he can pump iron to his heart's content, without being interrupted."

"Speaking of heart, I guess you know what has happened, because of Eric's recent behavior." I wondered with all the excitement of Christmas if Gavin had noticed.

"Girlfriend problems, I assume, from the long face and red eyes. In time he'll get over it. With Feather being gone, we have enough work to keep him from thinking about it too much."

"That reminds me. I need to call Feather and see how her granddad is doing. Maybe there's something that we can do. I shouldn't have waited this long," I said, going to the phone.

Her phone rang five times, and I was about to hang up when she answered. By her voice, it was obvious she was upset. "I don't know what to do. He won't eat and just sits in his chair all day. He's so weak, I have to help him up to go to the bathroom. I've begged him to eat something, but it does no good."

I felt terrible for her. Here we were, having a wonderful Christmas, and she was miserable, trying to care for the only family she had. "Feather, is there anything we can do?"

"No, I've tried to think of something else that might help but there's nothing. I'm sorry to be missing work, but I can't leave him."

"Goodness! Don't you worry for a minute about that. We're doing fine. Please call if you need us." We ended the call, with me thinking, *no one so young should have that kind of responsibility. She's a brave little girl.*

Gavin had listened to the call but wanted to know more. "It sounds like Lefty's not doing well. Is he even trying?"

"No. According to Feather he's given up. I wish there was something we could do, however, if he won't listen to her there's no chance we could influence him."

"You're right. Changing the subject, but I had an idea that might help Eric overcome his depression. I'm sure Cameron has never taught him to shoot. We have the 243 that Stacy hunted with. Maybe we could do some target practice and safety training. If he's interested, we might go hunting. It's been years since we've had venison. I haven't used one permit we've been given in the past sixteen years. There's still a couple of days of deer season left. What do you think?"

"Gavin, I think that's an awesome idea. If anything could get his mind off his problems that would have the best chance. When he comes in from his workout, ask him if he's interested."

"Unbelievable! Hallelujah! Praise JESUS!" I muttered to myself, celebrating Gavin's longest step toward restoration. Could I be dreaming? Am I building my expectations up, only to be disappointed? I didn't care. Encouragement had been too difficult to come by for the past sixteen years, and I was going to be joyful.

I was in the other room when Eric came in and Gavin propositioned him about learning to shoot. Eric accepted the offer but not with the enthusiasm I'd hoped for.

According to the information given to me by Eric, Riley didn't break off the relationship. She only gave Eric the impression that he wasn't that important in her life. I wished, for his sake, that she would just go ahead and sever their relationship, instead of dragging it out until he was humiliated. To her credit, she more than likely didn't realize she was the most important thing in his life.

When Gavin and Eric left the house for target practice, I couldn't be still. Cleaning the bathrooms, moping the kitchen, putting in a load of washing, and ironing still didn't diminish my excitement. I waited, anxiously, for them to return, praying that this miracle was real.

After what seemed like hours, they came in laughing. Meeting them, I couldn't wait to hear about the experience. "How was it?"

"Great. I held the scope too close to my eye and it socked me good with the recoil. It'll probably be black tomorrow. That's okay. It was fun."

"He's going to be a good shot. We started at fifty yards and stretched it out to a hundred after some practice. He was placing his shots in a six-inch group at that distance. Not bad at all. You better have the grease ready. We're going after a deer in the morning." Gavin was as excited as I'd seen him in many years.

The miracle was real.

GAVIN EXPLAINED their strategy the next morning while we were eating breakfast at five o'clock. "You know that hill about half a mile west of the pens? It's not much of a climb but it offers a perfect view of several hundred acres. Hopefully, we can catch them returning to their cover after feeding during the night. There's not much moon so that's good. The hill has a large rock with a good place to sit where you can rest your gun and have a steady aim. It was a favorite spot for me and Stacy when we hunted. She took several deer there. Another advantage is that we can drive right up to the area to load our deer if we're successful. I can just taste those fried venison steaks, biscuits and gravy. Do you remember how to cook those steaks, Luta?"

I smiled inside and outside. "You just bring me the meat and I'll show you."

"We better get a move on, Eric. We need to be in our spot an hour before daylight," Gavin said.

As they were driving off, it occurred to me to check and see if he had taken his nitroglycerin pills. I opened the cabinet door, and they were sitting on the top shelf.

44

ERIC

We parked on the east side of the pens at 5:30 so the truck wouldn't be in view of the area where we were hunting. It was dark and I had no idea where we were going. The flashlight Gavin carried was pointed down at the ground to prevent us from being noticed as we made our way to the spot. Gavin had a thermos of coffee and I carried the gun. It was clear and cold with no wind, according to Gavin, a perfect day. The stars sparkled. I'd never seen them appear closer or brighter.

The walking wasn't easy and we had to navigate over rocks and around thorny bushes. We stopped several times, and I noticed Gavin was breathing heavily. Once, he suggested that we sit down and rest. We reached the bottom of the hill and started climbing. We hadn't gone far when he stopped, saying he had to rest. We repeated this process of climb-and-rest several times before we reached our destination.

He showed me where to sit, and near as I could tell, we'd be looking south. Gavin sat down a few yards behind me, but I could still hear him breathing. It was cold and even with my heavy coat, gloves, and toboggan, I was shaking. It seemed like hours before it began to get light enough to make out images. I could tell the view was going to be good and a lot of country would be visible. Several times, shadows appeared that could've been deer, but were only bushes. As it became lighter, I strained to see any kind of movement. Just as the sun was coming up, I saw my first deer. Then another came into sight. My heart began pounding as I counted four, no five, moving toward me. They were still a long way off, but the last one had antlers that could be seen, even from this distance.

Placing my gun on the rock for support, I looked through the scope. The buck was big, moving along with his head to the ground. They were still too far, but now instead of the cold, I was shaking from excitement. I slipped the safety off my gun and waited. They stopped at the bottom of the hill, and the buck entered a brushy area disappearing. Taking deep breaths, I waited until he moved into view again. As I was about to aim, a moan from behind, startled me. Turning around, Gavin was leaned over—clutching his chest.

Crawling back to him, I asked, "Are you sick?"

"M-y ch-est. Ca-n't brea-the."

"Can you walk?"

"Do-n't th-ink so."

What am I going to do? No choice. I have to carry him. "Gavin, listen to me. I'm going to turn and sit down so you can put your legs around me. After that, hang on to my shoulders. I'll piggy back you down the mountain. Can you do that?"

"Tr-tr-y," he gasped.

It worked until I tried to stand. I made three attempts before realizing that leaning forward and getting to a squatting position before standing was the only way to get upright. Once up, we started down the mountain. I had to go slow because small rocks and loose dirt made it slippery. Gavin was heavy and several times I thought it wouldn't be possible to go any further. Images of walking across the ranch in the heat, escaping my captors, and swimming to shore after the boat sank, almost drowning, came to mind. I could do this—I would do this.

Reaching the bottom, I found a smooth place to sit Gavin down. "I'm going for the truck. I'll be back as soon as possible." He didn't speak only nodding and then lying down on his side.

It was at least half a mile to the truck, and I ran all the way. I stumbled and fell twice, skinning my hands and arms. I panicked at the truck, saying out loud, "Maybe he took the keys. Please GOD, let the keys be there." The keys were not in the ignition. My heart sank and then I saw them in the floorboard.

Within minutes, I was helping him into the truck and heading toward the house. He seemed stronger and was able to talk. "Your arm's bleeding."

"Yeah. It's not bad. I fell going to the truck."

"I don't know how you carried me down the mountain."

That was all he said until we arrived at the house. "I can make it inside now."

"You sure?"

"Just give me a hand. I'm already feeling better."

Dawn opened the door for us. "What happened?"

"I just got tired," was his response.

"He couldn't breathe and had chest pains," I explained.

She went to the kitchen and returned with a pill while I seated him in the den. He put the pill under his tongue and leaned back in his chair, closing his eyes. "Just let me rest for awhile."

Dawn motioned for me to follow her into the kitchen. "Eric, bring the car around to the front. As soon as the nitroglycerin pill takes effect, we're taking him to the doctor."

BY NOON, Gavin had been seen by a doctor in Alpine who did an EKG. He thought everything would take care of itself, with rest. He didn't need to be reminded overdoing it would result in another episode like the one this morning. That didn't prevent Dawn from lecturing him on the drive back to the ranch.

Gavin remained quiet until we drove through the arches at the ranch. "Looks like I messed up our chance for venison steaks. I didn't realize the effect that a little exertion would have on me. I'll know better next time. I still don't know how Eric was able to get me down the mountain."

"You're fortunate to have a strong, determined grandson," Dawn said.

"Yeah, that's right. We're going hunting again, but this time I'm staying in my pickup."

After getting Gavin settled back in his chair, I went to check on Arnold. Of course, he had turned over his water trough and wallowed around in the mud, even though it was still cold. He grunted as if welcoming me and nudged me on the leg several times. His self-feeder was empty and he wasn't happy about that. He kept going over to it and flipping up the lid.

I'd never had a dog, a cat, or any kind of pet. I was attached to this smelly pig and really believed that he liked me. When I brought him home, it wasn't as a pet but an FFA project, to compete at the local stock show and sell afterwards. The stock show was the first weekend in February which was only a little over a month away.

Gavin's dog, Jenny, was okay but she wasn't as smart as Arnold. It wouldn't bother me if we sold her. I liked her, but she'd never be special like Arnold.

I tried not to think about Riley. The hunting had helped somewhat, but the hurt returned when my mind wasn't focused on something else. Maybe everything would return to normal when the holidays ended. When Bruce came home there would be no reason for her to feel like he needed her.

After taking care of Arnold, I went to my weight room. I'd worked out twice and it'd helped get my mind off Riley. The room had light, a heater, and an old cushy chair. The guys who didn't play basketball had started working out three days a week after football was over. I'd followed the same routine the previous two days as the one at school. I would've liked to test my bench press strength but there was no one to spot for me. My best thus far was 220 pounds, but I had the upper body strength to do more. My greatest strength was in my lower body where no one came close to matching me in the leg press.

THE NEXT MORNING, true to his word, we were sitting on the east side of the pens, waiting for it to get light enough to see. We had the truck running with the heater on, and Gavin had leaned his head back and was dozing. No way could I find the rock we sat on yesterday, in the dark, without him guiding me. We'd decided that the best plan was for me to ease along at first light and try to reach the spot before the sun came up. That was going to be the best I could do.

I was able to reach the lookout on the side of the mountain before sunrise. Because of the sliding rocks I was causing, climbing silently was impossible. A deer would have to be senile not to hear me. Reaching my spot, I began looking for movement, with little hope.

There was a slight wind blowing in my face and even bundled up, it was still cold. I waited and watched for an hour, seeing nothing but a rabbit. The sun was shining brightly by now, and it was time to start back to the truck. I'd made too much racket.

The orange juice I drank at breakfast was going to force me to pee before going anywhere. I put down my gun and went about my business, but midway through the process, sliding rocks to my left, caught my attention. Glancing that way in my compromised position, I saw a buck coming down the mountain. I guessed him to be about a football field's length from me. I was helpless to move, halfway through relieving myself and could no way rush the process. Standing as still as possible and hoping he didn't see me, I finished and reached for my gun. The buck was still showing no signs of alarm and continued walking down the mountain. By the time I had my gun balanced on the rest to steady my aim, he was near the bottom of the hill. I slipped the safety off, found him in the crosshairs, aimed behind his shoulder, and squeezed the trigger. I didn't feel the recoil and was only vaguely aware of the sound. The buck took off running. How did I miss? I worked the bolt on the 243, ejecting the spent shell and shoved it forward, putting another in the barrel. Hopefully, he would appear and even though spooked, maybe another shot was possible.

I continued to scan the open country as far as I could see . . . nothing. How did he just disappear into thin air? Maybe, I wounded him and he's hidden in the brush. I moved down the mountain toward where I last saw him, rocks sliding, gun ready, hoping he would come into view. I reached the bottom and nothing. Starting back toward the truck and Gavin, I hadn't gone fifty yards when I saw him lying in a clump of brush. Reaching him, I was shaking with excitement. He had four points on each side, but his horns weren't as big as they looked in the scope. I'd taken my first deer. I had no idea what to do now. I hurriedly walked toward the truck, anxious to tell Gavin.

When the truck came into view, Gavin was standing outside and started toward me, asking the question when I was within hearing distance. "Did you get him?"

"Yeah," is all I could manage.

"Great!" he yelled, grabbing my hand and shaking it. "Let's go get him."

It took us several minutes to locate the buck. I'd been too excited to mark the location. He was heavier than he appeared, and it took an effort for us to put him in the back of the truck.

Gavin explained what we would do on the way to the house. "Most people field dress their deer on location. When possible, I like to hang mine and skin them first. That way, you get a much cleaner carcass, free of hair. It's a little more trouble but worth it. Another thing, many hunters will field dress their deer and don't skin it for a day or more. I never do that. The quicker you get the hide off, the easier it is and the better the meat."

"I thought I missed him. He ran when I shot."

"That's not unusual. With a bullet through the heart, most of the time that will happen. It was a good shot and I'm proud of you."

Did I just hear what he said? He was proud of me. Amazing!

45

FRANK

I t was not my favorite time of year. Christmas was over. We were back from visiting relatives, Julie had returned to work, and being without a hobby to fill my days, I was lost with nothing to do. I should be golfing, hunting, absorbed in creating a wooden cabinet, or following my favorite football team in the playoffs. None of these held any interest for me. Sadly, my work was my only hobby and school was out.

I received no sympathy from my wife as we had coffee the Tuesday morning after Christmas. "Frank, I have an idea. You can go to work for me, and I'll lounge around all day, maybe take an afternoon nap. That'll allow you to be busy and happy while I kick back and relax. What do you think?"

"You're making fun of me. I can't help it if I enjoy my work. Do you have a suggestion that might keep me occupied, at least part of the day? Maybe, like a hobby or something. I appreciate input from my best friend."

"You need more friends, Frank. Your social life is lacking."

"Riley has been spending most of her time with Bruce. Do you think that's good?" I changed the subject, becoming uncomfortable in the direction this was going.

"It's her way of grieving, Frank. She's a natural caregiver anyway, and this gives her a chance to channel her efforts at helping someone. I believe that's a positive characteristic of our daughter. I'm proud of her.

"Speaking of our children, wasn't that wonderful news that Coach Duncan and Vicky shared with us yesterday. It's sad they're leaving, but seeing them so happy was heartwarming. They'll be wonderful parents. You made a good choice when you hired him. He turned his life around."

"Yes, I'm glad it worked out, but now, what am I going to do for a coach?"

"What about moving Coach Adams up to head coach?" she asked.

"I've thought about that. He's done a really good job. He's mature for his age and has an abundance of enthusiasm. Being a local boy might not work too well. I've got to give it some more thought." I realized it might end up being my only choice. The phone rang before she could reply.

I answered it. "Mr. Mendenhall, this is Puckett. I'm going to visit some students today to weigh their animals. Would you like to go with me?"

I was surprised at the invitation, hesitated, and he continued. "We should be back by two o'clock this afternoon."

I couldn't believe this. Something to do. "Sure."

"Good. I'll come by in half an hour or so."

I told Julie about the invitation. "This is great. It'll give me a chance to get out of the house plus see some of this beautiful country. What should I wear?"

"You need to look professional for the animals, so maybe your navy suit and a striped tie would work?" She kept a solemn face, holding the laughter as long as possible.

"You're making fun of me again."

"Oh, Frank. You're so sweet. We need to get you some jeans, but it's too late now. All you have is your khaki pants that you wear when working in the yard. I wish you had some boots. We're going shopping and fit you out in some clothes that define West Texas. Now, get a move on. Mr. Puckett will be here and you won't be ready."

"Julie, did you notice after the funeral, how the students gathered around Puckett? Occasionally, one would reach out and touch him on the arm. It was like they were gaining strength and comfort from his presence. That says a great deal about this young man."

"Yes, I did see that. I thought it strange, but you're probably right. Get dressed now. I don't want him to have to wait on you."

I was ready when our ag teacher arrived. I felt like an underdressed sixteen-year-old going on my first date. I certainly didn't look like I lived west of the Pecos. Puckett had on jeans, a flannel shirt, and was wearing a cap. I took note, promising myself the next time a trip to the country was offered, I would look the part.

Our first stop was The Drug Store for coffee. We sat down at tables occupied by men, young and old, wearing jeans, boots—some with spurs—and cowboy hats. Puckett introduced me around, and I was greeted with strong handshakes from each, who looked directly into my eyes. *There was no shortage of honesty in this room. We could easily be back at the turn of the century,* I thought.

During our stay, Puckett downed at least half a dozen cups of coffee while I sipped on one. No sooner were we in his truck heading west, when he fired up a cigarette. "Does smoking bother you?"

"No," I lied, cracking my window. I wasn't used to cigarette smoke and probably was getting as much of it in my lungs as he was.

"You know everybody is always saying they'd like to quit smoking. I enjoy smoking and don't want to break the habit. Some people, especially those that smoke a pipe or cigars say they don't inhale. Why would you smoke if you don't inhale?"

This was not my area of expertise so I changed to another topic. "How many students do you have with projects?"

"All, thirty-one. A project is required to take ag. Of course that doesn't include those that are in 4-H. We all compete together at the local show in February."

"Do all your students keep their animals at home?"

"Have to. We don't have an ag farm which we need in the worst way. Some in-town students can't take ag because they have no place to keep an animal. An ag farm would help our program, tremendously."

"Why can't you have a farm?"

Taking one last drag on his cigarette, he put it out in the ash tray. "Don't have a place to put it."

"You mean with miles and miles of land, you can't get property?"

"That's right. Most of the large landowners won't give up an acre. It's in their genes to keep the ranch together. Something like an unwritten pledge to ancestors. I'm working with one guy whose land runs up to within two miles of the school. He's only been here thirty years or so and married the woman who owned the ranch. She passed away suddenly about two years ago, and he hasn't said no to my request for a three-acre block. I'm hoping he comes through. My students can do all the construction work for the barns and the fencing."

"I hope it works out. It surprises me that agriculture being so important to this area, landowners didn't see to it that the school had an ag farm long before now."

He lit another cigarette before commenting. "This is my sixth year, and it's been a good place for me and my family to live. I learned something several years ago that you need to know. Many of the landowners don't consider the Mexicans to be equal and that's not right, but it's a fact. Most of them don't expect or want any special consideration given to them in the classroom or otherwise. Translated, that means an ag farm is not a priority for them because most of the animals kept there would belong to Mexican students. They're good people but that type of thinking has been passed down from generation to generation."

"Is that why Loughton resented Luis taking over the quarterback position from Bruce?"

"Yeah, that's about it. Bruce is in my program and is as good as they come. Becky was one of my students. She was everything a father should want in his daughter. I don't know how he'll respond to her death. The best thing that could happen for this school would be for him to get off the board."

I ENJOYED the day and learned a great deal about the community and the school. We saw four students, weighed their animals and visited with their parents. I couldn't have asked for a better reception and was not surprised at the respect they showed Puckett.

As he'd promised, we were back in town before two o'clock. I thanked him for an informative and interesting day. His comment before leaving left me feeling good.

"You have a tough job, Mendenhall, especially here. I believe you're up to whatever comes your way. Keep doing what's right, don't change, and you'll be fine."

No one was home, so I walked over to my office. Sitting down at my desk, I reflected on what Puckett had told me. My goal, as a principal, was to implement programs that would help all students. I was going to run into opposition when I tried to increase opportunities for everyone, especially the low achieving ones, with many being Hispanic. A caste system had been in effect forever here, and anything that disrupted that was going to be opposed. How sad. A school should do whatever was possible to make all students successful.

Julie was right. I needed more friends. The town had a Lion's Club that met weekly, and becoming a member would allow me to meet more men outside of school. I did consider myself a nerd and reflecting on my actions, in school and out, others probably did also. Maybe, I needed to start smoking a pipe or even cigars. I shouldn't feel like a tie was necessary every day. I was going to get some jeans and flannel shirts. What if I grew a beard or a mustache?

The phone interrupted my thoughts, and it was Julie. "I figured you'd be at your office. How was your day in the country?"

"Good. I met several parents who were nice. Of course, being with Puckett, they wouldn't have been anything else. The house was empty. Where're the girls?"

"Bruce was being released from the hospital today, and Riley is at his place. Aubrey should've been at home. At least that's where I left her at noon. You might check the tennis courts."

"I'll call you back when I find her." After receiving that information, I ended the call, going directly to the tennis courts. They were empty. Anger, frustration, and then fear invaded my thinking. Where could she have gone? I drove to The Drug Store, hoping to find her there with friends. Several high school students were there but not Aubrey. When I inquired if she'd been there, they replied to the negative.

I hurried home, praying all the way that she'd be there. The house was still empty. I didn't know what to do, but wait. After half an hour, the phone rang, and I pounced on it. "Hello."

"Is she home, Frank?" Call it woman's intuition, but by her anxious tone, she already knew the answer.

"No. I checked the tennis courts and drug store. Nothing. I don't know what to do next, Julie."

"I'm coming home." The only other sound was a click.

AT FIVE O'CLOCK Aubrey was still missing, and we called Riley to come home. We then debated on whether or not to call law enforcement. From the shows on television, we'd have to wait twenty-four hours to report a missing person. Both of us agreed this was ridiculous. We called the county sheriff's office and reported Aubrey missing. The person taking the call was courteous and responsive even after telling him it had only been since one o'clock this afternoon. We gave them all the information requested, and they assured me they would notify law enforcement in the area.

Riley arrived, and after telling her we couldn't find Aubrey, I quizzed her for information which could give us some kind of clue as to her whereabouts. "Can you tell us anything that might help?"

Riley couldn't hide her emotions and her look conveyed fear and guilt. "I should've told you. One of the high school boys has been hanging around her. She's met him several times after school at the tennis courts. I warned her that y'all wouldn't approve. She becomes angry when I tell on her. I'm sorry."

"Who is the boy?"

"Devon is his first name. That's all I know. He's not in athletics. I'm sorry."

I immediately called Mrs. Kraal, and she gave me the boys full name and was even able to give me directions to his house. Her last comment was anything but encouraging. "I'm not surprised you're looking for him. This isn't the first time he's been in trouble."

Minutes later we stopped in front of Devon's house, and going to the door was meet by an elderly woman. I asked her if Devon was home.

"No. I expect him any minute. He's been gone all afternoon. He was supposed to be visiting a friend in Alpine. That boy is hard for us to keep up with. Me and my husband are his grandparents. Why do you need him?"

"My daughter and he are friends, and we can't find her. We thought they might be together. Do you have any way of reaching him?"

"No, not really. I don't even know his friend's name in Alpine." She didn't seem the least bit concerned.

I took out a piece of paper and a pen. "If I give you my phone number will you call me when he gets home?"

"Sure. I'd be glad to. He should be home anytime."

"How old is your grandson?" I asked.

"He's eighteen but is only a junior. He was held back in elementary," she answered.

Back in the car, I relayed the message to Julie. "I don't know anything we can do but go home and wait. Hopefully, she'll show up. I imagine she's with Devon. At least, I hope that's the case."

THE NEXT SEVERAL hours seemed like an eternity as the three of us waited. I called the sheriff's office and told them of the information we had. They knew Devon which only added to our anxiety.

At a few minutes after midnight, headlights appeared in the front of the house but immediately disappeared. The door opened and Aubrey came in. Her hair was a mess, her clothes were rumpled, and even from a distance . . . she reeked of alcohol.

46

ERIC

The excitement of hunting lasted only one day before my thoughts returned full time to Riley. I tried to call her every day but she wasn't home. I had enough manners not to ask where she'd gone. When I wasn't with Gavin feeding, my focus was the weight room, and Arnold, my pig. The stock show was coming up shortly and he'd gained so much weight, exercise was on the schedule each day the weather permitted.

The week seemed to drag by, and I was anxious to get back in school. Maybe Riley would, at least, be available to talk with me. I thought constantly about how to convey my feelings toward her. From information gathered by Dawn, Bruce was doing much better and would return to school on Monday of next week. Riley's work should be completed, and maybe things would return to normal between us.

Feather hadn't returned to work. Dawn had gone to see about them and came back, informing Gavin that Lefty showed no signs of recovering. Without her, our work load increased and much of the day we were gone. According to Gavin, we were having a mild winter which was good for the cattle.

. . .

MONDAY FINALLY ARRIVED, and leaving early, I was at school by 7:30. I waited anxiously for Riley outside. She was usually here at least fifteen minutes before the first bell. At a few minutes before eight o'clock, I'd decided she wasn't coming. Just as the first bell rang, she appeared in the parking lot, walking beside Bruce who was on crutches. With a sinking spirit, I waited, opening the door for them.

"Thanks, Eric," Bruce said.

"Hi, Eric." Riley moved past without saying anything else.

Now what? Stand here like the school doorman or follow along, hoping to get a word in to Riley? I chose the latter, trailing behind until we reached Bruce's locker. "Can we talk?" I asked, as she turned around.

"Maybe later, Eric. I have to help Bruce get to his first period class."

"I appreciate you coming to visit me in the hospital," Bruce said. "That was really thoughtful."

"No problem," I muttered, turning and leaving.

The remainder of the day was a repeat of first period with her reply being the same each time. "I have to help Bruce to his class."

Intercepting her as she was on her way to the gym, seventh period, I was determined not to be put off any longer. "Riley, what's going on? You've been avoiding me all day."

"I told you. Bruce needs my help. Surely, you understand what he's going through his first day back after losing his sister. There wasn't time to spend with you. I'm going to be late for practice."

"Can I call you tonight?"

She hesitated, taking a deep breath before answering. "Eric, I think it's best for us just to be friends. I've put off telling you which was not right. Please understand, and don't be angry with me. Now, I have to get to practice."

I felt like a fool. She's been telling me this for weeks and instead of taking the hint, I hung on, hoping it wasn't happening. She finally gave up, coming right out and telling me it was over. I should've known it was too good to be true. It was never going to last.

I went to athletics and the weight room in a trance, not being aware of anything—only going through the motions. Coach Adams asked me if anything was wrong and I ignored him, continuing my workout.

After school, I practically ran to my truck, being one of the first to leave. On the drive home, unable to control my hurt, I cried. "Stupid, stupid, stupid. Whatever made you think it was possible? It was bound to happen." I screamed, "Get over it!"

Reaching the house, I ignored Dawn's greeting and went directly to my weight room. I changed into some warmups, kept there to work out in. An hour later, drenched in sweat, and gasping for breath, I collapsed in my soft chair. Now the hurt had turned to anger. Why did she lead me on? She let me believe that she cared. After all, I'd have never in a hundred years thought there was a chance she could be my girl. Now, she ended it, just like that. I hated her!

Looking at my watch, it was after five and time to feed Arnold. At least he cared about me. Not only that but he depended on me. He was at the fence, grunting his usual greeting. I began scratching his back and he lay down. I continued to rub him to the sound of his feeble appreciative grunts that actually sounded somewhat like moans. When I stopped, he became silent. Resuming my massage, he started his noisemaking again. Finally, he became silent, and I knew that meant he was asleep. When I poured pellets into his feeder, he woke up, waddled over, and began eating.

"Eric, you must've had a dreadful day," was Dawn's welcome when I went into the house. "What happened?"

I didn't want to talk about it but decided I might as well get it over with. "Me and Riley broke up."

"Oh, I'm sorry."

Pride put the lie on my tongue. "No big deal."

"I'm sure there are other girls waiting to go out with you."

Now, I had her telling untruths. "I'm not hungry tonight. I have some studying to do and will be in my room."

"If you change your mind, we're having venison steaks, potatoes, and cream gravy tonight. Oh, and homemade biscuits."

I went on to my room determined not to come out until morning. While my bath water was running, I looked at my image in the mirror.

Shirtless, muscles had replaced the stomach flab and my arms were larger as well as my neck. Coach had called it a bull neck. My friends in San Antonio wouldn't recognize me.

After my bath, I decided to eat supper, but left immediately afterward to return to my room. I went to bed early hoping to put Riley out of my mind. I dreamed of seeing her and Bruce together everywhere with them pointing and laughing at me. I could go nowhere—there was no escape. I woke up sometime in the early morning, whimpering softy, lying there wondering how long this was going to last. I finally drifted off to sleep, again interrupted by dreams. However, this time they were different. Small wispy shapes in the distance were singing, "You Are My Sunshine." I strained to see and, at first, thought there were three shapes then could see there was only two. The young girls' voices were soft and the song was beautiful. I woke up, confused but feeling better. It didn't take long for my depression and hurt to return.

THE REMAINDER of the week was the worst since the beginning of school. No matter the effort, I kept meeting Riley in the hallway between classes. She didn't attempt to avoid me and seemed happy. Most of the time Bruce was with her, still on his crutches. In the three classes we had together, I sat as far away from her as possible.

The only class I looked forward to was Mr. Puckett's Vo-Ag. I was learning to use a cutting torch and to weld. Mr. Puckett was my favorite teacher, and maybe it was only my imagination, but he spent more time with me than the other students. I'd received even more attention from him this week, afraid the other students would be jealous. At the end of his class on Friday, he asked me to stay a few minutes.

"Eric, this is a small school with few secrets. I know about your disappointment, but you can handle it. You're a different person since school started, and this may be a little setback for you, but you'll come out of it stronger. You have my word on that. Now, stay busy this weekend, and if the opportunity arises, help someone else with their problems and get your mind off yours. That always helps me."

"Yes sir, I'll try," I replied, amazed that a teacher could care about my problems.

I left school feeling somewhat better, but it didn't last long. By the time I was at the ranch, the sadness and hurt had returned. I just couldn't get my mind off Riley. We had a home basketball game tonight, and I couldn't decide whether to go or not. It was a district game and important. Luis had asked me today if I was coming. Mr. Puckett advised me to stay busy, so it would probably beat sitting around and feeling sorry for myself.

I worked out again, knowing if I was exhausted, sleep would come easier tonight. After feeding and watering Arnold, I told Dawn of my intention to attend the games.

"Good. You need to get to bed early, though. Gavin has a lot of work lined up for you tomorrow."

I left the house feeling a little better, once again. The girls' game had just begun when I arrived. It was close throughout but Riley made two free shots with five seconds remaining and we won 42-41. People flooded onto the floor offering congratulations and of course, my eyes were focused on one player. I watched as Bruce hobbled out to meet Riley, who threw her arms around him. Before she let go of him, I was already at the door, leaving.

On the drive to the ranch, I said aloud, over and over, "It doesn't matter. Why punish yourself for something that can't be changed. It was now Riley and Bruce instead of Riley and Eric. I'd suspected this was going to happen but wouldn't admit it . . . fool."

It was only eight o'clock when I walked into the house. Going directly to my room, I went to bed, hoping sleep was possible and would blank out my mind. Two hours later and wide awake, the faint ringing of the phone reached me. Several minutes later a knock on my door and Dawn's voice. "Eric, I need to talk with you."

"Okay. Come in." Maybe it was Riley calling to apologize, was my first thought.

"Feather called and her granddad is bad. She was upset, and someone needs to be with her. Gavin has overdone it this week and shouldn't go and I'm afraid to leave him. Would you go?"

"I guess. Are they at home or at the hospital?"

"Hospital. The ambulance took him just before she called. I feel sorry for her. She has no one to depend on. You can take my car if you like, it has plenty of gas."

FORTY MINUTES LATER, I was parked in front of the hospital, wondering if Feather would even want me around. In my depressed state, I wasn't the best person to be providing comfort to anyone.

At the front desk, I was told that her granddad was still in the emergency room. They pointed me in the direction of that area, and I found Feather sitting with her face in her hands. She raised her head when I called her name, and it was obvious she'd been crying.

"Eric. I didn't expect you. Thanks for coming. Pops is bad, really bad. He had some kind of spell and passed out. I called 911, and the ambulance brought him. I haven't talked to the doctor. I tried to get in touch with my parents but wasn't able to reach them."

She seemed so small and helpless, like an animal caught in a trap. I had no idea what to say. "Is there anything I can do for you?"

"I haven't been able to eat in a long time. Could you get me something to drink and some chips out of the vending machine? I didn't bring any money."

I left and returned a few minutes later with a Coke and package of Cheetos. "Will this be okay?"

"Perfect. Thank you."

We sat in silence as she ate her snack and drank the Coke. She'd lost weight and had dark circles around her eyes. The work clothes were too large for her and just hung on her tiny frame. I tried to think of something to say but everything that came to mind seemed frivolous. Eventually, I asked about her horses.

"They're doing good. Getting fat since I haven't been riding. How's everything at the ranch? I've missed coming to work." She perked up and I realized horses were the perfect subject to get her mind off her Pops.

"We're making out, but we missed having your help. I got a deer last week. An eight-point buck," I said, hoping that information would continue the conversation.

"Really? I didn't know you hunted."

I commenced to tell her about Gavin getting sick and having to carry him off the mountain, not going into detail about the next day when I killed the deer. I did describe the delicious venison steak that Dawn had cooked. She seemed interested, listening intently and then I noticed her eyes blinking, indicating she was drowsy. I asked her how long it had been since she'd slept.

"I've sat up with Pops every night. I sleep whenever he sleeps which is not much. I'm so tired."

"Just relax. If a doctor comes in with news, I'll wake you up." She needed no further encouragement, leaning back in her chair. Within minutes she was asleep and had leaned her head over against my shoulder. I dared not move, afraid she would wake up.

We stayed in that position for two hours, with my arm and shoulder becoming numb, until a doctor came into the waiting room, approaching us. "Is this the granddaughter?"

"Yes," I said, moving as gently as possible to keep her head from falling over. She woke up, looking confused. "Feather, the doctor is here." Her eyes cleared and she was instantly alert.

He spoke directly to her. "Your granddad is very sick. He has heart failure and fluid on his lungs. He's weak and we're doing all we can. We have moved him to ICU. We will notify you if there is any change. He is not conscious, but you may go see him for a few minutes if you wish."

"Thank you. I'd like to see him. Eric, will you go with me?"

I nodded, getting up and following her to ICU. We entered and I was shocked at the sight of her Pops. He looked like a skeleton with skin. His mouth drawn tight and his eyes sunken in—he lay motionless. As we stood by the bed she took his bony hand in hers, mumbling, "I love you, Pops. Please try to live. I need you."

We returned to the waiting room and took our seats. "Would you like to go home for awhile? I can stay and call if anything changes."

"Yes. I need to bathe and put on clean clothes. It shouldn't take over an hour. Thank you, Eric."

After she left, I found an *Outdoor Life* magazine. By the time I'd read most of the articles that interested me, the doctor appeared. "Where is she?"

"She went home. I can call her if you have news about her granddad."

"I do, but it might be best if you told her in person. We did everything possible for him, but he passed away. I'm sorry."

47

LUTA

E ric had called that Lefty had passed. Gavin was visibly upset. "I'd known him most of my life. He was an honest horse trader which is unheard of today. I was riding a horse that he sold me for $75 when your dad hired me."

"I worry about what will happen to Feather, now that he's gone."

"Luta, we're going to see to it that she's taken care of, whatever it takes."

"Eric told me when he called that he was going to stay with her through the weekend, at least. I'm proud of Eric for being there for Feather. I can't believe her parents just deserted her."

"When Eric came out here, I didn't believe there was a chance he'd last. I guess he has some of his old granddad in him after all. He's turned out pretty good considering everything."

"What about his old grandmother? Does she get any of the credit?"

He laughed, with a twinkle in his eyes, which I hadn't seen in years. "A little. I haven't forgotten how much patience you had with the both of us that first several months. Had it not been for you, he'd have gone home with his tail between his legs."

"Do you think we should drive over to Alpine and see how they're doing?" I asked, not knowing if he felt like going.

"That's a good idea. The Loughton place is not much out of the way. We might stop in and pay our respects. It's been three weeks since they lost their daughter, and maybe they're up to having visitors."

I was surprised and pleased at Gavin's suggestion.

WE WERE DRIVING through the bump gates of the Double L by midmorning. The house was a half-mile off the highway but was visible from the entry. The land was flat and better than most in the area. A bunkhouse was located a couple of hundred yards to the right of the main house. It was common knowledge that half a dozen hands worked year 'round with more hired during busy times of the year. Slade's mother and dad were no longer living. They were kind and generous and had been friends of the family for many years. After they died we had very little contact with Slade and his wife.

When Gavin rang the doorbell a young Mexican girl opened it. Gavin asked if Slade was home and received no answer. Switching to Spanish, he asked, "¿Está Slade en casa?"

"Sí," she answered, smiling. "Le diré que tiene una visitante." (I will tell him he has a visitor).

We stood outside the door until Slade appeared. "Gavin, Luta, come in. We're in the kitchen having another cup of coffee."

Following him into the kitchen, Nadine met and hugged me. "It's good to see you, Luta. Would y'all like some coffee?"

We both declined, with her inviting us to sit down. "We're being lazy today. It just seems like we have a hard time getting started after . . ."

When she hesitated, I picked up. "It's Saturday, Nadine. It supposed to be a day off for most people."

She wiped away a tear. "I know. It's just hard."

"We came by to let you know we're thinking about you." Gavin was interrupted before he could continue when Bruce came in from outside.

"Have you finished working with that colt?" Slade asked his son in a rough voice.

Bruce answered without looking at his dad. "Not yet. I'm taking a break."

"You've been trying to break that colt to ride for six months. At your age I would've had it done in half that time."

"Slade, please, not now," pleaded his wife.

"Well, it's true. I'll get one of the other boys to start on the colt Monday."

Bruce turned and glared at his dad as he was leaving. "That's fine with me."

It was an awkward moment, but Gavin continued where he left off. "We're so sorry for your loss. Is there anything we can do?"

"No, there's nothing anybody can do," Slade answered, angrily.

Nadine wiped away a tear. "Everybody has been so nice. I don't know what Bruce would've done if not for that sweet little Mendenhall girl. She has truly been an angel."

The room went silent with her comment. I looked at Gavin, hoping he would know what to say. Evidently he thought changing the subject would improve the atmosphere. "How's your stock holding up this winter? It's been one of the mildest I ever remember."

"Better than usual. I'm thinking that the market might improve in the spring. Maybe, it's just wishful thinking, but it sure would help. We were disappointed this fall when we sold our calves." Slade's voice had returned to normal. Gavin was successful in bringing up the ranch as a topic of discussion.

Slade continued to talk about the ranch and the visit became friendlier, the longer we were away from the tragedy. Nadine added little, content just to listen and probably thankful that Slade's anger was gone. We stayed another half hour never returning to the topic of their daughter.

They went to the door with us, and after hugs and goodbyes, we started out. Slade had one last comment as we were leaving. "Luta, it worked out for the best that Carter is leaving."

Gavin stopped, but grabbing his arm I herded him to the car.

.   .   .

ERIC AND FEATHER weren't at home when we arrived. We assumed they were in the process of making funeral arrangements for Lefty. It was a mild day, and we sat in chairs on the porch and waited for them to return. We didn't have to wait long until they drove up in Eric's pickup.

Feather came straight to me and fell into my arms, sobbing. I held her, not saying anything until she could talk. "Thank you for coming. We've been making arrangements for the service. Pops had already paid for his funeral." She began crying again, and I continued to hold her.

"Have y'all had anything to eat today?" Gavin asked.

"Just donuts, this morning," Eric said.

"Let's load up and find a place to eat. Feather, where's a good place to go?"

She suggested a little family owned café on the east side of town that served a daily lunch. Feather smiled a tiny smile reflecting on a memory. "It was Pops and my favorite place to eat."

She was able to talk now without crying. "We're going to have graveside rites for Pops. He didn't go to church. It worries me. Do you think he'll go to heaven?"

Gavin had a smile as big as Texas. "Honey, I have no doubt that Lefty will go to heaven, and he may be the only horse trader there."

It was the perfect response from Gavin and brought smiles to all of us. Eric hadn't said two words since meeting us. I finally asked him how he was doing.

"All right. Not much sleep, but I can catch up later."

Feather reached over and touched his arm. "I couldn't have made it without Eric. I still haven't been able to reach my mom or dad."

My heart went out to this brave little girl. "Feather, when will the funeral be held?"

"Monday morning at ten o'clock. I called, Larry Gill, the only preacher Pops knew. He would come by occasionally and visit with him. He holds most funeral services for those that have lived here but didn't attend church. I don't know what this community would do without him."

"You've taken care of everything that can be done here. Why don't you come to the ranch and stay with us 'til Monday morning? We can all come back for the funeral."

"Thank you. I appreciate it. If Eric stayed with me this afternoon, we could come over later in the evening. I'd like to get in touch with some of Pops' friends. There's one in particular that I need to call. Bob Matthews, who has a ranch in New Mexico, has bought horses from Pops for years. They've been friends ever since I can remember."

"That name's familiar," commented Gavin.

"You may have heard of him through his grandson. I went with Pops to a match roping in Hobbs, New Mexico, several years ago. Cody Lowe who was from Pecos, was matched against Matthews' grandson, Bo Skinner. It was a big deal with lots of money bet on Lowe by Texas people. Pops said a lot of Texas money stayed in New Mexico that day. I was about twelve and remember that Bo Skinner, who was in college, was the best-looking thing I'd ever laid eyes on."

"I remember now. Everyone in this part of the country knew about that match roping. It was supposed to match the best in Texas to the best in New Mexico. Rumor has it that Lowe never got over that defeat and is still bitter. I was never a fan of his and remember being glad he lost," Gavin said.

With the memories, Feather's grief lessened, and before we left the café she was doing better.

ON THE DRIVE back to the ranch from Alpine, I couldn't get my mind off Slade Loughton. He was angry and was taking it out on anybody who was convenient, including his son, Bruce. How sad he would react in such a way to the tragic loss of his daughter. Was it guilt over how he had treated her or was it just his way of grieving? Gavin had been difficult to live with for many years, but it appeared that he would be no match for Slade.

Slade's mention of Coach Duncan was a surprise. But shouldn't have been. It was just another way to remind me that he'd won. Gavin was about to go back, for a confrontation when I led him to the car. That would've solved nothing and only embarrassed Nadine.

With Eric coming to live with us last year, our lives had changed. It had taken time, but Gavin was returning to his old self. Feather coming to work at the ranch had also been positive. Hopefully, she would stay until the fall when Cameron's stock was sold.

Gavin interrupted my thoughts. "Do we need to stop in town for anything?"

"Eric and Feather will be here for supper. What would you like?"

"I keep waiting for a cold spell so we can have some of that home-made chili. I've about given up on the weather, so let's have it anyway," he suggested.

"That sounds good. We can stop in at the grocery and get what I need."

Within minutes we were at the store, and Gavin went in with me, which was unusual. Most of the time he would remain in the car while I did my shopping. The store wasn't large, and I always ran into someone I knew. Today was no different.

"Luta and Gavin, how nice to see you," greeted Pastor Jacob.

He and Gavin shook hands and we visited briefly about the weather, with him also giving us an update on some of the church members who were ill. We were about to move to the checkout when Gavin gave me a shock.

"Pastor, I'm coming to church with Luta tomorrow. I don't wanta hear any of that hellfire and brimstone stuff either. Hit us with something to make us feel good."

48

FRANK

W e were horrified at Aubrey's appearance. We were so glad she was home we did nothing. Had we tried to talk with her, it would've probably done no good since she was drunk. While Julie put her to bed, I called the sheriff's department and told them she was safe. Afterwards, we sat hand-in-hand on our sofa discussing preliminary plans about what we should do.

"I don't know what to do, Julie. We could file charges against the boy since he's eighteen, but what good would that do? She went with him on her own free will."

"We have to talk with her before we take any action, although it's doubtful she'll be truthful. Regardless, the boy has to be held accountable. The least he did was provide a minor with alcohol. I hope and pray that's all he's guilty of." Her face reflected as much anxiety as I'd ever seen.

"You're suggesting that I file a complaint against the boy?" I clarified.

"Yes. You can't take any action yourself, as the high school principal. Turn it over to the law. I'm sure this isn't the first time an incident of this kind has occurred involving this young man."

My next question brought out the worst of our fears. "Should we take her to the doctor for an examination?"

She frowned. "It depends on how believable she is when we talk to her. The problem is going to be how much she remembers of what happened. Unless we're both convinced nothing else was involved other than the alcohol, we'll need to get an appointment in Midland with a doctor."

"What did we do wrong, Julie? Surely, we're not that bad of parents. I keep asking myself, what could we have done differently?"

"I don't know the answer to that. She's always been beautiful and has used it to get attention, from the time she realized it. Now, of course, it's the wrong kind of attention."

It was late when we went to bed and neither of us slept well. I was up early, making coffee when Riley came into the kitchen. "Is she okay?"

"You saw the shape she was in last night. Your mother put her to bed. We're going to talk with her this morning."

"I know Devon. He's in some of my classes. It's hard to believe that Aubrey would have anything to do with him. I'm surprised he hasn't been sent to your office for discipline. He has a terrible attitude. And is rude to just about everybody, including his teachers.

"Would you want me to talk with Aubrey? She's going to come nearer telling me the truth than she would you and Mom."

"Maybe. I'll ask your mother what she thinks." I thought Riley was probably correct.

THE INTERROGATION, which is the only word to describe it, started later in the morning. We expected to see Aubrey cry and beg forgiveness, but she surprised us. She remained calm and answered our questions as if there was nothing unusual about running off with an older boy to a party and drinking.

She was defiant. "Devon asked me to go and I accepted. I knew it wouldn't do any good to ask you. Riley goes places all the time, and I just stay home. It's not fair. All we did, was go to a party in Alpine." In her stubbornness she considered her conduct justified.

"Were there adults at the party?" Julie asked.

"I didn't see any."

I interrupted. "Didn't it bother you that we would be worried?"

"I never thought about it. I knew you'd be mad," she answered.

Julie leaned forward. "What did you do after you left the party?"

"Came home, I guess. I don't remember anything after we left the party until we got home."

"What did you do at the party?" I asked.

"Danced and drank punch. Some watched TV. Others just sat and talked. Devon had lots of friends there. Some of them go to school here."

Julie and I looked at each other with both of us thinking—we're not getting anywhere. I instructed Aubrey to go to her room. "What're you going to do, ground me forever?"

"We don't know yet." Julie answered honestly because we had no idea what we were going to do.

After she was gone, I could see that Julie was as confused as me. "I didn't expect that."

"Me neither. Riley's in her room. I'll tell her to see what she can get out of Aubrey. I'm going to make her a doctor's appointment. You can go ahead and file a complaint with the sheriff's office. She's different this time, Frank. We have to do something."

What a mess, I thought. Never would I have guessed it would come to this. I'd expected problems with Aubrey but nothing to this degree, especially this early.

THE REMAINDER of the week was spent trying to work on our problem. I filed a complaint against Devon for providing liquor to a minor. Riley had no more success with her questioning than we did. Julie took Aubrey to a lady doctor in Midland for an examination which was inconclusive. We grounded her indefinitely. We informed her the duration of the punishment would depend on her future conduct. She continued to show no signs of remorse.

I was glad for school to resume on January 3 and was in my office early. At least there would be something else to take up my time and thoughts besides my youngest daughter. The morning was uneventful, and I spent most of the time going through my mail that had accumulated over the holidays.

A few minutes before the lunch bell, Mrs. Kraal informed me Devon's grandparents were here and wanted to talk. They came in and sat down without an introduction. I assumed since she had talked with me previously none was needed. They were older than I thought, and it was impossible not to feel sorry for them.

The granddad spoke softly as if he had memorized his speech. "You filed charges against our grandson. Devon has to appear in court Monday of next week. We're worried about what'll happen to him. We didn't know what to do except come talk with you. Is there anything we can do to change your mind to drop the charges?"

"My name's Frank. What can I call you?"

"Eli will do."

"Eli, Devon took my fourteen-year-old daughter to a party without our knowledge. When he brought her home at midnight, she was drunk. My wife and I were worried out of our minds, not even knowing where she was."

"Did he force her to go?"

"No, but that's not the point. She's only fourteen, and your grandson is eighteen. He's an adult, and she's just a child."

"Devon brought her by the house before they left for Alpine. We had no idea she was so young. She looked more like his age. If we'd had any idea she was that young we'd have said something to Devon," said the grandmother.

"Has this type of incident happened before?" I asked.

"No. He was picked up for a DWI and another time for an assault charge. The judge warned him he didn't want to see him in court again. We understand your feelings, but we don't want to lose our grandson. This time he might go to jail. We're asking you to drop the charges." His grandmother pleaded, on the verge of tears.

I didn't know what to say. These poor people were trying to raise a grandson that probably the parents had abandoned. There'd be no way they could afford a lawyer. I felt sure it took all their income to get by. They were neat and well groomed, but he had on a pair of overalls and she a faded dress. "Let me talk to my wife, and we'll get back to you."

"Thank you. Would you like to talk to our grandson? You're welcome to do that. He's ornery, but I've never caught him in a lie. He'll usually confess to whatever he's done."

"Yes, but not during school hours. I have to separate my job as principal from being a father. If you'll have him come to The Drug Store at six this evening, we can visit there."

Eli looked at his wife for the answer. "He'll be there."

I shook hands with Eli and they left. I called Julie and asked her if she could come home for lunch. She agreed and within fifteen minutes we were at the kitchen table. I told her about my meeting with the grandparents. Before I could complete my account of the meeting, Aubrey came busting through the door, running to her room, crying.

I looked at Julie. "Now what's that all about?"

"Don't have any idea but we better find out," Julie said, getting up and heading for Aubrey's room, with me following.

Julie sat down on the side of the bed. "What is it, Aubrey? Why're you so upset?"

She had her head buried in a pillow. She said something but we couldn't understand her, only garble. Unable to breathe, she came up for air. "Th-ey call-ed me a slut! N-ot going b-ac-k."

"Who called you a slut?" I asked.

"Th-ey d-id."

Julie reached over and smoothed her hair. "Who're 'they'?"

She sobbed. "The g-irls in m-y class. The-y we-re chant-ing it in th-e cafeteria."

Julie motioned for me to leave. I waited on her until she came back into the den. "I don't know what else to do. She brought this on herself by her Devon escapade. Word has gotten around and some of the junior high girls are not going to miss any opportunity to hurt someone, especially a classmate as pretty as Aubrey. She's just going to have to live with it. I suggest we let her stay home this afternoon. When she calms down, we'll talk to her."

I finished telling her about the meeting with Devon's grandparents. She wasn't as sympathetic. "Frank, he has to be held accountable. He knew it was wrong. I feel sorry for his grandparents, but if something isn't done to stop him, it could be repeated."

"Would you go with me to talk to him?"

She was emphatic. "Sure, but it won't change my mind."

WHEN WE ENTERED The Drug Store at 5:55, Devon wasn't there. At 6:10, he still hadn't shown up. Ten minutes later we decided to leave. We stood and that seemed to be his cue to come through the door. Of course, I'd seen him at school in the hallway, but he'd never been in my office. He was wearing a long sleeve shirt with jeans and tennis shoes. He seemed younger than I remembered. He came directly to our booth.

"Devon, this is my wife, Julie."

He sat down across from us. "What's this about?"

"I think you probably already know, but I'll refresh your memory. You took Aubrey, our daughter, who is only fourteen years old to a party and brought her home drunk. At eighteen, you're considered an adult. I filed a complaint against you for providing alcohol to a minor. We're concerned about what else might have happened. Aubrey said she remembered nothing, after leaving the party, until she arrived home."

He grinned, which infuriated me. "Are you going to believe me? It looks like you've already made up your mind."

"Try me." I gritted my teeth.

"First, Aubrey told me she was sixteen. When I questioned why she was only in the eighth grade, she said her parents held her back. She sure doesn't look like she's fourteen," he said, smiling again.

"What's so funny?" blared Julie. "I'd like to slap that smile off your face!"

He raised both hands as if to protect himself. "She told me you'd given your permission for her to go with me."

"I don't believe you!" Julie boomeranged.

He continued to smile that devilish grin. "I could care less what you believe. It's the truth."

"You gave her alcohol," I accused.

"No. I didn't give her anything. No one offered her booze. She found the punch bowl all by herself." He stated as a matter of fact.

"What happened from the time you left the party until you brought her home?" Julie asked.

"I drove—she slept. Out like a light. Even snored," he said, smiling again.

I quickly responded, afraid Julie was going over the table after him. "Your grandparents said you had always been truthful to them. I hope you're not lying to us."

"Nope. I wouldn't take advantage of a girl who was passed out. Not my style. Anything else?"

I looked at Julie whose face had turned from a golden brown to a fiery red. "I guess that'll be all unless my wife has something else to say." When she didn't reply, I told him that was all.

After he left, Julie delivered the verdict. "He's lying."

"At least we listened to his side of the story. We can ask Aubrey if it was true or not."

AUBREY DIDN'T COME out of her room for dinner that evening. I asked Riley if she'd heard about the incident.

"Sure, everybody has. Some of our students were at the party in Alpine and saw Aubrey. They know Devon's reputation. Word spread quickly. This is a small school. The girls are jealous of Aubrey and they jumped all over it. I feel sorry for her, but it's her fault."

"I thought you would be more sympathetic," Julie said.

"You've tried to tell her. I've tried to tell her. Maybe she needs to learn the hard way." This was a first. Riley had always taken up for Aubrey, no matter what the issue.

Julie and I went to Aubrey's room, knocked, and entered. We spent the next half hour, questioning, comforting, advising, scolding—ending the session with a prayer.

As Aubrey answered questions, Julie's face turned white, as she learned that Devon had told the truth, at least about Aubrey lying about her age and having permission to go with him. There was no reason to believe he wasn't telling the truth about the ride home. We informed her that she was going to school tomorrow and face whatever was waiting. Maybe Riley was right after all.

The first thing in the morning, I would go by the sheriff's office and drop the charges against Devon.

49

ERIC

I waited outside for Feather to return, trying to decide how to tell her that her pops had died. I didn't have much time to think about it before I saw her coming. Seeing me, she realized the news was bad, coming hurriedly to me. "I'm sorry, Feather."

She fell to her knees, crying softly. I reached down and taking her by the shoulders, lifted her up. I held her closely, while she continued to whimper, with her head on my chest. We stayed that way for several minutes until she stepped back—wiping her eyes on her sleeve.

"Thank you, Eric. On the drive back from the house, I had a bad feeling. At least, now, he's not suffering. I loved him." She began to sob again.

"Let's go back to the house. Did you feed your horses while you were home?"

She shook her head. "I didn't think about it. We need to see about them."

Maybe, asking her about the horses was the right thing to do because she stopped crying and was able to talk on the drive back to her house. "I have to make some decisions. I haven't been able to get in touch with my parents. Will you help me?"

"Sure. I'll do what I can."

"After we look after the horses, we'll go to the funeral home and make arrangements. I'm so glad to have you here with me."

We stayed busy the rest of the morning. I was amazed she was able to complete plans for her pop's service and hold it together. When we arrived at Feather's house, Gavin and Dawn were waiting on us. During lunch in town, Feather agreed to stay with us until the funeral.

Late Saturday afternoon. Feather was restless and wanted something to keep her mind off her pops, so we rode around the ranch. I tried to keep from thinking of Riley, but the image of her hugging Bruce at mid-court wouldn't go away. I tried to talk to Feather but would lapse into silence for long periods.

"What's bothering you?" she asked, as we were driving through the east part of the ranch.

"Riley broke up with me."

"When?"

"Yesterday. She's more interested in helping Bruce after his sister was killed in the wreck."

"Just wants to be your friend, huh?"

"Yeah. How'd you know?" I asked.

"That's what they always say."

"Has it happened to you?"

"Sure. Most everybody has heard that line at one time or another. I guess your heart's broken, but you'll get over it. You sure she's only interested in helping Bruce? Maybe it's developed into more than that."

It didn't seem like she was interested in providing sympathy for me the way this was going. "I think she really liked me."

"You think so. Let me ask you this. How did she kiss you?"

"What do you mean?"

"You know. Quick or slow? Closed or open mouth? How long did the kiss last? I mean it didn't have to be like kissing a four-inch pipe, but did she part her lips or just pucker? I guarantee you, it makes a difference."

"That's a personal question."

"Sorry. I was just trying to help. Eric, you lost something that you cared about, but you won't know real sorrow until you lose something that you loved and that loved you back. Remember that."

"You mean like your pops?"

"Exactly."

THE GRAVESIDE RITES for Feather's granddad were held Monday morning at ten o'clock. Feather and I went in my truck while Gavin and Dawn took her car. We arrived early at the cemetery and only a few people were there. By the beginning of the service, a crowd of about thirty were present. The minister read several scriptures, said a few words about Lefty, and closed the service with Lefty's favorite song, *Ghost Riders in the Sky*, played on a tape player.

Feather held up well until some of her pop's friends came by to offer their condolences. It was just too much for her and she broke down again. Most of the people left but a few stayed around to visit. When a break occurred in those waiting to offer their sympathy, I guided her to my truck, thinking it would be best if she got away. She didn't resist and within a short time, we were on our way to her house.

I waited while she packed, since the next week would be spent at the ranch. I was in the den when she came in carrying a black felt hat. "Eric, I'd given this new hat to Pops for Christmas. He'd never worn it. Would you like to try it on?"

"Yeah, I guess." The hat was a perfect fit and felt good.

"What do you think? It looks good on you." Her big blue eyes affirmed what her lips were saying.

"I like it."

"It's yours. At least someone will put it to use. Now, you have a hat to go with your boots."

"Are you ready to leave?" I asked.

"Just as soon as I hook on to my trailer and load the horses. It worked out that we only had two. We always kept at least half a dozen up until about a month ago. I believe that Pops knew he didn't have much time left."

We left for the ranch, with me following her in my truck. It was a

forty-minute drive which gave me too much time to dwell on Riley. I
dreaded going to school tomorrow and seeing her in the hall with
Bruce. Having three classes with her would be difficult, too. I kept
thinking about what Feather said. She was probably right about Riley's
interest in Bruce being more than just helping him. I was sure of one
thing—it was going to take me a long time to get over Riley.

When we arrived at the ranch, I helped her pen and feed the horses
and then checked on Arnold. Of course he'd turned over his water and
was almost out of feed. He greeted me with a series of grunts and
rubbed up against my leg when I got in his pen. I could always depend
on him to welcome me. I'd never thought in a thousand years a pig
would be my best companion. He continued to nudge my leg with his
nose until I scratched his back, causing him to lie down.

Feather came up, surprising me. "That pig is something else. He
seems almost human. I've heard how smart pigs were and now he's
proven it. It's obvious that he knows you, Eric."

"Most people would think I'm crazy, carrying on over a pig and
treating him like a pet. I didn't mean to become attached to him. He's
the only thing that ever depended on me to survive. I provide feed and
water which he couldn't do without. Maybe if I'd ever had a dog or
even a cat to take care of it would be different."

"I feel the same way about my horse. It might be a little strange
that your loyal companion is a pig, but hey, don't worry about it."

By the time we entered the house, Dawn had supper on the table.
Feather was quiet throughout the meal, going to her room before we
had finished eating.

"It's going to be hard on her for a long time," Gavin stated.

"I wish there was something we could do for her," Dawn said.

"The best thing to do is keep her busy. I found that to be helpful.
Reminding her about caring for her horses, got her mind off her pops,
after she learned of his passing."

"That shouldn't be a problem since you'll be going back to school
tomorrow. The weather forecast is calling for some bad weather the
next couple of days. We'll be feeding tomorrow," Gavin said.

The next day was even worse than I expected. It seemed that I ran into Riley and Bruce in the hall at every turn, in addition to seeing her in the classes we shared. It was obvious, they were a couple. I tried not to look at them but it was impossible. She was always smiling. Had she been that way with me? It didn't get any better the next day or the next.

It was a relief to get back to the ranch each day. I would immediately go to my weight room and work out for as much as an hour, furiously. I would then feed and water Arnold and spend time with him. Exhausted, I would return to the house, take my bath and by then, it would be time for supper.

Feather was grieving less, and after eating, we would watch TV. Friday night, after Gavin and Dawn had gone to bed, she turned down the volume on a movie. "Are you getting over Riley?"

"No. I'm trying but it just gets worse. You were right about Bruce."

"Do you think she worries about how you're feeling?"

"Of course not, that's a stupid question."

"What good does it do to grieve over her?" she asked.

"None, but I can't help it." I was getting tired of the questioning. It looked like she could show me a little sympathy. I also got tired of her always being right.

She turned the volume back up on the movie, but I still heard her last comment. "Well, I don't feel sorry for you. She didn't love you back. Get over it." I got up, without responding, and went to my room.

THE NEXT DAY WAS SATURDAY, and Gavin had the day planned for us. While eating breakfast he gave us our orders. "It's too cold for me today. I'm staying by the fire. I've accounted for most of the stock but not all of them. We haven't covered the far western part of the pasture. I believe some of the cows are staying there. I've neglected it because it's rough country. There's a dirt road that you can drive up and go into our land. It's not much of a road and is not maintained, but if you drive slow you can make it. Trailer your horses over there, and you'll have less ground to cover. Luta will fix you a lunch, and I'd like for you to go over as much of the area as possible. I think you'll see cattle that haven't come up when we fed."

"How do we find the road that we need to take?" asked Feather.

"It's easy. When you leave the front gate, turn west, look at your odometer and go exactly five miles. You'll see a narrow dirt road off to the left. Take that road and go another five miles and you'll come to our gate. Just drive inside and unload your horses. You can't drive far since there's no road. Be careful with your horses. It's the roughest country on the ranch. You'll also need to keep your bearing so you won't get lost. You're going to earn your money today. Dress warm."

Gavin was right about it being cold. There was no sun, and by the time we reached the gate to the area we were to ride over, I dreaded leaving the warmth of the pickup. I had said little, still angry over Feather's comments the night before.

We unloaded the horses, tightened our cinches, and rode off to the east. At first the brush was thick with large rocks determining our path. Eventually, the terrain became clearer and the travel easier. We found bunches of heifers and had counted forty-two head by the time we stopped for lunch. We found a wind break among a group of cedars and dismounted, tying our horses. Both of us were frozen.

"Eric, let's build a fire and try to get warm. I brought some matches, and while you gather wood I'll find some kindling. Just make sure the wood is dead."

Still pouting from last night, I walked off, mumbling to myself, "She's still ordering me around like a child. She could've at least asked me about a fire."

By the time I returned with an armload of wood, she had a small fire going, and was feeding it with small sticks. I dumped the wood down. "Here's your wood. I hope it suits you."

She stood up, coming closer. "Eric, you were good to me when Pops passed. I shouldn't have said what I did last night. It was just that I'd lost someone dear to me, and you were grieving over losing a girl-friend that didn't care much about you. I should've been more sympa-thetic. Now, we have a long difficult day ahead of us. Let's be civil to one another."

She extended her hand, I accepted it. "The fire looks good. I'll go for another load of wood and maybe we can get warm."

When I returned, she had a nice fire going and it did feel good. My hands, face, and ears were numb. We sat by the fire, ate sandwiches and cookies that Dawn had fixed for us and talked about our strategy for the afternoon. I felt better after her apology and had gotten over my ill feelings. It was, with reluctance, that we put out our fire and rode off to the east.

By midafternoon, we decided to circle back toward our truck. We'd been able to count another fifteen heifers. We figured it to be at least a three hour ride back. The route took us further away from the mountains and was easier traveling. We were shocked to find a dead heifer that was partially decomposed. We couldn't find any reason for her death. We came upon another one that had recently died and then another.

"What happened to them, Feather?"

"I would guess they ate something that poisoned them. I heard Pops talking to ranchers about how some plants at certain times of the year will kill horses or cattle. I think we should gather some of the plants that are growing and take them back to Gavin. Since it's winter, we shouldn't have a problem deciding what is growing and what is dormant."

We did what she suggested, gathering several different species and putting them inside our coats to carry. When we reached the truck, the count of dead heifers was up to five. It was getting dark as we loaded our horses for the drive back.

"Gavin's going to be upset with the news," I said.

"Yes, Eric, I dread telling him."

The first thing I did after unloading the horses was to check on Arnold, who needed more feed and water. Feather fed the horses. Darkness followed us into the house. We told Gavin the news immediately, giving him the plants we had recovered.

Gavin sat silently for a full minute before responding. "Garbancillo. We had a wet winter with a lot of cloudy and cold days. It thrives in those conditions. Cattle that are raised here, usually leave it alone but that's not the case for ones brought into this area. We have to get the heifers out of that pasture as quickly as possible and that's not going to be easy. In the process, we can expect to find more dead ones.

50

LUTA

After Eric and Feather left the supper table to watch TV, Gavin expressed his fears. "Luta, this could ruin Cameron's chances of paying off his debt. In many ways this country is unforgiving. If it's not loco weed, it's some other villain. We haven't had a problem with Garbancillo in years. Of course, we haven't had cattle in that pasture for a long time. I should've thought about it, with this wet winter. We've got to move those heifers into another pasture closer to the house and do it quickly. Lord knows how many dead ones we'll find. We need several more hands, and I have no idea where to find them."

"Cameron said he would be out by tomorrow afternoon when I called him. How much extra help do you think we need? I hate to do it, but we can take Eric out of school for several days. He's a good student and can make up his work," Luta said.

"With Feather, Eric, and Cameron we would still need at least three more. I just can't do it. If I get out in the cold for just a little while, I start hurting and become short of breath. I can drive and honk up as many as possible. That's about the limit of what I can do." Thank goodness, Gavin was being realistic about his condition.

"I can ride Casper if Eric can ride your horse. That would give us one more and just leave two we would need. Maybe I can locate a couple of men that day work in this area."

I called two of our neighbors who gave me the names of several men they used for day work. I spent the next hour on the telephone with no success. They either had jobs or weren't interested. I'm sure the weather had something to do with it. Spending all day in the saddle with the temperature below freezing for $25 was not a very inviting proposition.

Gavin suggested that tomorrow we honk up as many as possible. A good number of the heifers stayed close enough to where we fed to come to the horn. He said that Eric and Feather could ride the area west of the pens and drive in whatever they found. I hated to miss church, but we really didn't have a choice.

"At least we have a plan." I told Gavin.

He didn't speak for a minute, and I was surprised at his response. "You know, Luta, we've got our work cut out for us this week, but I feel more alive than I have in years. I'm just sorry it's not possible for me to do more. Maybe when the weather warms up that will change. Now, I'm going to bed. We have a long day tomorrow."

I went into the den and told Eric and Feather our plans. They were involved in watching a show, and I thought they didn't hear me at first until Eric responded. "I'm still not thawed out from today. I've never been that cold. What's the weather forecast?"

"More of the same. In fact, the cold is supposed to be here until at least mid-week," I announced.

Feather laughed. "No problem. We're tough."

"I can miss school Monday, Dawn. My grades are good, and it won't be hard to catch up."

"Thank you, Eric. Gavin and I had already talked about that. We have a challenge for next week, and it's a blessing to have you and Feather here with us. Your dad will be here late tomorrow evening to help out, also."

"You mean he's actually going to come out here? I can't imagine him taking off work," Eric said.

"I'm going to bed now, and it would be a good idea for y'all to turn in early. We need to leave at first light."

Gavin was already asleep when I went to bed. Lying there in the quiet, I thought what a change in our lives since Eric had come to live with us. First Gavin was terrible and Eric wasn't much better. Then Eric, with the encouragement of Coach Duncan and Mr. Puckett started to change. Of course, Riley also had a positive influence on him. As Eric changed, Gavin's attitude improved. That coupled with Cameron's bad investment, which provided a challenge for us, turned the tide. Now, we were facing that challenge together. I said a prayer for all of these blessings and drifted off to sleep, wondering how I was going to manage being on horseback all day in the bitter cold.

My ALARM when off at five o'clock. I had to get busy in order to make something for us to take for lunch and to cook a good breakfast. I made ham sandwiches along with peanut butter and jelly. I made two pots of coffee. One would be for breakfast and we would fill a thermos with the other one to take. I'd mixed together the dough for cookies last night and put two dozen in the oven to bake while I started breakfast.

"Good morning." Feather startled me. "What can I do to help?"

"Oh, Feather, you're up early. You can get the eggs out of the fridge and beat up a dozen and a half for us to scramble. There're a couple of cans of green chilies in the cupboard you can add to them. After that you can open three cans of biscuits to put in the oven when the cookies get done. I'm frying sausage and will have gravy to go with it."

"Luta, I know it's going to be a terrible day to be on horseback but I'm excited. Does that sound strange? Most people would want to stay inside by the fire."

I laughed at her observation. "You're eighteen, Feather. When you're fifty-five you may feel differently. At your age everything excited me, even hardships. I'm dreading today, worrying about being able to make a small contribution. I keep wondering if I can make it." Before I could continue, the phone rang.

It was one of the cowboys that turned me down yesterday, saying he had reconsidered and would like to work a few days. He asked if he could bring a friend. Controlling my excitement, I told him to come on and bring his friend. We could use the extra help.

"Good news, we're going to have a couple of cowhands assist us. It couldn't come at a better time. That'll make five of us, and with Cameron coming this afternoon, we'll have six by tomorrow. Things are looking up, Feather."

BY EIGHT O'CLOCK we were at the West Pasture, saddled and ready to go. The two men who joined us seemed willing enough. It was bitter cold with a north wind that seemed to cut right through you. I'd put on several layers of clothes plus my heaviest coat. We spread out about 200 yards and started moving east, making as much noise as possible, hoping to push whatever cattle we encountered west toward the holding pens. This was the densest part of the pasture, and likely, would be where most of the cattle were.

Within two hours we were in open country and had thirty or forty head moving ahead of us. By noon we had increased our number by another twenty. We gathered behind a group of large rocks that offered a wind break, and I passed out the sandwiches and chocolate chip cookies I'd brought in a sack tied to my saddle horn. We returned to our position and ate our dinner, moving forward, afraid some of the heifers would turn back if given a chance. I was already stiff from riding and the cold made it worse.

I was in the middle, with Feather to my left and one of the men who came to day work on the other side of Feather. Eric was on my right and the other man on the right of him. At midafternoon Feather rode over to me. I knew something was wrong by her expression.

"Luta, he keeps coming over and talking to me. I'm afraid we'll miss some of the cattle. I've told him to stay in his position several times but it does no good. What should I do?"

I didn't like the man's look when we were introduced. Maybe it was just woman's intuition. "Let me trade with you, Feather. I doubt if he'll want to talk with me."

That solved the problem. He didn't come close to me, and when we drove the cattle into the trap behind the pens, he stayed as far from me as possible. Gavin came over before I could dismount. "I counted sixty-two. That's more than I expected you to get. I honked up over a hundred so we're off to a good start. I bet you're about froze."

I swung my leg over the saddle to get off and my other leg buckled. Had Gavin not caught me, it would've been a nasty fall and probably resulted in a broken bone.

He laughed, still holding on to me. "Looks like I'm good for something. You poor thing, let's get you in the pickup and thawed out."

"I'm sorry. My leg wouldn't hold me. I'm numb from cold and sitting so long in the saddle. Thank you for catching me."

The pickup was warm. I didn't know heat could feel so good. The others also tied their horses to the holding pen fence, and since Gavin's pickup was an extended cab, we were able to squeeze everyone in for the ride back to where we left the other vehicles. After that we could return for the horses.

Feather rode in the front with us and Eric in the back seat with the other two men. Gavin let me off at the house to put something together for supper. The phone was ringing when I entered. It was Cameron and he had to stop in Ozona due to the icy roads and wouldn't be here until tomorrow.

I'd cooked a whole ham yesterday and only used a small portion for the sandwiches today. To go with it, I'd cooked a large pot of red beans. I put potatoes in the oven to bake and that was going to have to be it. I could barely get around and could only imagine what it would be like in the morning. I smiled. *How could I feel this good to be in my condition?*

I expected them back long before the headlights announced their arrival. In fact, I was getting worried that they might have encountered problems. When Gavin came in, I knew something had happened. Eric and Feather were not with him.

"Luta, we had a little problem. Let's sit down at the table, and I'll tell you about it. When we reached the West Pasture, Eric stayed in the pickup a few minutes talking with me about tomorrow. Feather went to her pickup as did the two hired hands. We heard Feather scream and both of us bailed out, headed full speed to her. Of course, Eric got there way ahead of me. The sight I encountered was something to behold. Eric had one of the men pinned down hitting him in the face. Feather was trying to pull him off but wasn't having any effect on stopping the fight. Did I say fight? It was more of a beating. I'll never know how he got him down that fast. The other man just stood there watching as if he couldn't believe what he was seeing."

"How did you get him stopped?"

"I don't know. I grabbed him by the shoulders and pulled, calling him by his name. It was like he was in some sort of trance. I tell you, Luta, when I grabbed him, it was like getting hold of a rock. He finally got up and went to Feather who was still crying."

"What did you do about the man?"

"I asked Feather what happened, but she just shook her head and wouldn't answer me. I had a pretty good idea. I wrote them a check for the day's work and told them not to return tomorrow. They didn't argue. The man was bleeding pretty bad and may have needed stitches."

"I'm not surprised. I had to trade places with Feather to get him away from her this afternoon. Is Eric all right?"

"His knuckles are skinned up some but that's all. They stayed at the barn under the pretense of looking after the horses and feeding his pig. Really, I don't think either of them wanted to tell you what happened. If it's okay, let's not say anything about it."

"Absolutely."

When Eric and Feather came in, they had little to say and we ate supper in silence. After finishing, they left for the den to watch TV.

"Gavin, I don't know if I can ride tomorrow or not. I can barely get around and my legs have already started cramping. It looks like the weather will be even worse after the news from Cameron."

"No problem. You can go with me in the pickup and hopefully Cameron will be here in time to help."

I took my bath after doing the dishes, and soaking in the hot water was pure heaven.

51

FRANK

I usually put the coffee on around six in the morning and Julie would come in half an hour later. We'd drink our coffee and visit until the girls were up. This morning was Tuesday, January 11 and it was cold. I'd gone outside to check for ice, wondering if school would be canceled. It appeared that the roads were clear, even though ice had collected on the grass and sidewalk. Mr. Cleburne was going to be forced into deciding whether or not to run the buses. He probably would have to confer with several board members to make a decision or maybe just one.

Julie came into the kitchen wrapped up in her housecoat, shivering. "Frank, it's freezing in here. Is the coffee ready?"

"It is. I lit the stoves, but it will take time for the house to heat."

A knock at the door startled us, and we looked at each other, wondering the same thing. Who would be wanting something this early on such a dreadful day? I went to the door, opened it and saw an elderly man.

"What do you need?"

"Frank Mendenhall? I'm Gavin Sager. Could we visit?"

"Certainly. Come in. You're Eric's granddad, aren't you?"

"That's right," he replied, coming in and removing his hat.

"My wife and I are having coffee. Would you like to join us?"

"I really don't have time. I have a problem, and hopefully you can help me. I need one of your students to work for me on my ranch today."

He then explained his situation, asking for Luis to be excused from school. It was difficult to believe that this man, who was much more important in the community than me, was standing here asking my permission for anything. Here he was, with his hat in his hand, asking me if I could help him.

"Have you asked Luis or his dad about this?"

"No. I came to you first. If you agree, I'll go by their house and get Luis. He's a good hand and has worked for me in the past. His dad works for a ranch and will understand."

"Mr. Sager, I doubt if we'll even have school today because of the weather, however, if we do, Luis will be excused from school. I'm sorry for your problems. Hopefully everything will work out for you."

He stepped forward extending his hand. "Thank you. I've heard good things about you and evidently they're true."

Returning to the kitchen, I explained to Julie what had occurred. "I hope it was the right thing to do. He was courteous, making no demands, only asking my approval. That kind of respect for a principal is unusual."

"Frank, of course, it was the right thing to do. School attendance is important, in fact it's the law, but this is an emergency and you made an exception. Whether or not you realize it, you always make the right decision. I don't understand why you ever doubt yourself."

She was correct. I wasn't comfortable making decisions in my new role as a principal. I needed to stop second-guessing myself and just do what I thought was right. Maybe in the future that would come easier. Gavin Sager was impressive in his hat with boots tucked into his jeans, but that's not the reason I made my decision.

"Do you think the worst is over for Aubrey?" she asked.

"It can't get much worse. She's gone to school crying every day and comes home crying. Those junior high girls are relentless." I didn't expect it to get any better, but hopefully it won't go any further.

"Do you see any good coming out of the experience she's had?"

"I hope so, Julie. If not, then nothing will change her behavior."

I hadn't said anything to Julie, but now was as good a time as any to put another worry on her. "For the first time in her life, I'm concerned about Riley and this relationship she has with Bruce. They're together every minute possible at school and then after basketball practice. It started out with them supporting one another in their grief over Becky but has gone beyond that. I think it might be a good idea to find out how serious this relationship is."

She frowned. "I didn't realize they were together that much at school."

"Before school, between classes, lunch, and after basketball practice. I may be concerned for nothing but would you talk with her?" I hated to put this on Julie, but she would be much better at this than me, trying to be both a principal and a father.

"Certainly. You think it might be serious? Maybe too much so?"

"Watching them together, leads me to believe that could be the case," I replied.

"Maybe we should've had boys, Frank. Parents don't spend as much time worrying about their love life, which is not fair. Why didn't you tell me sooner?"

"I had doubts and didn't want to worry you. Yesterday, I saw them kissing just before he left for home after basketball. That convinced me to tell you."

"Oh me, Frank. Surely we don't have to worry about Riley making a bad decision. She's never come close to being serious about a boy."

The phone rang before I could respond. Answering, it was the superintendent. "Frank, have you checked the roads?"

"No. They look clear though. However, my sidewalk does have ice on it."

"I've had several board members call and asked me if we were going to have school. Maybe, you better drive around and see what you think. Get back to me and we'll decide something. It's already time for some of the buses to leave."

Unbelievable! An hour before school starts and he's calling *me* to check the roads. I hung up after agreeing and left the house. I found a few slick spots in town but overall the roads were fine.

Returning to the house, fifteen minutes later, I called and told him my opinion.

"Good, that's what I thought. I'll tell them you checked the roads and everything was fine. School will begin on time. Thanks, Frank," he said, hanging up.

"Great," I muttered, "if someone has a wreck on the way to school it'll be my fault."

BY TEN O'CLOCK THAT MORNING, the sleet began coming down. An hour later the roads were solid ice. The phone was ringing constantly with parents expressing concern about getting their children home. It was almost time for lunch, and we had an open campus. Many of the students went home or to town for lunch. I knew they couldn't be allowed to leave school.

I went into the outer office. "Mrs. Kraal, we're going to close campus for lunch. Hopefully by the time we let out, the streets will be improved. Let the parents who call know the plans. We can't stop them from picking up their kids if that's the choice they make."

I made the announcement over the intercom before going to the cafeteria, informing them to prepare extra food. After that I called Cleburne and told him the plans. His response was not a surprise.

"Looks like it was the wrong decision to have school today. My phone has been ringing off the wall."

Bad thoughts went through my mind but didn't make it out of my mouth. "Yes, it didn't work out. Maybe the weather will improve before school is out."

It didn't get any better when Mrs. Kraal came into my office. "Slade Loughton is on the phone and wants to speak with you."

I picked up the phone, said hello, and listened to him rant and rave about my stupid decision to have school. I just listened, knowing it would be futile to put up any type of defense. His final statement deserved a response. "Your contract comes up next month. I'll remember this decision that you made to put kids in danger."

"You do what you have to, Mr. Loughton." That ended the call and I thought, how can my day get any worse? Fortunately, it didn't. The students accepted the closed campus for lunch as did the parents. The ice storm continued, but we were able to get everyone home. Thank goodness, school buses do well on ice, and we had good drivers. No accidents were reported. By six that evening, still in my office, I was exhausted, stressed to the max. I was about to leave when the ag teacher came in.

"Bad day, Mr. Mendenhall."

I laughed. "You could say that, Mr. Puckett."

"I hate to bother you this late in the day, but our county show is coming up in a few weeks. I wanted to give you details about our schedule and what we'll need from you."

For the next twenty minutes he gave me a full description of the annual county ag show and sale. Throughout, I kept wondering, how a young teacher could be this more organized and efficient than the person who led the school district. I actually felt better after he finished describing this event that was important to him, his students, and the community. When he rose to leave, I thanked him for the information.

"You have a tough job, Mr. Mendenhall. Working for someone who has crap in their backbone makes it even harder. Most of the people in the community realize this as well as the faculty. Continue to stand up for what you believe and everything will work out."

I thanked him and after he was gone, thought—*I needed that.*

ERIC

"I can take care of myself."

"It didn't sound like it when we heard you screaming," I reminded her.

"He caught me by surprise. I wasn't expecting him to be so bold and aggressive. I would've been all right. Anyway, thanks for helping me."

She was driving and I noticed her right hand was trembling on the steering wheel. "What actually happened?"

"He came on to me, and when I didn't cooperate, he grabbed me and tried to kiss me. That's when I screamed. I can take care of myself," she repeated.

"Really? How much do you weigh, Feather?"

"You're not supposed to ask a girl her weight. It's not appropriate."

"I bet you don't weigh a 100."

"You're wrong, I weigh 101," she replied, angrily.

"That's probably with your boots on and a pocket full of rocks."

We were getting close to the ranch and Feather asked. "What're we going to tell Dawn?"

"Nothing. Gavin probably told her anyway. Are you mad at me? It seems like it."

"No, Eric. I just don't want to be in a position where I have to depend on someone. I could never count on my parents for anything. Pops is gone so I have to look after myself from now on. Your hand's bleeding. Does it hurt?"

"Not much." I lied.

We drove past the house to the barn, where we unloaded our horses. We stalled them and while she fed, I took care of Arnold. Just one time, I'd like to go to his pen and not find the water trough turned over. It seemed that he'd get cold wallowing in the mud but evidently that wasn't the case. He met me with a series of grunts. "I'm not scratching your back today. I've been thinking about a warm fire all day and that's where I'm headed."

Feather joined me and took hold of my arm on the way to the house. "I'm sorry, Eric. He scared me. I don't want to be helpless, however, if you hadn't been there he wouldn't have stopped. I-I'm still shaking."

When we entered the house, I was expecting my dad to be there. Dawn explained his absence and strangely, it was a relief. Supper wasn't ready so I went to my room to get cleaned up. While I was soaking in the hot tub, it occurred to me that Riley hadn't been in my thoughts much today. Maybe, concentrating on looking for cows, and freezing, didn't leave room for much of anything else.

I thought of the horrible dream several nights ago when Riley and Bruce were laughing at me. Strangely that same night, the dream that followed of the young girls singing "You Are My Sunshine" had a soothing effect on me. I even knew the words to that song. It was one we sang on the way home when we were celebrating a win. I'd seen and heard them several times in my dreams and, at first, it frightened me, thinking it was the twins. That was ridiculous. I was only a few months old when they died. My thoughts turned to the incident involving Feather.

When she had screamed it didn't take but a second to know she must be in trouble. Arriving on the scene, I don't remember much of what happened until Gavin was calling my name and pulling me up. My reaction, thinking back, surprised me. Why would I take up for her? She was a know-it-all pain in the butt. I must've felt sorry for her. Suddenly, I wondered what Riley was doing. Probably with Bruce or maybe she was home by now. Did she ever think about me? "No, stupid. Why would she think about you?" I mumbled.

DRYING OFF, I studied myself in the mirror. Was this the same person that stood here six months ago? It couldn't be. The fat stomach was gone, replaced by a smaller and firmer waist. The scales read 174 last week in the field house. I'd bench pressed 275 that day, thirty pounds more than anyone else. I hardly noticed the resistance offered by the man I threw to the ground and started punching. What would I have looked like if not for coming to live with my grandparents and being introduced to the post hole diggers and football?

Would my dad treat me differently now? Maybe even say something nice to me. He would be here tomorrow and I'd find out. A knock interrupted my thinking.

"Eric, supper's ready," announced Dawn.

I was warm and hungry. I put on some warmups and socks before heading to the kitchen.

I WOKE up early the next morning, wondering what the weather was going to be like today. Maybe it would be warmer. I'd slept good, after eating two bowls of chili with beans and cornbread last night. I got out of bed, determined that Dawn wouldn't have to come to my room. I was going to miss school again today. It would be better riding all day in whatever weather we had, than seeing Riley and Bruce together at school.

I dressed for the cold, not taking any chances, putting on two pairs of socks, a heavy flannel shirt, and getting a sweatshirt with a hood to take along with my heavy coat and gloves. I'd wear the hat that Feather had given me, with a heavy scarf tied around it that covered my ears.

In the kitchen, Dawn was sitting at the table drinking coffee. "Eric, you're an early bird this morning. Get you a cup of coffee and sit down. We've got a big day. Gavin left me a note. He's gone to town, probably to find someone to replace me. I can hardly get around."

I'd just recently started drinking coffee. My taste buds were gradually adjusting, and in the cold weather it seemed to be the thing to do. I sat down at the table after filling a cup and added plenty of cream and sugar. "You're not going with us today?"

"Oh, me. I can barely get around, Eric. I don't think another day would be possible. Your dad should be here sometime today and take my place. I'm going with Gavin and maybe help him."

"What's the weather like today?"

"Worse, if possible. Something's been falling and it's still below freezing. We gathered less than 200 head yesterday. Hopefully, with the weather, they'll be in bunches, and we'll do better today."

I couldn't imagine it being worse than yesterday. "Gavin sure has changed. He's been much different toward me. What caused it?"

"I can't say for sure. Probably the two biggest reasons were you and Feather. I think having the challenge of caring for the heifers has helped also. It could have just been time for a change. You know, Eric, even a cactus, full of thorns, blooms."

"I'm just glad he's nicer to me. I wonder if my dad will treat me better?"

"I'm sure he will," she said. "Now, I've sat here long enough. Breakfast isn't going to fix itself. Today is pancakes and sausage. Would you knock on Feather's door, and tell her it's time to get up?"

Feeling good about being up before her, I went to her door and knocked . . . nothing. I knocked again, loud . . . nothing. I cracked open the door and could see she was still in bed. I went in, reached down and shook her. "Feather, get up."

She whispered, "What time is it?"

"After six. Time to get a move on."

"I'm so tired and warm. Would you bring me some coffee?" she mumbled.

Unbelievable. I wasn't her servant.

"Please?" she asked.

Well, since she said please. That was a first. I went to the kitchen and a few minutes later returned with coffee, laced with cream and sugar. "Here's your coffee."

"Just leave it on the night stand and thanks. Pops used to bring me coffee every morning."

It looked like I was replacing her pops, I thought, returning to the kitchen and finding Gavin was back with Luis. Surprised, I hadn't considered him as a possibility for helping.

"Morning, Eric."

"Luis, you going to miss school, too?"

"Yeah. If we even have it today. It's sleeting and the roads may get too bad. I don't care. Working is better than going to school, even in this weather."

Breakfast was on the table, and we were eating when Feather came in. She was already dressed for the cold with only her face visible. She must've had on at least three layers of clothing.

"What's the plan for today?" She sat down next to me.

Gavin stopped eating and put down his fork. "Yesterday, the heifers would come to the horn but wouldn't follow me very far. Today, maybe y'all can get behind them, and we can get them to the trap. I do know this. Whatever we end up with today, we have to move into the pasture closer to the house. We have to get as many as possible out of this pasture and away from the Garbancilla weeds. We've already found sixteen dead heifers, and we can't afford to lose any more. I'm sorry for having you to get out in this terrible weather, but we have no choice."

IF YESTERDAY WAS BAD, today was worse. It started sleeting at midmorning, and the cold, with the wet, made it almost unbearable. We did have more success, and by the end of the day, we'd penned about 200 more cows and heifers in the trap behind the holding pens. Still that was only half of the cattle we needed to move.

We penned the last group of cows an hour before dark and gathered at Gavin's truck. "We did better than I expected. We'll move these in the morning before we do anything else. By my calculations we have well over half of the heifers. I don't mind leaving the older cows here. They won't eat the Garbancilla. You did good today. Let's go to the house, get warm, and have a hot meal."

Feather had taken her truck and trailer, however, she wasn't able to drive. I could hear her teeth chattering on the drive to the house. She rode in the middle and Luis by the window. Reaching the house, Luis left immediately for home leaving us to take care of the horses.

"Eric, I'm sorry. I can't help you. My arms and legs just won't work. I've never been this cold in my life."

"No problem. You stay in the truck, and I'll put the horses in the stall and feed."

"Thank you."

After feeding the horses, I looked in on Arnold and for once, he hadn't turned his water trough over. He was actually under his shed. Before leaving, I gave him a belly scratching just to show my appreciation before returning to the truck.

At the house I heard my dad before I saw him. "Just how many did I lose?"

"We've found sixteen dead heifers," Gavin answered.

"Sixteen! That's unbelievable! Why'd you put them in the pasture with the poison weeds?"

"Cameron, we didn't know Garbancilla was growing there."

Dawn defended Gavin. "We're doing the best we can."

"I can never pay off the loan with that kind of losses."

I guess my dad realized how unappreciative he sounded because he calmed down and asked what the plan was. Gavin explained what we were doing.

"I'm sorry. It's just that I could be ruined by this situation. I know it's my fault but surely we can do something to prevent me from financial ruin."

During this exchange, my dad didn't even acknowledge my presence. *Nothing has changed.*

We ate the enchiladas and beans in silence before going to our rooms. My dad was sleeping in my room in one of the twin beds. We exchanged few words before retiring for the night.

.   .   .

THE WEATHER IMPROVED and for the next three days we gathered and
moved the heifers and cows. Friday evening by Gavin's count, we had
462 heifers moved to a twelve section pasture that ran right up to the
house. It was appropriately named the House Pasture. My dad left for
home, never once expressing interest in me or what was going on in
my life. Confused and angry, I kept telling myself it was not a big deal.
Repeating it so many times—I almost believed it.

53

LUTA

I t was Monday, January 17, Eric had left for school, and Feather had stayed inside to help me with the breakfast dishes. Gavin had gone to town to get a load of range cubes so we were alone.

"I have an idea, Feather. We worked hard all last week in freezing weather. Today is nice and sunny. Let's make a trip to Alpine and buy you a new Sunday dress. We'll have dinner and just enjoy the afternoon. We can go by your house and check on everything. You probably need to pick up some personal items anyway. I'll leave Gavin a note. Maybe we'll meet him coming home on the way in. How's that sound?"

"Great. I do need to go by my house."

"It's settled then."

A half hour later we were on the way to town when Feather asked, "Why does Eric's dad treat him the way he does?"

"I'm having trouble with it, also, Feather. I thought when he came this time, it would be different. Eric wants his approval so badly. Cameron was in a panic the whole time he was here over losing the heifers. He couldn't seem to get it off his mind."

"He doesn't even seem to view Eric as his son," she replied. "Has it always been that way?"

"More or less. To my knowledge, he's never spent time with him or paid much attention to him except when Eric got into trouble."

I wanted to move on to something more positive. "Feather is a beautiful name. I've never heard it before."

"They named me that because I was so small and light as a feather. I'm still small. My classmates started calling me Mouse when I was in grade school and it stuck. When I went to live with Pops it was wonderful to leave that name behind. Do you think I look like a mouse?"

"Of course not! You're beautiful."

"Well, I've sure not generated much interest from the boys, except that creep who tried to force himself on me the other day."

"Gavin told me about that. He was surprised at Eric's reaction and impressed. Both of us were glad Eric took up for you."

"You know, it's strange. Eric and I don't even get along very well. He thinks I'm a know-it-all. We argue almost every time we work together. He actually likes that pig more than me," she added, "maybe more than anything."

"I know. It worries me that the stock show is coming up soon and his pig will be leaving us."

WE FOUND her a cute spring dress that the store had just recently received. We were fortunate they had the dress in the smallest lady's size on the market. Coming out of the dressing room, she resembled a life-size doll.

We had lunch at a nice restaurant before going by her house. We both ordered the special, which consisted of chopped steak with brown gravy, greens, and mashed potatoes. I tried not to think about my girls when looking at Feather, but it was impossible. She reminded me of Stacy, the way she walked and especially the way she rode. I kept telling myself that the twins would be in their early thirties, now.

While we were eating, I had the urge, for the first time in my memory to talk about my little girls to someone. "Feather you remind me so much of one of my girls. She loved horses and the outdoors. I try not to compare the two of you, but it's impossible."

"Thank you, Luta. I consider that a compliment. Tell me about them when they were growing up. I imagine you have some wonderful memories."

"Yes. They were beautiful little girls and talented. Beginning at about age four they would sing "Jesus Loves Me." Everyone who came to see us had them sing. They could harmonize even at that age. They began singing in church by the time they started to school. It was unbelievable. The pastor would beg them to sing specials. He said if people knew they were going to sing, his attendance would increase. I miss them so much."

"Eric told me what happened. I can't imagine you and Gavin having to go through something so horrible."

"Sometimes, as I look back it just seems like a nightmare. Gavin and I seldom talk about it. Maybe if we reminisced more about the happy times when we had them it would help. I don't know. The manner in which they were taken from us made us want to wipe out all memories of the past. You know—they never caught *him*. Oh, there were rumors and stories about serial killers that confessed but none related to our girls. I've often wondered how it would affect us if *he* were caught. I keep praying that *he* will so another child will not be taken from their parents. I tried praying to be able to forgive *him* but it was useless and I stopped. The mystery is how he even got close to the girls. We had warned them since they were small never to have anything do with strangers."

"Did they continue singing when they got older?" Feather asked, knowing I was about to break down talking about *him*.

"Oh, yes. They even started singing some country songs by the time they were seven or eight. Their favorite was an old time Jimmy Davis number, "You are my Sunshine."

WE DROVE to Feather's house after leaving the restaurant. Driving up, there was an older car parked in front. I noticed her stiffen as a man came out of the house.

"That's my dad."

She made no move to get out. He came to the car and opened the door. "There's my little girl. Get out here and give me a hug. It's been a long time."

She sat still not moving toward him. I reached over and nudged her toward the door. Moving slowing, she got out, with him doing most of the hugging. She stepped back from the embrace, pointing to me. "This is Luta Sager. The lady I work for. This is my dad, Richard Jackson."

"Glad to make your acquaintance, Mrs. Sager. Thank you for looking after my little girl."

"Actually, she's been a God-send for us. We couldn't have done without her."

He turned back to Feather. "Your mother will be glad to see you. She hasn't been feeling well and is asleep now. We hadn't heard about Lefty passing. We came by to see you. When no one was home we talked to a neighbor who told us the news. Your mother was upset of course to hear about her dad."

I couldn't believe this. Poor Feather. She just stood there as if waiting for the next lie. His next statement brought her out of the trance. "You can stay here with us. We plan on being around for awhile. It'll be nice to spend some time together."

"No. I live at the ranch with Mr. and Mrs. Sager, now. I work full-time for them. I came by to get some more clothes and personal items. I tried to get in touch with you when Pops passed."

"We've moved since last talking to you. We'll need to stay around until we take care of Lefty's estate. I haven't talked to your mother about what she wants to do with the house. She'll probably want to sell it as soon as possible since you're not living here. It's not good for the house to remain vacant."

I held my breath, wondering what Feather's response would be. She'd told me that her pops had left the house and all his belongings to her. She turned and looked at me, as if for support, before addressing her dad. "Pops left everything to me."

"What?"

"I said, Pops left all his belongings to me, including the house."

He looked surprised. "Did he have a will?"

"Yes. He had a lawyer draw up a will. The original is in his lock box at the bank. I have a copy."

"I see. That's a surprise. I'd have thought his only daughter would inherit his estate."

"Well, she didn't. Now, I'll get some of my things from the house and be on my way." After that she didn't move but was looking at me.

That was my cue she wanted me to accompany her into the house, which I did. Her dad followed along behind us. I stayed right with her as she put together some clothes and other items which required only one trip to the car. We didn't see her mother, and her dad remained silent the entire time. As we drove away, he watched us leave, not offering any type of farewell.

"When's the last time you spoke with your mom or dad?" I asked, on the drive to the ranch.

"It's been almost a year. Growing up, my parents weren't around much and were drunk or high when they were. They did pay attention to me, especially when I was younger. The older I became the more they were gone. An elderly neighbor who was a widow took care of me when my parents weren't able, which was most of the time. I don't know what would've become of me if not for her. She passed two years ago."

I noticed she was wiping away tears. "What're you going to do with the house?"

"Nothing right now. Maybe later. I don't know. I can't see myself living there. I need to be thinking of my future. I love horses and the work on the ranch, however, there has to be more for me, down the road. I'm not interested in going to college so that's out. I appreciate you and Gavin giving me a place to live and the job on the ranch. More important, you have become the family I never had."

Now, I couldn't stop the tears. How could any parents not love this precious little girl? "You'll always have a home with us, Feather. I hope you stay at least a year or two on the ranch. You're a big reason for the change in Gavin and have been worth any two hands we could've hired."

Gavin was home when we arrived and I had Feather try on her new dress for him. His face lit up when she walked into the room. "If that's not something beautiful . . . my, my, my. You look, more like a princess than a cowgirl."

She beamed. "Thank you, it's a beautiful dress and it just fits. I'm going to wear it to church Sunday, even though spring isn't here."

She returned to her room to change, leaving us alone. I told Gavin about her parents and the conversation with her dad concerning Lefty's estate. His response was not surprising.

"I'm calling the bank and telling them not to allow either of her parents access to the lock box containing the will. I wouldn't put nothing past them. We also need to probate the will has soon as possible. I'll get in touch with a lawyer and set up an appointment. We're not going to let them near that will.

"I hope she stays with us for a while, at least. I do have an idea about a future for her, and when the time is right, I'll tell her." He smiled. "Now, it's just going to be my secret."

THAT AFTERNOON, while Gavin and Feather were gone, I received a call from Landon Elmore. He was the local pharmacist who was on the school board. He asked if he could have a few minutes of my time this evening to visit. After ending the call, I remained puzzled the remainder of the day about why he wanted to talk with me.

When Gavin came in, I explained the call and he too was at a loss as to the reason for the meeting. "Maybe it's something about Eric?"

"I don't think so. If that was the case, the principal would be coming to see us."

At six o'clock, the time set for the meeting, he arrived with his wife. We invited them in and after moving to the den, he got right to the point. "Luta, our school is in a bad situation. Slade is practically running it. He has three board members that will vote with him on any issue. The other three of us don't have a chance because Slade will always be the decisive vote and get his way. Mr. Cleburne is useless. He will not take a side on anything and just sits there.

"I thought losing his daughter might change Slade, but he actually seems worse now about getting his way. Our new principal's contract comes up next month, and Slade is determined not to renew it. Mr. Mendenhall is the best thing that's happened to our school since I've been on the board."

"What's this got to do with me even though I do agree with you about Mr. Mendenhall?" I was still confused about the reason for the visit.

"That's easy. Slade is up for re-election this year, and we want you to run for his place. Now don't say no until I explain. The three of us have talked it over, and we believe that you're the best candidate for the job. You're well liked and respected in the community. Your family has been here over a hundred years and that counts, as you know. Most important, everyone knows that you have common sense and will make decisions based on what's best for the school. Also, you have a vested interest now that your grandson is attending school here."

Too shocked to reply, I sat in silence. Gavin spoke up for me. "I agree with you, Landon. Luta would be an excellent board member."

"We think so. You can beat Slade, Luta. He believes everyone agrees with what he's doing. No one in the community he talks to will challenge his opinion, he's so aggressive. I've never known a better example of a bully than Slade Loughton."

Of all things, I never expected this. Me—running for the school board? This was too much to digest. "I need some time to think about it. When is the filing deadline?"

"You have over a month. We've agreed that it would be better not to let it out in the community that you have considered challenging Slade. One reason is Slade, himself. We don't know how he'll react. The other reason is that people in the community would put additional pressure on you to accept. Most of the community feels the same way we do."

"I'll consider it but will not make any promises. I can't see myself as a member of the school board."

54

ERIC

The County Stock Show was approaching, and I was spending a lot of time with Arnold. I was walking him every day and brushing him which suited him fine. He weighed 221the last time he stepped on the scales that Mr. Puckett brought to the ranch. That was perfect for him to be classified as a Heavy Weight Cross. Mr. Puckett said he looked fit and ready for the show ring.

Vocational Agriculture had become my favorite class, which was strange since I had lived in the city my entire life before coming to the ranch. I'd learned to use a cutting torch and weld among other skills needed for living here. I was anxious to demonstrate my skills to Gavin, who not only was decent, but actually seemed to like me. The dog, Jenny, that had been given to Gavin when leaving the hospital, didn't replace Max. In fact, he was becoming more of Dawn's dog and followed her everywhere.

The last several weeks it continued to be difficult seeing Bruce and Riley together. I would lay awake at night, hoping and even praying that our relationship would resume. Admittedly, I did think of her less often as time passed but getting over her totally seemed impossible. Working out for an hour each day after school was one way I dealt with the grief. The extra work paid off as I had benched pressed 300 at school this week, sixty pounds better than anyone else.

Weekends, Feather and I continued to ride the Mountain Pasture, looking for heifers we had missed earlier. With some success, we penned and moved an additional thirty-five to the pasture behind the house. I was actually enjoying riding and was at ease in the saddle. Feather continued with the encouragement and compliments. We were getting along better and had fewer arguments.

SATURDAY, February 5, the day of our stock show, was cold but with sunshine. Gavin helped me load Arnold in the stock trailer and we were at the show barn early. I put him in a pen filled with straw, watered and fed him. I was excited about competing and felt good about his chances. For the most part, lambs, steers, and pigs made up the animals involved, however, there were a few students that showed chickens.

I stayed at the pen with Arnold but Gavin went back home. The swine show wasn't scheduled to start until eleven o'clock, and he assured me he'd be back in time. Mr. Puckett came by, and again commented on how good Arnold looked. Feather had assured me that she would be here, also. Now, all we had to do was wait.

Time dragged by and it seemed like eleven o'clock would never get here. The schedule called for the Duroc Class to go first, followed by the Hampshire, York, and then the Cross. I watched the other classes, wanting to get an idea about what I should do in the ring with Arnold. It was strange the way each of the boys and sometimes girls, herded their pig around the ring, guiding him with a stick, looking at the judge. The judge, with a frown, studied each of the pigs, indicating how difficult his decision would be. Finally, he would say a few positive things about each, as well as point out flaws. Eventually, he would announce a winner to the applause of the crowd.

When it came time for the Cross Bred Class, I opened Arnold's gate and moved him in the direction of the show pen. All the pigs ahead of him walked into the pen—not Arnold. When he reached the gate, he ran in and made a circle around the pen with me chasing him. Laughter erupted from the audience, and I was embarrassed, wanting to go hide somewhere. I finally was able to get him contained in a corner of the pen. From there he stopped running but continued to move around the pen, bumping into the other ten pigs. The crowd continued to laugh, and I just wanted it to be over.

The judge motioned several of the pigs out of the ring, and I kept hoping he would signal me to remove Arnold. Eventually there were only three of us left, but Arnold still hadn't run out of energy. I was worn out from chasing him.

Taking the microphone, the judge announced. "We have three outstanding Crosses in the ring. They would show good anywhere. It's a tough decision but the fresh pig has them beat." He pointed at Arnold.

I couldn't believe it! We'd won. Suddenly, I wasn't tired anymore, as the applause was like music. Evidently, Arnold liked the applause, also, because it took me several minutes to get him out of the show ring headed back to his pen. Gavin, Dawn, and Feather were waiting on us.

"Congratulations, Eric, I'm so proud of you." Dawn hugged me.

"That pig is something else!" Gavin exclaimed, presenting his hand.

"You did good," Feather said, reaching down and scratching Arnold's back.

Mr. Puckett walked up, congratulating me. "Good job, Eric. Now you need to get ready for the championship drive. The top two pigs in each class will compete for the grand and reserve champion. Maybe, after being in the show ring, your pig will settle down."

Arnold continued to move around too fast during the championship drive but not quite as bad. The judge took forever to make a decision but finally he pointed out Arnold as the Reserve Champion and the York as the Grand Champion. More celebrating occurred when I took him back to his pen.

"Eric, he should sell really good at the auction tonight, being the Reserve Champion." Gavin announced.

"That's unbelievable to do so well your first year," Dawn said.

"We have time to eat before the sale starts. All this excitement gives me an appetite. We'll eat in town," Gavin said, "and I'm buying."

I couldn't believe it. Arnold was Reserve Champion. I stayed behind when everyone left to put out extra feed and scratched his back until he lay down, grunting his approval. "You did good, Arnold. We showed them, didn't we? I'm proud of you."

I WAS nervous waiting to take Arnold into the sales ring. It seemed forever, but my time finally came. True to form, he scampered around the ring, never standing still like the other pigs. The auctioneer started the bidding at $400 which went to $450 and $500 and finally to $875. I was amazed! Eight hundred and seventy-five dollars! I was rich! I heard him call out the First National Bank as the buyer. I was ecstatic as we went back to his pen. That was a lot of money. What would I do with it? No one was around so I talked to Arnold. "You did good again. You made me all this money." I started scratching his back and he lay down. Seeing Feather coming, I stopped and met her.

"He sold really good, Eric. That's a lot of money for a pig."

"He's a special pig, though. I bet he's the smartest pig in the world. I hate to give him up but the bank bought him. He'll have a good home."

Feather remained silent as I told Arnold goodbye. He grunted and rubbed against my leg as if he understood me. She was riding home with me instead of Gavin and Dawn.

We were halfway to the ranch before she spoke. "Eric, don't you understand what will happen to your pig?"

"Sure. The bank bought him. I guess they have a place to keep him or maybe turn him out."

"I'm sorry but that's not where he's going. Somebody should've explained it to you before now. The bank paid that money to you in support of the FFA program. They, in turn will sell him to a packing plant for market price just as all the other buyers will do."

"Maybe all the other pigs but not Arnold. He's too smart. Arnold is not an ordinary pig." I began to feel concern.

"No, Eric. He will be sold along with all the other animals. I'm sorry, but that's the way it is."

"You mean he . . ." I couldn't finish.

"Yes."

"No. I don't want that to happen! I'll give them back their money!"

"Listen to me, Eric. I'm sorry. I should've told you instead of assuming that someone else would. There's nothing you can do."

I couldn't believe this! They were going to kill Arnold. I wasn't going to let that happen. I would give them their money back and get my pig and take him home. I stopped in the middle of the road and turned around. I had the check in my pocket and could give it to someone in exchange for Arnold.

"What're you doing, Eric?"

"I'm going back and get my pig. They're not going to kill him."

"Eric, please be reasonable. That's just the way it is. He's only another pig."

"No! He's not just another pig. I love him and he loves me. I have to take care of him."

Within fifteen minutes we were back at the show barn. I jumped out of my truck and hurried to the loading dock. The animals were being pushed into trucks and I approached a man who appeared to be supervising. "There's a pig being loaded that I want back. I have money to give you for his release."

"What do you mean? These animals are heading to the packing plant. I can't just give one back to someone." He looked at me like I was crazy.

"I have money! Eight hundred and seventy-five dollars. It's yours if you give me my pig back."

"Son, you must be out of your mind. This truck is leaving, heading for Odessa. Now, go away and leave me alone."

Just at that moment, I saw Arnold being driven up the ramp into the truck. I begged the man, "Please . . . mister, give me my pig back."

He ignored me—I sat there crying—as the truck pulled away.

55

FRANK

I enjoyed the stock show and was surprised at the interest it created in the community. From what people told me, the sale was good, and most of the students came out at least even on their project. I was especially pleased for Eric's pig being named the Reserve Champion. He'd come a long way since I first met him.

Julie went to the show and sale with me. Aubrey was there also, but she kept her distance from us. She'd suffered greatly at the hands of the other junior high girls which might have had a positive benefit. She talked less about boys and actually had been avoiding them. Of course, Riley was with Bruce who was showing a steer.

Julie had told me about her conversation concerning Bruce. "I didn't get much out of her. She kept saying that Bruce needed her. When I asked her how serious the relationship was, she clammed up, which isn't like her. She actually became testy with me when I mentioned the goodbye kiss at school. She said something to the effect that we shouldn't be spying on her. Maybe this is a wake-up call for us. We always assumed Riley would make good decisions and took it for granted. Now, Bruce comes along."

I'd avoided talking with Julie about the threats made by Loughton. My contract would be coming up at the board meeting next week. I didn't know what to expect other than Loughton opposing the renewal. I'd only been given a one-year contract which, at the time, didn't concern me. Of course, I had no idea that a Slade Loughton would be on the board, running the school. I'd get no support from Cleburne. I'd hoped to one day be a superintendent and was learning, first hand, what constituted poor leadership. You should learn by observing good leadership skills but in my case, the opposite was true.

If not for Loughton, my year would be going fine. The teachers for the most part had accepted my philosophy and responded in a positive manner. I was most proud of Mr. Kelly, my new hire. He had already selected a show for the One-Act Play Contest, and I'd attended several rehearsals. He was brilliant and his students adored him. Of course, you can't fool kids, and they saw immediately he was a special teacher, and they did everything possible to please him. No matter how bad a day I experienced, going to his rehearsals lifted my spirits.

THE BOARD MEETING WAS TUESDAY, which was the first day of February. I tried not to think about it but found myself wondering, throughout the day, what would happen. Surely they'd give me more than one year. I kept expecting the superintendent to call and ask for my presence at the meeting. It didn't happen.

I stayed up late, waiting for word from Cleburne but none came. I finally went to bed after midnight, spending a sleepless night, tossing and turning.

I HADN'T BEEN in my office but a few minutes the next morning when Mrs. Kraal informed me that Cleburne had called and wanted to see me. Five minutes later, I was sitting in his office observing the worried look on his face.

"Frank, it didn't go well last night. I'd warned you that the ranchers wield a great amount of power in this community. Slade Loughton was determined your contract not be renewed. There was quite a discussion which became heated at times. Three other board members defended you and questioned Slade's motives, which was unusual in itself. The other three members were going along with him, regardless. Of course, he got his way with a 4-3 vote. I'm sorry Frank. There was nothing I could do. Of course, I'll give you a good recommendation."

I sat there stunned but not surprised. I was going to have to move my family again because of one person. I hadn't carried out his demands and this was the result. Rather than say something I would be sorry for later, I rose and left. Cleburne said he was sorry again as I walked out of the room.

I didn't go back to my office, instead going to my truck and driving out of town. I took the highway south and drove for half-an-hour wondering how Julie and the girls would respond. The scenery was beautiful this morning, reminding me that I had grown to like this country and most of the people. The school was improving under my leadership, and now a new principal would come in and shake things up. Students didn't respond well to changes, especially in a short period of time.

I'd need to begin looking for another job. I tried to focus on the positive. Being early in the year, it would give me at least three, maybe four months to find something. We'd been able to sell our house in Fort Worth which would enable us to buy a house wherever we went. My thoughts kept returning to Julie, and I felt an urgency to let her know the bad news.

I was at the bank within the hour and seeing me come in, she knew something was wrong, meeting me in the lobby. "What is it, Frank?"

"Could you get off a few minutes to talk?"

"Sure. It's slow this morning. No one is in the lounge. We can talk there."

It was my first time in the lounge and it was nice, as probably all banks were. I sat down, and she brought me a cup of coffee. "It must be bad. You look like you just lost your last friend."

I told her what happened at the board meeting and my visit to Cleburne's office. "I'm sorry, Julie."

"Frank! Don't say that. You did nothing wrong. That man is terrible. Everything will work out. It always does. We'll find a place where everyone appreciates your professionalism and leadership."

I should've expected this response from her. She never faltered in her support of me. "I hate to think of moving you and the girls again."

"Look at the positive, Frank. We can buy a larger house wherever we move to. We're worried about Riley and her relationship with Bruce. Distance between them will be good. Aubrey can get a new start and not be bullied by girls in her class. We have to look at this as an opportunity to improve our current situation and not sit around and be depressed."

"You are amazing. How do you stay calm when I just lost my job?"

"Easy. I know a good man when I see one. This will be a great day for some school in Texas even though they don't realize it now. It's time for me to get back to work. Remember, stay positive."

We hugged and I left, feeling better, but still guilty over letting my family down.

WHEN I WALKED into the building, the smell of smoke hit me. I knew, seeing Mrs. Kraal smiling that the building wasn't on fire. She must not have heard the news yet.

"Good morning, Mr. Mendenhall. You had visitors this morning. If you'll go into your office, I'll explain what they were doing here."

She followed me in, along with the smoke and closed the door, continuing to smile. "The word's already out about the board meeting last night. My phone's been ringing constantly this morning with irate parents. But that's not all the news. Luta Sager, came in this morning, accompanied by Gavin and his cigar. She filed for the school board, running against, you-know-who. I can't tell you how pleased this makes me."

"That's good news, but I can't wait around until the school board election before looking for another job."

"I don't believe that will be necessary. Being new to this community, you are not aware of the people. If I was asked to name the most respected person in the community it would be Luta Sager, hands down. She's loved and revered by everyone, except maybe Slade Loughton, who is going to be rabid when he finds out. I expect this to happen when the word gets out; at least one and maybe more of the board members that went along with Loughton will change their vote. They will know what's going to happen. Luta could run for mayor and be elected. She might even be elected to the state legislature. I admit that Gavin frightens me and probably most everyone else. Loughton better tread lightly and be careful about saying anything about Luta.

"I'm sorry for the action the board took last night, however, I can't stop smiling, thinking what's going to happen. Loughton and his cronies grossly underestimated the respect that you already have in this community. Now, it's going to come back and bite them in the rear. What's about to happen needed to occur years ago."

"I hope you're right, Mrs. Kraal."

"If I was a betting woman, I'd wager everything it will play out this way."

"I appreciate your confidence. It does cause me to feel better."

She returned to the outer office, closing the door behind her. I was anxious to tell Julie about the latest happenings. It was still two hours until lunch, but I could call her and ask that she come home on her break.

I DID everything possible to conduct business as usual for the remainder of the week but discovered it wasn't going to happen. Parents kept coming to the office interrupting me to offer their support. The students were circulating a petition demanding that I be reinstated. When they submitted it to Mrs. Kraal on Friday, there were 146 signatures.

She brought it into my office and plopped it on the desk. "This has got to be a first. A popular high school principal. We have 151 students in high school but five were absent today. Notice, the signature down toward the bottom on the first page."

Scanning down the page there it was . . . Devon Roberts.

56

ERIC

"Did you not have any idea about what would happen to your pig?" Feather asked me on the drive home.

"No. I hadn't thought about it. If I had he'd never been put in the sale."

"Just what would you have done with him?"

"Kept him at the ranch and took care of him." I answered without hesitation.

"That's not realistic, Eric. Just consider what Gavin would think of that."

I tried but couldn't stop the tears, thinking about what was going to happen to Arnold. I was ashamed and embarrassed not to be able to control my emotions.

"Do you want me to drive?" she asked.

I didn't answer, but pulled off to the side of the road, got out and went around to the passenger door. She took my place behind the wheel, adjusted the seat, and pulled back onto the road.

She stared ahead but started talking. "I'm going to tell you something that you're not going to like, but it needs to be said. You've been anything but sympathetic to others experiencing grief. For instance, you didn't understand Gavin's sorrow over losing his beloved dog. You didn't express any sympathy toward Bruce when his sister was killed. Instead you were occupied with Riley and y'all's relationship. When Pops passed you did try to comfort me and I appreciated that, however, I didn't feel like you were sincere nor able to understand my suffering. Now, you're the one hurting. Remember what I told you. You don't experience real grief until you lose something that you love and loves you back. Hopefully, from now on you'll be more understanding of others who are mourning. Now, I've said it and hopefully you'll not be angry at me."

I didn't respond. That's what I despised the most about her—she was always right.

SEVERAL EVENTS RECEIVED the most attention the next three months. Dawn was running for the school board which created excitement. Mr. Mendenhall had been fired by the school board at the February meeting then rehired at the March meeting. Everybody was saying it was because of Dawn and that she would trounce Bruce's dad in the election which was coming up next week.

I'd helped Feather make posters encouraging people to vote for Dawn. We placed them in people's yards after asking permission, which was always granted. Of course, Feather provided me with detailed instructions on my part in making the posters. If I messed up, we did it again.

Gavin continued to be civil and even was beginning to make some jokes. Most of them were corny, but we laughed anyway. It was amazing how much he'd changed, but I kept expecting a return to his old ways.

My dad had come out several times, concerned about the number of heifers that had died from the poison weed. Feather and I continued to find more strays and to date had accounted for 456, total. That still left 44 that were either missing or dead. Gavin wasn't concerned about his own cows, saying that being raised in the area they wouldn't eat the weed.

I'd gradually come to accept the fact that Riley was history, and time spent thinking of her was wasted. Everywhere you saw Bruce, you saw Riley. I tried to avoid them as much as possible, which was difficult, since we had several classes together. They were friendly, in fact too much so. It would've suited me fine if they ignored me.

I continued to work out at school and at home. My weight had stabilized at 175, and I was now wearing a size 32 pant. Working out, enabled me to eat all I wanted without gaining.

The Junior-Senior Prom was coming up soon, but I'd decided not to attend. Most everyone would have a date and besides, I couldn't dance. That meant standing in a corner watching everyone have fun. I made the mistake of mentioning it to Know-It-All, who of course started right in on me.

She flapped her arms, squawking, "Chicken."

"Why are you so mean to me?" I asked.

"Eric, here you go feeling sorry for yourself. You've turned into quite a hunk. Lots of girls would like to go with you to the prom, but you'd rather mope around and think 'poor pitiful me.' "

"I can't dance. What would I do while everyone one else was dancing?"

"People don't dance all the time. They stand around and visit. You wouldn't be noticed because you didn't dance."

"Nope. I can't dance. No reason to go and feel like a fool."

She just stared at me. I hated that look. "Eric—Eric—Eric. You poor thing. I'll teach you to dance. Some girl is going to miss out being escorted to the prom by a good-looking young man because he can't dance."

"And have you laugh at me? No way."

"Have I ever laughed at you?"

She had me there. She was a know-it-all but she hadn't made fun of me. "No, but I don't know the first thing about dancing."

"Just give it a try. We'll stop anytime you want to. I'll just teach you the two-step. It's easy and you'll be doing it in no time. What do you say?"

"You promise that we can quit any time?"

"Sure. No problem. Now, do you have someone in mind to ask to the prom?"

"Of course not. I didn't plan on going," I replied.

"Name some prospects."

"I've got to think about it. Give me some time. Don't be so pushy."

AFTER OUR EVENING MEAL, we moved the kitchen table and chairs against the wall to give us room for my lesson. We found a country music station on the radio, and my instructions began. We didn't get off to a very good start. Of course, I was clumsy, and she was bossy. I stepped on her toes several times and was on the verge of giving up when things began to improve. Gavin and Dawn came into the kitchen offering encouragement as they watched.

"Eric, you're doing much better than me when Luta taught me to dance. I gave up several times but she stayed after me. I couldn't follow the music and had two left feet. It took a week before we were doing anything resembling dancing."

"He's not exaggerating, Eric. It's a wonder he didn't cripple me for life. We eventually became pretty good, and went to many dances."

"You got to hold her closer. What's a girl to think if you dance at arm's length? This is country music. Slow music means . . . hold me close," Gavin demanded.

"I tried, but he keeps pulling away, like he's afraid of me," Feather said.

I couldn't take it anymore! "Y'all are making me nervous. I'm doing the best I can."

"Okay, we'll leave. You got a good teacher, Eric. She reminds me of Luta at that age. A little bossy but worth it."

Half an hour later, I pulled her closer and we did better to Crystal Gail singing "I'll Get Over You." It seemed like an appropriate song for us to end the night on. I have to admit; it was nice holding her close. She sorta melted into my arms, so small and fragile.

"You did okay, Eric. Tomorrow will be better. Now, you need to start thinking about who you're going to ask."

"It's still a couple of weeks until the prom. I have plenty of time."

Miss bossy continued. "No, that's not right. All the good ones will be taken."

"It's bedtime for me." I knew the only way to get away from her demands was to leave.

"Okay, but you start thinking of someone."

Once in my room, I relaxed, lying down on the bed staring at the fluffy stuff on top of the bed. Mercy, she was a pain in the butt. She must think she's my mother. No, my mother wouldn't have cared if I attended a dance or not. She was gone most of the time and when at home, ignored me. Ethan cried when she left. Not me. I didn't mind seeing her go. Good riddance. My most vivid memories are of lying in bed at night, hearing them scream at one another. After she left, I thought my dad would pay more attention to me, which didn't happen. Now, after being here less than a year, this seemed more like home. I was actually happy and was treated better than at any time in my memory. I had friends at school and was looking forward to my senior year and football.

I felt better about myself and had more confidence. Spending so much time horseback, I'd become a better than average rider. Even Gavin bragged on me. Feather had been trying to teach me to rope, but thus far it was hopeless. She kept telling me that I roped like a girl. Luta had an old milk can that we used for practice. It was frustrating watching Feather, who never missed and made it look easy.

For the next week we practiced every night after eating. I became more comfortable and actually looked forward to the lessons. It was less than a week until the prom, and I still hadn't asked anyone for a date. Feather was right. Most of the attractive girls already had a date. She continued to nag me every day to ask someone before everyone was taken.

With only three days left she really lit into me. "You've put it off and now it's too late. I've wasted my time teaching you to dance. I should've known you wouldn't ask anyone. You're still so hung up on

Riley who never gives you a thought."

I was stunned at her anger and didn't respond until she ran out of breath. "I'm sorry. You're right. Of course, you're always right. Don't you ever get tired of being right? Wouldn't you like to be wrong just once? I'll go to the dance by myself. There'll probably be some other boys without dates and we can hang out. I might even dance with someone else's date. I bet Luis would let me have a dance with his girl."

She didn't answer, stalking out of the kitchen to her room and slamming the door.

"Well, that's that," I mumbled.

I was totally confused when it came to Feather. Sometimes, she was nice, but mostly she just ordered me to do this or do that. In one sense she seemed older, but again, she was so small she could've been younger. Regardless, I was sure of one thing—I did want to please her.

The next morning was Thursday and only two days until the prom. I arrived at school early and went directly to the principal's office. Mr. Mendenhall wasn't in so I waited in the outer office, making small talk with Mrs. Kraal. I'd rehearsed my speech on the way to school but was still nervous. He came in a few minutes before the bell rang.

"Morning, Eric. What can I do for you?"

"Could I talk to you?"

"Sure. Come on into my office."

My hands were sweating when I sat down. "I need to ask you something. It's about the prom, Saturday night. Would it be possible for me to bring someone who isn't in school here? I mean, she graduated in January from Alpine. She stays with us at the ranch and works there."

"I see," he said.

"She's a nice girl. She doesn't smoke or drink or anything like that. She wouldn't cause any trouble."

"I see," he repeated. "Is she pretty, Eric?"

"Sorta. I hadn't really thought much about it." I wondered what that had to do with it.

"If you could go with anyone in the school to the dance would you still want to bring this young lady?"

"Yes. She taught me to dance. I wouldn't want to dance with anyone else."

He burst out laughing. "I'm sorry, Eric. I just had to have a little fun with you. Of course, you can bring this young lady to the prom. I look forward to meeting her."

57

LUTA

I knew there was nothing left to do. So, I decided to make the commitment to challenge Slade Loughton for his position when Mr. Mendenhall was fired. Mr. Mendenhall had helped Eric, and according to everyone I talked with was a good man plus being an excellent principal. Now the election was next week, and I couldn't help but be nervous about the outcome. People kept assuring me I would easily win. I still wasn't convinced.

Our home was a much happier place now than it had been since we had lost the twins. Both Gavin and I enjoyed Eric and Feather. We had almost become what you would call a make-shift family. Watching Feather teach Eric to dance caused Gavin to laugh like he used to do many years ago. Cameron continued to be the problem. He would show up every other weekend complaining about the lost heifers— always worried. I kept telling him, we were fortunate to find the number we did. He and Gavin didn't argue like they used to, but there still was no father-son closeness.

It would soon be time for the heifers to start calving, and we still hadn't hired additional help. I reminded Gavin but he kept putting me off. Overall, we had a mild winter and the heifers looked good. We'd already had some spring rains and the country is beautiful when the cactus blooms.

Jenny, Gavin's dog had become my dog. She followed me every-where. I didn't expect her to replace Max but thought she would at least take up with Gavin. We let her stay in the house at night and she slept on the floor on my side of the bed. The main problem was that she wouldn't mind anyone but me. I was the only one she would obey. She would stand and stare at them like she didn't understand.

ON MAY 2, Gavin and I left early to vote. I was nervous and didn't want to discuss the election so we talked about Eric and Feather.

"I'm confused about their relationship. It seems to be more of a brother-sister thing," I said.

Gavin laughed. "The way she orders him around it could be a mother-son relationship. She's even more bossy than you were at her age. Remember how angry I used to get when you told me what to do?"

"Was I that bad? It seemed to me, I was only making suggestions."

He laughed again. "Well, Luta, you made a lot of suggestions in those days."

"Back to Feather and Eric. Do you think that she'll stay here another year or so?" I asked.

"No, afraid not. I'd like that but we have to do what's best for her. She has no future here, and it would be selfish of us not to help her find a career. I have an idea about something that would suit her to a 'T.' "

"Okay. Enough of the suspense. Let's hear it."

"I'm not ready to share it with her. Not yet anyway."

"I'll keep your secret. Now you have my curiosity up."

"At Lefty's funeral, I met one of his longtime friends that Feather had mentioned. He was also concerned about Feather's future. It was Bob Matthews from Lincoln, New Mexico. He and a friend of his, Tom Warren, have several race horses they run at Sunland Park and Ruidoso. Knowing Feather's love of horses, I asked him if he might be able to use her as an exercise rider and maybe later a jockey. He was enthusiastic about my idea and told me to let him know when she could go to work. I know that he'll take care of her and can be trusted. I'd like to wait until the end of the summer to tell her. Of course, we need her on the ranch but the main reason is Eric. I prefer to wait until he starts school in the fall. He's going to miss her and after making such a change for the better I think that would be best for him."

It was impossible to hide my enthusiasm. "That's a wonderful idea. I hate to see her leave but she'll love it. She can come back to the ranch in between race meets."

"What makes it even better is the young man who will be helping her. Bob said that Jimmy Light, who trains for him is the best man with a horse he's ever known. Bob's grandson, Bo, also helps with the horses. It'll be a perfect environment for Feather and a dream job for her."

Thank you, Jesus. He's come full circle to thinking of others and not just himself. "Thank you, Gavin. You did great. Feather will be thrilled."

By this time, we were driving up to the court house where we'd vote. I asked Gavin if he had his voter registration card. "Of course not. They can look me up on the roll sheet for this precinct."

We voted. And were back home by eight o'clock. The rest of the day I tried to stay busy so as not to think about the election. It was one of the longest days I remember, but at seven that evening the polls closed. It would take a few hours to count the votes then we'd know the results.

Gavin smiled. "What if you lose?"

"I'll just lose. I wouldn't be surprised."

"You wanta make a wager?" He had a gleam in his eye.

"You know I don't gamble."

He was trying to keep a serious look but wasn't being successful. "What about me doing the dishes for a month if you lose and you cooking me an apple pie if you win?"

"Okay. I'll make this one exception."

"With ice cream to go with the pie?" he asked.

"Don't push it. One dip and that's all."

He smacked his lips. "I can taste it already."

The phone rang at 9:05. Gavin picked up. "Yes. That's the final results? I appreciate you calling." He turned to me with a frown. "Well, it looks like I don't get a piece of apple pie with one dip of ice cream."

I tried not to sound disappointed. "See, I told you so."

Then bending over double with laughter, he finally got it out. "I get the whole pie plus a gallon of ice cream. Luta Sager, 236 votes; Slade Loughton, 38 votes."

THE NEXT WEEK, at a special board meeting that Slade Loughton didn't attend, I was sworn in as a new member. Mr. Cleburne couldn't have been nicer, going out of his way to say how pleased he was for me to be on the board.

There were several other items on the board agenda to be approved. The first was the schedule for summer maintenance which was to begin shortly. "I need to know what rooms should be painted this year and if we should redo the gym floor."

An awkward silence followed Mr. Cleburne's statement, forcing him to continue. "We generally make a schedule at this time of year. I need to know what you think needs to be done this summer."

Landon Elmore, who had asked me to run for the board spoke. "Mr. Cleburne, you know more about what needs to be done than we do. We're not around the school enough to make those kinds of decisions. I suggest that you make out a summer maintenance program and then throughout the summer you can report to us on the progress being made."

Mr. Cleburne's look reminded me of a child being caught stealing from the cookie jar. "I-I don't know about that. T-he board has always come up with a plan. It's worked well in the past. I'm not s-sure this would work."

The frustration was evident in Elmore's reply. "No, Mr. Cleburne, the board has not always told you what to do. That would be Slade Loughton, who is no longer on the board. Your salary if I remember correctly is a little under $40,000 a year. I'm only one board member, but in my opinion, it's time you start earning that pay."

More awkward silence followed and then he continued. "Once again, it's just me talking, but I see this as a different school board beginning tonight. We've all sat by and watched Slade virtually run this school. I'm not blaming him. We let it happen. He just exploited our weakness with his strength. Now, I may be out of line, since I haven't talked to any of the other board members about this. Someone else, please speak up if this is the case."

Another member responded to his statement. "I make a motion that Mr. Cleburne develop a summer maintenance schedule and report progress to us at the June, July, and August board meetings."

"Second the motion," added another member.

"All in favor," announced Landon, and seven hands went up.

ERIC ARRIVED at home on Thursday, May 12, in a good mood. I could always tell how his day went, when he walked in the door.

"Hi, Dawn. Where's Feather?"

"She's gone with Gavin to pick up a load of range cubes. You should've met them on the way home."

"Must have missed them. When will they get back?"

"It shouldn't be long. They've been gone about an hour. Do you have something important to tell her—like you have a date to the prom? That would probably stop an argument tonight."

"Nope. Nothing like that. I'm going to my weight room and work out. When she gets back will you tell her where I am?"

"Sure." I wondered what was going on that was so important that he see Feather.

He left and I went back to work cleaning the stove, still confused about Eric's behavior. A short while later, Gavin and Feather arrived home. I told Feather what Eric had said.

"What's the deal? He must've gotten a date for the prom and wants to tell me."

"No. I asked him that."

"Well, I'm not interested in hearing what he has to say." She headed toward her room.

"What's for supper?" Gavin asked.

"Salad. After you ate that apple pie last week we're back on our diet."

"Ah, Luta. I can't survive on rabbit food."

"I'm kidding, a little anyway. We're having baked chicken and vegetables with jello for dessert." I wasn't exaggerating. He had eaten most of the apple pie last week.

"That's a little better. Of course, I'd rather have a medium rare T-bone with a loaded baked potato."

"Eric's in his weight room. Will you go tell him that y'all are home? He has something to tell Feather. What, I have no idea."

"Sure."

I sat down at the table with a glass of iced tea and waited for their return. They came back within a few minutes. "She's in her room, Eric. She wasn't interested in talking to you when I told her you didn't have a date."

He went directly to her room, pounding on the door. "Get out here Miss Know-It-All."

She came out of her room and walked by him without saying a word. She poured herself a glass of tea and took a place at the table while Eric remained standing.

"I didn't get a date to the prom but you already know that. You know why?"

"Yeah. You put it off too long and there's nobody left to take."

"Wrong. For once you're wrong. Hallelujah! I had someone in mind the whole time but was afraid to ask Mr. Mendenhall. I finally talked to him today. He gave me permission to bring *you* to the prom as my date. So, will *you* go with me?"

She had her glass halfway to her mouth but put it down. She sat there a full minute and then began to cry, rose and went back to her room.

"Now, what'd I do wrong?" He turned and looked at me.

I went into her bedroom, and she was sitting on the edge of the bed still crying. "What's the matter, Feather?"

Sniffing, she tried to explain. "I've never been to a prom. Boys asked me but I had nothing to wear. I was so shocked that Eric asked me, I couldn't handle it. All the time he didn't ask anyone, and I was giving him the third degree—he was just waiting to ask me."

"Hadn't you better go back in there and accept his invitation?" I asked.

Rather than answering, her head bobbed up and down.

THE NEXT MORNING AT BREAKFAST, I broke the news to Gavin. "Feather and I are going to Odessa shopping today. We'll be late getting home so you and Eric will have to fend for yourselves. Eric has a new suit to wear, but Feather needs a prom dress and matching shoes. I'm telling you right up front. We're going to spend a lot of money."

His response was surprising. "Do what you have to. I want her to be the prettiest girl there."

Eric didn't respond but was smiling from ear to ear.

58

FRANK

J ulie said everything would work out. She was right. Luta Sager filed for the board and everything changed. I was re-hired soon after my contract was terminated. And, it was extended for another two years. From that time on, my life improved considerably.

The highlight of spring was Mr. Kelly's One-Act Play which advanced out of district for the first time in twenty years. Two weeks later in mid-April the regional contest was held in Odessa. We took a good crowd from the community, and when *King Stag* was announced as one of the two advancing shows to state, you would have thought we had won the state championship in football.

Mr. Kelly had our students dressed nicely for the awards ceremony with the boys wearing dress pants and ties and the girls their Sunday outfits. Our students made me so proud. Their conduct was exemplary, putting the other participating schools to shame.

Problems always confront high school principals in the spring and mine could've ruined my entire year. Of course, it concerned the cheer-leaders and tryouts for the 1977-78 school year. They were scheduled for the week after our success with the one-act play. The tryouts were held in the gym and included the eighth-grade class since they would be in high school next year. Aubrey was one of the eighth graders trying out even though she continued to suffer from the episode with Devon in January.

I didn't change the procedure used in the past. The girls would perform in front of the student body and faculty. When the students exited the gym, they would be given a ballot to vote and turn it in to their next period teacher. It seemed to be a simple process.

One thing I learned the hard way. Girls are fanatical in their quest to become a cheerleader. I can't explain it but believe me it's true. All we heard at home leading up to the tryout was Aubrey attempting to determine her routine and hoping she would win. Julie had been a cheerleader, and she helped her develop a routine. On one hand, I hoped she was successful, but it was not going to disappoint me if she wasn't selected. It seemed to me there should be a great deal more important things to do than jumping up and down, hollering.

Fifteen girls had signed up and only six could be selected. The tryouts were held fifth period right after lunch. That would give Mrs. Kraal and the junior high secretary time to count the votes and announce the results before the end of school. I had several teachers on duty outside to prevent any of the students from skipping out during the tryouts.

Everything went fine as each of the girls had their turn of performing in front of the audience. I couldn't help but notice that Aubrey received limited applause after her turn. It wasn't that warm but all the girls were red-faced after their performances, probably because of the excitement. There wouldn't be much learning happening the remainder of the day.

After the last girl performed, the students filed out of the gym receiving their ballots. I stood in the hallway as they returned to class, chattering away and discussing who they thought should win.

Ten minutes later, Mrs. Kraal went by each classroom for the ballots. The junior high secretary followed the same process in her building. They returned to the counselor's office where they would count the ballots. The office phone rang continuously for the next hour, with parents wanting to know the results.

Finally, Mrs. Kraal returned with the results informing me they'd counted the ballots twice. I looked and sure enough, Aubrey had not won. All that was left was informing the girls of the outcome. The counselor, Mrs. Fields, assembled the girls in a vacant classroom and gave them the good news or bad depending on whether or not they'd been selected as a cheerleader. I could hear the wailing from my office when she announced the results. Thank goodness, she had the common sense to allow the losers to remain in the room for the remainder of the day.

Well, that's over, I thought, closing my door and propping my feet upon my desk. A knock at the door interrupted my after-cheerleader-tryout bliss. "Come in."

Mrs. Kraal entered looking as if she'd just witnessed a multiple homicide.

"Is there a problem?" I asked.

She opened her mouth but nothing came out.

"Is there a problem, Mrs. Kraal?" I repeated.

"Yes, Mr. Mendenhall. I happened to count the total number of ballots. We have 142 students present today and 170 ballots were turned in. I'm sorry. We should've done that before we announced the results."

Suddenly, I felt nauseated. "That can't be right. Are you sure?"

"Yes. I counted the ballots three times. Evidently, someone got ahold of additional ballots and filled them out."

My nausea increased. I couldn't speak for several minutes. She continued, "It's all right to cuss, Mr. Mendenhall. I've been doing it since the first count."

"We'll have to vote again. Would you have Mrs. Fields come into my office?"

I told the counselor what had happened and asked her to reassemble the girls who tried out and inform them we would have another vote. She was calm and attempted to reassure me that every-thing would be okay. That's why I loved counselors. They were always so positive.

Ballots were delivered to each classroom and under strict supervision, a vote was taken again. Once again, a count by Mrs. Kraal and the junior high secretary. Hoping and praying that the outcome would remain the same, I waited—and waited some more. Finally, Mrs. Kraal gave me the results. My nausea returned . . . three fold. There was a change. Aubrey had won by one vote, eliminating one of the previous selections.

The outcome couldn't have been worse. Now what? Announce the results, creating a situation involving the principal's daughter, that moved her into a cheerleader. I sat in my chair staring at the wall for fifteen minutes before a knock at my door. Mrs. Kraal entered.

"What now, Mr. Mendenhall?"

"Tell me about the girl that Aubrey will replace."

"She'll be a senior next year. She is shy but has tried out each year, not winning. She's an excellent student but so quiet you wouldn't know she was around. You saw her in tryouts. She's awkward and didn't do very well, however, I believe she received votes because she didn't give up, even though three times she was rejected."

How could it be any worse? I was hoping she might be a discipline problem or a poor student. I took a deep breath and exhaled. "Do you have any suggestions, Mrs. Kraal?"

"It's a no win-situation. We could say the second voting didn't result in a change but that wouldn't be the truth. I know that wouldn't be acceptable to you even though it would be the easiest. We could increase the size of the squad to seven, but everyone would know that your daughter was the reason. How compassionate is your daughter? I mean is she anything like Riley who wants to help everyone?"

"No, to the last question. A big NO. She's probably the most self-centered student in this school. I do agree, since she will only be a freshman that it'd be great for her to accept the first count. I don't have the least bit of confidence in that happening but it's worth a try. It's only twenty minutes until school is out. We have to do something fast. Call junior high and have her sent over here."

How was I going to approach this? Appeal to her conscience? Talk about doing the right thing? Before I could decide, she was sitting in my office, eyes still red from crying.

"How're you doing?" I asked, which was a stupid question.

She replied in a broken voice. "I wanted to win."

"When the votes were counted a second time you did win by one vote," I explained, watching the change in her expression.

"Really! I knew something must be wrong. I did good with my routine. Thank you! Thank you!" she exclaimed, getting up and coming around to hug me.

"Now please sit down and let me tell you the rest of the story. You defeated a girl who will be a senior by one vote." I continued to relay what Mrs. Kraal had told me about the girl Aubrey would replace. When I finished her expression had become more serious.

"Are you suggesting that I let her have it even though she didn't win? I won, even though it was only by one vote."

"Please think about what it will do to her, Aubrey. She's tried out three years and lost. Finally, she's going to be a cheerleader. This was her last chance and she believes a successful one. Put yourself in her place for just a minute and think what it would do to you." I pleaded, watching her tear up again.

"I have to think about it," she said.

"No. We don't have time. I need to announce the results before school is out." I held my breath.

She burst out crying, unable to talk. I sat there and watched for several minutes until she could finally speak. "Go ahead and tell them there wasn't a change. I can try out again next year."

This time, I rose, went around my desk and hugged her. "I'm so proud of you, Aubrey. You understand this has to be our secret. You can't tell anyone."

"Not even Riley?"

"Yes, of course Riley and your mother." I hugged her again.

On Wednesday the fourth of May, we left for Austin for the State One-Act Play. Our show wasn't until tomorrow but it was at least an eight-hour drive. The girls and Julie went also and were excited about the trip. Mr. Kelly had put a banner across the hallway reading, *Austin is beautiful in May.*

I had insisted to Mr. Kelly that he get the cast a nice hotel. Most of the students had never been to Austin, and it was going to be a life-long memory. Mr. Cleburne didn't object to spending the money but wasn't planning to attend the contest. Several parents and grandparents were going. For the first time in the history of the school, the community was talking about an academic event.

Mr. Kelly reserved rooms at the Hyatt for his students. I told him to also reserve me a room, but since I was taking my family, to make a separate billing. Arriving that afternoon, I couldn't believe the traffic. I thought Fort Worth was bad but it was nothing compared to Austin. We found our hotel, checked in, and ran into Mr. Kelly in the elevator.

"This is a nice place," I said.

"It's my favorite place to stay in Austin. We had a terrible rehearsal this morning but that doesn't bother me. The kids are so excited, I expected it. They want to tour Sixth Street this afternoon. If it's okay with you, I'm going to take them. In the daytime, there shouldn't be any problems."

"Sure. I know that's the area most talked about when Austin is brought up. Would it be okay if my daughters went with you?"

"No problem. We're going to leave in about an hour and return before dark. Have them meet us in the lobby," he replied.

In our room, the girls couldn't wait and went down early. It gave Julie and me a chance to talk privately. I sat down in a cushiony chair and propped my feet up.

"You look comfortable," Julie observed.

"I deserve to relax after the cheerleader elections. Talk about stressful."

"I still have a hard time believing Aubrey gave up her spot. It was wonderful but so unlike her."

"Julie, she gave us hope. I was pleased. Aubrey demonstrated something to us that was a long time coming—compassion. It wasn't easy for her to do. Isn't it amazing that something good could develop out of a wrecked cheerleader election?"

"I've noticed she's been different since then. Maybe it's the praise she received from us. She has a better attitude," Julie said, "and is more optimistic about most everything."

"Now, Julie, what about our other daughter who has always been perfect. It appears we may have traded one problem for another."

"I know. Riley has changed and not for the better. Bruce is a nice boy, but he seems to have brought out the worst in Riley even though it wasn't intentional. I never thought she'd be defiant. When you told her that Bruce couldn't accompany us, she tried to argue. That was so unlike her. I noticed the change when she showed little sympathy to Aubrey," Julie commented, "even when she came home crying every day, after being ridiculed."

"We can hope that Bruce goes to college—far away," I said.

She smiled and shook her head. "Boys would've been easier, but it's too late to think about that now."

OUR SHOW WAS outstanding the next day, and filled with pride, we waited anxiously for the result which seemed to take forever. When the All-Star Cast was announced, we were pleased to have three on the Honorable Mention and two on the All-Star Cast. Third place was announced first as we sat on the edge of our seats with fingers crossed. When we were identified as taking second place our students and fans erupted in excitement, hugging one another. I congratulated Mr. Kelly who remained calm as if he'd expected the outcome all along.

59

ERIC

I was only halfway through my breakfast when Dawn and Feather left for Odessa Friday morning. I didn't understand what the big hurry was and expressed this to Gavin.

"When women have shopping on their mind nothing else matters, Eric. You need to understand that right away. Don't ask me to explain it. The thought of spending money excites them like nothing else. I learned many years ago not to get in their way. It wouldn't surprise me if they didn't get home until late tonight. We might as well figure on looking out for ourselves today. I'll buy your dinner if you'll meet me in town. Just tell me what you want, and I'll order for you and have it waiting. That will give you time to eat and get back to school."

"Sounds good. Just get me whatever the lunch special is. I should be there by 12:10. Friday is hamburgers in the school cafeteria and they're pretty dry. It's a good day to miss," I said, pleased at his offer.

"What was Dawn like when she was Feather's age?"

"She was the prettiest thing you ever saw. Small, but full of life and confidence which made her bossy. Ordered me around like I was a stepchild. I'd get mad sometimes, but it didn't take me long to get over it. She would smile and say, 'Gavy, don't be mad . . . you know you love me.' She called me Gavy for a long time, up until we lost the girls.

She stopped then. I guess because nothing seemed to be appropriate that wasn't serious.

"Luta thinks Feather reminds me of the twins, but actually she reminds me of her at that age. Feather does love horses and the outdoors like Stacy but her actions speak to Luta."

"Feather told me the saddle you got her for Christmas was the best gift she'd ever received. I guess she's had a pretty hard time, with her parents being the way they are."

"No doubt about it," he affirmed.

"It's time for me to get going or I'm going to be late. See you at noon."

MOST OF THE talk at school was about the prom tomorrow night. I met Luis at the flag pole before school. "You have a date for the prom?" he asked.

"Yeah. I'm bringing Feather."

"Does she have a dress? She seemed to be all cowgirl."

"Sure. In fact, she and Dawn have gone to Odessa to buy her a new prom dress," I said.

"She was so covered up when I came to the ranch, it wasn't possible to see what she looked like. Is she as pretty as Riley?"

I was getting uncomfortable with the questions. "What's the deal, Luis? You'll see her tomorrow night. You decide." I was getting tired of all his questioning.

"Don't get your feelings bent out of shape. I was just curious."

Thank goodness, the first bell rang and we went inside. I hoped the questions didn't continue throughout the day. I went out of my way to avoid Riley, afraid she might question me about tomorrow tonight. No doubt, she'd be with Bruce.

Everything went fine the rest of the morning, and I met Gavin at the downtown café for lunch. The fish, fries, and coleslaw went down much better than the dry hamburger.

That afternoon it clouded up and looked like rain when we went to the weight room to do our Friday testing. I guess it was our imagination, but on cloudy rainy days everyone seemed to improve on their bench press. Today was no exception, and I pressed 315 pounds to everyone's applause. The next best performance was 250 pounds. It felt good to be able to leave my shirt off and not be ashamed about how I looked. In fact, I went shirtless as much as possible now.

I left school glad the day was over and no one else had questioned me about the prom. On the drive to the ranch, I wondered what everyone would think about Feather. She wasn't beautiful like Riley, but she was cute, and I could dance with her. Besides, I had a date and it wasn't anybody's business.

When I arrived at the ranch, a strange car was parked in front of the house. When I went inside a man and woman were sitting in the den with Gavin. Silence greeted me, and I noticed Gavin's scowl, similar to the one that welcomed me almost a year ago. "Sit down, Eric, and meet Feather's parents." He nodded toward them.

"Be reasonable, Mr. Sager, we only want what is rightfully ours. My dad had no other children, and I deserve to inherit at least part of his estate. Since Feather is staying here, you can influence her to do what's right."

Gavin had a cigar in the corner of his mouth but it wasn't lit. He spoke without removing it. "Just why in the hell do you think I would help you? This remarkable little girl you have ignored most of her life is going to get all of what her granddad left her."

The man looked at her and said, "Honey, this isn't getting us anywhere. We need to get a lawyer and settle this thing."

Gavin removed his cigar. "Let me tell you something and listen carefully. I don't have a lot of money, but my credit is good. I'll spend a hundred times the value of Lefty's estate to see that you don't get one dime. Now, you remove yourself from this house, and I don't want to see you again." He rose and left the room.

We sat there several minutes looking at each other before they left. I went into the kitchen but Gavin wasn't there. I checked the bedroom and found him lying on the bed, rubbing his chest. I went back to the kitchen, opened the cabinet, and took out a pill. I returned to the bedroom taking a glass of water.

"Here, Gavin." I handed him the pill which he accepted. After placing the pill under his tongue, he lay back down.

"I'll be okay. Just need to rest a few minutes. Did they leave?"

"Yeah."

"If that's not the scum of the earth, I don't know what is. Thank goodness, your grandmother and Feather weren't home."

I left and went back to watch TV and waited for them to return. I couldn't concentrate, thinking of Gavin's response to Feather's parents. It scared me to see him that way, reminding me of his attitude toward me the first several months I was here. I waited an hour then went back to check on him, and he was asleep.

Dawn and Feather were home by late afternoon and came in talking, telling me all about their shopping trip and asking if Gavin was home. I told them he was asleep causing them to lower their voices.

"Eric, we did really well. You're going to be proud of your date to the prom. We found the perfect dress. What did y'all do today?"

I didn't dare tell her about the visit from Feather's parents, instead saying we had eaten lunch together in town. I also told them about my record-setting bench press. Gavin came in and they started telling him about their trip to Odessa.

⁂

THE NEXT DAY I started having doubts about my decision to attend the prom. Maybe I shouldn't have asked Feather then it would have been possible to change my mind. Riley would be there with Bruce and watching them dance would be depressing. I still thought about her every day and hadn't given up on us getting back together. Maybe when Bruce left for college it would happen. As the day progressed my doubts became stronger, and I started thinking of ways to get out of my commitment. I could suddenly become ill, or hurt my back while working out in the weight room. No way could I attend a dance if unable to walk.

My conscience kicked in before making a decision. Feather was looking forward to the prom. She'd spent hours teaching me to dance. Her parents were horrible, and she'd just lost her pops. I couldn't back out now. I would tolerate the evening and maybe we could come home early. It wasn't that I didn't want to take Feather. I was more comfortable with her than anyone. I just kept remembering last year when everyone made fun of me.

Dawn and Feather left after lunch for her hair appointment in town. I worked out in my weight room to relieve some of the stress. I had to pass Arnold's pen on the way, and like every other day, I refused to look at it. I spent the remainder of the afternoon watching TV after my workout. Dawn and Feather were home by four o'clock and she went directly to her room to begin getting ready.

"What's the deal, Dawn? The prom doesn't start until seven."

"It takes us girls a little longer to get ready," she explained.

"Two and a half hours?"

"At least, Eric. Do you have a shirt picked out that needs ironing? I guess you'll wear the new suit you bought for Lefty's funeral. What about a tie? You can borrow one of Gavin's if you like."

"I've never had on a tie."

"The prom is formal. All the boys will wear ties. Pick out your shirt, and I'll get a tie to match."

This was getting worse by the minute. I went to my room and chose one of my long sleeve Sunday shirts. My suit was dark blue and it had to be altered to fit. The pants were too large but the coat was perfect. Of course, last year the pants would have fit also. I gave Dawn the shirt and she nodded her approval.

Time dragged by. I was hungry but we were going to eat in the cafeteria at seven, and the dance would start an hour later in the gym. I finally gave in and put peanut butter on a slice of bread to hold me. At 5:45, I took my bath, shaved, applied some after shave, brushed my teeth, and was dressed by 6:05, except for the tie. I'd heard it thunder while getting dressed, so we were probably going to get wet. Lately we'd experienced several storms.

I sat down in the den and watched the weather report on the Odessa-Midland channel, which was forecasting storms for this region. I heard her come in but didn't look, occupied with the television.

"Eric. You need some help with your tie?"

"Yeah," I said looking up. Stunned, I just stared with my mouth open. Wow! She looked great. Her dress reached all the way to the floor. It was shiny and brown with no sleeves. It fit perfectly. "How're you going to Two-Step?"

Then . . . she turned around. "See this little boxy thing starting at the waist? It's a pleat, one big one which allows me to move."

"Oh, I see," I said, trying to sound normal. The dress had no back except two straps coming from the shoulders and making an X. The front was beautiful, the back took my breath away, causing my heart to race.

Poking a tiny turquoise shoe out from under it, she continued. "Luta thought this color would complement the gown, so she let me borrow her turquoise jewelry and bought these shoes to match."

"You-you look really good," is all I could get out. I went to stand and my legs were weak. I had no idea she would look like this. That backless thing was awesome.

Before leaving, Luta had to take a bunch of pictures. We were going in her car and it was in the garage. Before backing out of the garage, Feather moved over next to me. I was still having trouble breathing, and this didn't help anything.

"It looks like it's going to rain," she said.

"Yeah," is all I could think to say.

"Do you really like my dress?"

"Yeah, you look really good."

She took hold of my arm and put her head on my shoulder. "Thank you for taking me to the prom."

"No problem." What a stupid response, I thought. "Are you hungry?" I was in a panic to say something appropriate.

"Not much. I'm too excited to think about eating."

The remainder of the trip we rode in silence. Arriving at school, it was lightning and thundering but not raining. I found a parking place and went around to open the door for her. At least, I knew that much.

"Thank you, Eric." She took my arm and added, "You have big muscles."

I didn't reply. We were on time and at least half of the students were already there. When we entered noise greeted us, everybody seemed to be talking at once. Then suddenly it was silent, and I realized we were the center of attention. Mr. Mendenhall came over and introduced himself.

"So this is the young lady you asked to bring. My, my, Eric, you have excellent taste."

"Thank you for allowing Eric to bring me," Feather said.

"You're welcome. I believe you'll enjoy our prom."

The cafeteria had decorations hanging from the ceiling as well as on the tables. We found a place to sit and glasses of water were already at each site. I started fiddling with my water glass unable to think of anything to say.

"The decorations are beautiful. Somebody went to a lot of work. Are you going to introduce me to some of your friends?" she asked.

"Sure." No sooner had I replied, when Luis came over.

"Hi, Eric. See you made it. I see you brought your cowgirl. She looks more like a princess than a cowgirl." His eyes were glued to her and he hadn't even seen the back of her dress.

"Thank you, Luis. I guess that's a compliment," Feather responded.

After Luis left, a steady stream of my friends came by to meet Feather. All boys. The girls stood off at a distance and stared. I began to feel good with more confidence as the evening progressed. The meal was served which consisted of roast, creamed potatoes, and green beans. I wasn't hungry but was able to eat what was on my plate.

Throughout the meal, I kept glancing at her, thinking, she's never looked like this. Surely, I'd have noticed it if she had. Then a voice spoke inside my head. *Stupid, you didn't see anyone but Riley.* I'd spotted Riley and Bruce earlier and looking at her, thought she doesn't look as pretty tonight as she usually does.

Mr. Mendenhall went to a podium and said a few words of welcome, encouraging everyone to enjoy the evening and then said the dance would start immediately in the gym.

We didn't have to leave the building to reach the gym, which was fortunate since it had starting raining. The gym was decorated even more than the cafeteria with colorful streamers hanging from lines stretched across the building. A Disc Jockey was set up and music was playing. We took off our shoes, leaving them under chairs that were lined up against the wall. Refreshment tables were set up along the other side, containing bowls of punch, cookies, and nuts.

The DJ was playing pop music but few couples were dancing. That changed when he put on a country song. We took the floor and with the lights dimmed, it was easy. The practice paid off and I was relaxed. He continued to play country music and we danced to the next three songs before he switched to pop.

"You did good, Eric. That wasn't hard was it?"

"No, it was fun. Would you like some punch?'

"That would be great."

I walked around the gym to the punch bowl, filled two cups, and noticed a boy talking to Feather when I started back. He was a senior and one of the linemen on our football team. "How's it going?" I asked him, giving Feather her punch.

"Okay. I'd like a dance with your date, but she said I needed to ask you," he said.

"It's not country. That's all I dance to. It's fine with me," I said.

"Eric, I love the Bee Gees. He's playing their songs. It's about the only pop music I like. You sure it's okay?"

"Yeah."

Watching them dance, I was amazed. She could move. When the song ended, she returned. "You can dance to pop music."

"Sure. This isn't my first rodeo. I like country music much better, though."

The remainder of the evening followed the same pattern. We danced to almost every country song. Some we two-stepped, others required a waltz, which we had practiced also. Boys continued to ask her to dance when we sat out Pop music, and she always referred them to me. I never refused, always leaving it up to her.

At 11:55 the DJ announced, "Grab your favorite girl because I'm puttin' on Loretta Lynn and "Love is the Foundation." Hold her tight now, like you mean it."

She molded up against me and whispered, "I had a wonderful time, Eric. Thank you so much for bringing me."

"It was my pleasure," I said, pleased with my answer.

The song ended. We put on our shoes and going to the door, found the exit crowded. Someone said, "It's raining cats and dogs."

Peeping out the window of the door, she was right. It was pouring down and water was standing in puddles all over the parking lot. I looked down at Feather. "You want to make a run for it?"

"I can't run in these shoes. Besides, it would ruin them."

No one had left. We might as well go for it and be the first, I thought. "Here's what we'll do. Take off your shoes, and I'm going to bend down and you get on me piggy back, and we'll go to the car that way. I don't mind getting my shoes wet. What do you think?"

"Sounds like a plan. Let's go for it."

I bent down, she jumped on my back, and someone opened the door for us. She had her arms around my neck and we left, headed toward the car, which was a good distance away. I jogged at first but slowed to a walk it was raining so hard.

Halfway to the car, she bit my ear, laughing and saying, "Giddy up horsey, you can do it."

We got in the car, soaked and laughing. We noticed other couples leaving the building. She moved over next to me and squeezed my arm. "Look what we did. If not for us they might have stood inside all night."

It was still raining when we arrived at the ranch. I started to pull into the garage, which was connected to the house, so we wouldn't get wet again.

What are you doing?" she asked.

"Parking in the garage."

"No, that won't work. You have to walk me to the door. That's the proper thing to do."

"But we both live in the same house." I argued.

"Doesn't matter. I want you to walk me to the door. Then you can park the car in the garage."

"That's crazy, Feather. I'll get soaked again."

"Doesn't matter," she repeated.

Giving up, I backed out and parked in front of the house, got out, went around and opened the door for her. We were drenched again when we reached the front porch and dry territory.

"Now what?" I asked.

"We say goodnight. It was one of the best evenings of my life. Thank you again," she said, reaching up and putting her arms around my neck pulling me down to her.

Her lips reached mine, slightly parted, and I felt the tip of her tongue and at that moment, nothing else seemed to matter. After several seconds she released me and said goodnight, going into the house. I turned, starting back toward the car, but missed the steps and fell off the porch into the mud.

60

LUTA

I woke up early, wondering about the prom. I meant to stay up until they came home but gave up and went to bed at twelve o'clock. I eased out of bed to keep from waking Gavin, and went to the kitchen to put the coffee on. I let Jenny out to potty, noticing the stars were shining, announcing that the rain had passed.

Getting my coffee, I returned to the porch and selected a dry chair to sit in. It was going to be a beautiful day. The air smelled fresh and clean. I said a prayer of thanks for the blessings that had been abundant the last six months. Gavin and I had suffered so long after losing the twins and for the first time our lives had resumed to a semblance of normalcy. No doubt, Eric was a big part of that change.

After they left last evening, we talked about the twins and the fact they'd never attended a prom. As we watched Eric and Feather prepare to leave, our hearts were filled with long denied joy and our minds with memories. We talked about the fact that we'd never get over the death of our girls but would see them again one day. We discussed Eric and his future, wondering if he'd ever return to his dad, not admitting it but both hoping that he would stay at the ranch. What a change he'd made since coming to live with us. What a difference he'd made in our lives. I'd come close to giving up on Gavin. Now, I felt as if he and I were beginning a new phase of our lives.

The door opened. I expected Gavin but was surprised to see Eric. "Good morning, you're up early after a late night."

He sat down. "Woke up and couldn't go back to sleep."

"How was the prom?"

"Awesome. We had fun."

"What about Feather?"

"Amazing. Everyone wanted to dance with her. The boys stared at her and the girls glared. I guess they viewed her as an intruder."

"She was beautiful."

"Yeah. I never realized it until last night. I guess it was the clothes."

"The inside of her, Eric, makes her even more beautiful."

He smiled. "I guess so. The outside of her sure looked good last night."

We talked until Gavin appeared after getting his coffee. Eric got up and gave him his chair saying he was going to his room. "I may see if it's possible to sleep awhile longer."

Gavin and I talked the next half hour about the future, especially the heifers that were due to start calving in another month or so. Time was running out, and we needed to hire additional help which I reminded him of once again. "Do you have any ideas about where we might find several men for the summer?"

"I've been thinking about that and have come up with an idea. Why don't we just see if Luis and a couple of other high school boys would work for us this summer. They, along with Eric, should be enough. I could show them how to pull a calf when the heifers are having trouble. I believe they could do it."

"That's a good idea. I'm sure they would jump at the chance to have a full-time summer job. They've been dependable in the past."

"Now, since we settled that, I'm hungry. You may have to cook breakfast in shifts today."

"That's no problem. You sit here and enjoy this morning air with your coffee and I'll get started." The phone was ringing when I opened the door heading back into the house. It was early for a call, I thought, answering it. The person asked for Gavin. I went back out to the porch and told him.

I had the bacon frying and the biscuits in the oven when he came back. I could tell by his expression; it wasn't good news.

"I knew everything was going too well, Luta. That was Bob Matthews, the man I met at Lefty's funeral who was interested in helping Feather. He and his partner, Tom Warren, are in a bind at Ruidoso with their race horses. They're finding it impossible to hire help. They want Feather to begin working for them. I couldn't say no. It's too good of an opportunity for her."

"We can't feel bad, Gavin. It's best for her and would be selfish to keep her here. I know these are good men and will take care of her. When do they want her in Ruidoso?"

"Immediately. We have to talk with her. Of course, it's going to be a surprise since we haven't mentioned anything about it to her. We'll tell her about the offer today and then call Bob back this afternoon. I know she's going to be excited."

AN HOUR after Gavin and I had eaten, Feather came in, followed a few minutes later by Eric. Feather was talking non-stop about the prom, and it was difficult for anyone to get a word in. I started the second breakfast, and we continued to listen as she went into detail about the dance.

"I enjoyed every minute of the dance. My feet are sore today but it was worth it. I was proud of Eric. He didn't step on me one time. The DJ played great music and alternated between country and pop. Of course, he played more country songs. Did Eric tell you he had to carry me to the car so I wouldn't ruin my shoes?"

I turned and looked at Eric. "No. He left that out."

"Did he tell you he walked me to the door when we got home?"

"No, he didn't tell me that either?" Again, I looked at Eric whose face had turned crimson.

"Oh, well. He was sweet, and I had a wonderful time."

Gavin cleared his throat, indicating he had something to say. "Feather, I have some news for you. I know you're going to have questions, but let me finish before you start asking them."

He started with talking to Bob Matthews at her pop's funeral. He covered everything up and through the phone call this morning. She sat and listened, her eyes lighting up the longer he talked. When he finished, he leaned back in his chair. "Okay. Now, what do you think?"

"You mean they would pay me for working with their horses?"

"That's about the size of it. They need help desperately."

"I can't believe it. It would be a dream job. Maybe becoming a jockey someday. I would love it!"

He took out a cigar and lit it. "So, you would accept the job?"

"Of course. But it would mean leaving the ranch. Don't you need me to work here this summer?"

He removed the cigar. "Luta and I have a plan that'd allow us to get by."

"When would I start work?"

"As soon as possible. I'm going to call him back with your answer and tell him when you'll be in Ruidoso."

"Today's Sunday. I'll be there Tuesday. I can't believe this."

I'd watched Eric's expression grow more solemn, the longer they talked. He rose and left the table, going to the door and leaving, without saying a word.

Feather got up and started toward the door. "I'll talk to him and try to make him understand why I have to take this job."

I stopped cooking and turned off the burner and oven. "Did you see this coming, Gavin?"

"I suspected it but was hoping he'd understand. Eric's matured some, but he still has a ways to go. One of these days he'll see things from the other's perspective and not just his."

"I believe you're right. The question is how long that will take."

THEY RETURNED HALF AN HOUR LATER. I continued cooking breakfast as they sat down. "Are y'all hungry?"

"I don't know about Feather but I am."

"Me too. We have it worked out. We're going to talk on the phone at least once a week. Eric's going to come see me when school's out. It's a five-hour drive, but he can leave early and be there by noon."

"I know she has to take the job. It's just that I've gotten used to her being here. It won't be the same without her. She seems like a sister."

"Oh, Eric. You didn't seem to think that way last night when I kissed you goodnight and then you fell off the porch. I heard you and looked through the glass in the door, seeing you getting up out of the mud."

Eric looked shocked and had trouble getting words out. "Y-ou, Y-ou, shouldn't be telling that."

"Why not. It's the truth. If you had a sister, I can't see you letting her kiss you like that."

Eric was suffering more each second, and I thought he might get up and leave again so I changed the subject. "Feather, are you going to take your horse to Ruidoso?"

"I don't know. Maybe Gavin can ask Mr. Matthews if I need to bring him when he calls. I'll probably be too busy to ride. Of course, I might need him to use as a pony horse."

We continued to visit as they ate breakfast about her new job. Eric joined in and seemed to be doing better with Feather leaving. How long that would last is anyone's guess.

Gavin called Bob Matthews back and told him of Feather's decision to be in Ruidoso Tuesday. Her living accommodations hadn't been discussed, but during the conversation Matthews told him she would be staying in a house owned by his partner in Ruidoso. He also told Gavin she'd need to bring her horse.

She was pleased upon hearing the news about taking her horse. "Now, since that is settled, I still have another problem. What should I do about the house in Alpine? I really don't want to sell it now."

"I have an idea. Gavin and I could advertise it to rent to someone. We could look in on it occasionally, collect the rent, and save it for you."

"That would be great. I wouldn't have to worry about it then. I just hope that my mom and dad aren't a problem."

I noticed Gavin stiffen up. "Honey, don't give them another thought. I'll take care of anything that comes up."

THAT AFTERNOON FEATHER and I went into town and bought her some clothes. She needed a light weight jacket since the mornings in Ruidoso would be cool. We found some long-sleeved shirts on sale and were able to purchase three pairs of jeans that fit her. Gavin told me that since there was not a place to buy a hat in town, he would give her the money to buy one in Ruidoso.

It was midafternoon before we started home and I noticed she had become quiet. "Is something wrong, Feather?"

"No. I'm excited about my new job but sad about leaving. I'm going to come back as often as possible, however, that may be difficult. I'd need to have at least three days off. Will y'all come to see me?"

"Certainly. I love Ruidoso and it gives us a chance to get away from the ranch. Eric's already said he'd be visiting you."

"Eric. Oh, me. I'm going to miss him. He thinks I'm bossy, which is true. But he needs direction. I've become fond of him. I guess more than any other boy I've known."

I suspected that Eric would finally notice someone besides Riley. It took that backless dress to redirect his attention. I didn't express it but both Gavin and I would miss her also—more than she realized. With her in Ruidoso it would be much easier to get Gavin away from the ranch.

AFTER BREAKFAST TUESDAY MORNING, Feather and Gavin hooked on her trailer and loaded Glo. Eric and I carried her luggage out front to load. She got out and came around to tell us bye.

"Thank you for everything. I'll miss you. You've been so kind to me. I couldn't have done without you." She hugged me and I cried. I couldn't stop the tears. She went to Gavin and hugged him. He couldn't stop the tears either.

"Eric, come around and open the pickup door for me and you can tell your sister goodbye."

They weren't completely hidden and we saw the goodbye. It definitely wasn't a brother-sister embrace.

EPILOGUE

One Year Later

They left early for Ruidoso with Eric driving and Gavin in the front seat. Luta was in the back. It was the opening race weekend in Ruidoso. Gavin and Luta had promised Feather they would be there. They hadn't seen her since Christmas but Eric had made three trips to El Paso after the first of the year.

He'd graduated last Friday night, ending a wonderful senior year. Being on the school board, Luta was allowed to present him his diploma when he walked across the stage. They were all proud of the young man he had become. After an outstanding year in football, he had agreed to attend school at Sul Ross on a scholarship. Coach Duncan had been to their house several times in the spring, encouraging him to come to Sul Ross.

Eric and his granddad had become close. According to Gavin, Eric could do little wrong. Cameron was a disappointment to Luta and Gavin. After two grueling months they had calved out the heifers. They ended up with 341 pair which wasn't bad for first year heifers. A buyer came to the ranch last November and offered $125,00 for the pairs and heifers that hadn't calved. That also included the bulls. Both loans were paid off. To date they hadn't received a dime of the approximately $47,000 profit for the pasture they provided or for their efforts. Cameron hadn't mentioned it in his infrequent calls and had not been back to the ranch.

It had been a good year. Mr. Cleburne had resigned in March, taking a job with the Service Center in Midland. He'd never become comfortable having to make decisions. Mr. Mendenhall was moved to the superintendent's position and it had worked out great. He was dedicated to the students and always had a recommendation on issues that came before the board. He was seen throughout the district daily and stayed informed on happenings in each of the buildings. In fact, it was difficult to catch him in his office.

THEY WERE STANDING at the rail as close as possible to the track. The bugler blared out the call to the post and the horses started onto the track. She was riding number 7, a black filly who was dancing sideways, and lunging forward every few steps. The rider on the pony horse had her snugged up as close as possible, and was still having troubling controlling her.

THE ANNOUNCER WENT DOWN the list of riders and horses beginning with number 1. When he came to the 7 horse he had several additional comments. **Ladies and gentlemen, Miss Bo Black is owned by Bob Matthews and Tom Warren of Lincoln, New Mexico and is trained by Jimmy Light. Up on her is the leading jockey for the Spring Meet at Sunland Park, Feather Jackson, affectionately known as "The Mouse" by her fans.**

Smiling and waving, she spotted them immediately when she drew even with them. She dropped one hand from the rein and blew a kiss to Eric, who blushed of course.

Someone called Gavin's name and turning around it was Bob Matthews accompanied by another man and a little girl.

"Gavin, glad you could make it. I want you to meet my friend and partner, Tom Warren. Tom this is Gavin Sager and his wife, Luta, the couple who sent us Feather."

"It's a pleasure Gavin and Luta. Feather is something else. We have all fallen in love with her."

"B-Boy, aren't you going to introduce me?"

"I'm sorry, honey. Gavin and Luta, this is my granddaughter, Tommie Rose, who you can see is not bashful. Bo and Lexie are here somewhere trying to corral the twins but she wanted to come with me to the rail. She adores Feather and follows her around like a puppy. I guarantee you if we go to the winner's circle for a picture, she'll be on the filly with Feather.

"Eric, I'm sorry to have ignored you but it hasn't been long since we've seen you. You've become sort of a temporary fixture around here. You've met Tom and Tommie Rose. Feather talks about you constantly. She tells me you're going to Sul Ross on a football scholarship."

"It looks like that's the plan."

The announcer directed our attention to the starting gates.

Ladies and gentlemen, it's post time. The horses are entering the gates. The number 3 horse is causing some problems—the rest of the horses go in peacefully. They're all loaded. They're off, and it's a good break for all . . .

Made in the USA
Columbia, SC
28 January 2023

10595999R00233